PASSING THE 8TH GRADE CRCT IN GEORGIA STUDIES

Kindred Howard
Ernest Everett Blevins
Sandra Bassett
Meredith Barr
Joshua Williams
Jeffery Wells
Michael B. Cassidy
Susan J.E. Illis

American Book Company
PO Box 2638
Woodstock, GA 30188-1383
Toll Free: 1 (888) 264-5877 Phone: (770) 928-2834
Fax: (770) 928-7483 Toll Free Fax: 1 (866) 827-3240
www.americanbookcompany.com

ACKNOWLEDGEMENTS

The authors would like to gratefully acknowledge the formatting and technical contributions of Marsha Torrens.

Graphics are the expertise of the very talented Mary Stoddard.

This product/publication includes images from CorelDRAW 9 and 11 which are protected by the copyright laws of the United States, Canada, and elsewhere. Used under license.

Printed in the United States of America

07/07

Preface xi

Diagnostic Test 1

Evaluation Chart 12

Chapter 1 Native American Cultures and the First Europeans 13

1.1 Native American Cultures 13
- Paleo Indians 13
- Archaic Peoples 13
- The Woodland Peoples....14
- The Mississippians 15

1.2 The Europeans Arrive 16
- Spanish Exploration of Georgia 17
  - Hernando de Soto 17
  - Spanish Missions 18
  - The End of the Spanish Missions 19

Chapter 1 Review....20

Chapter 2 Great Britain and Colonial Georgia 23

2.1 The Founding of British Georgia 23
- James Oglethorpe and the Charter of 1732 23
  - Reasons for Founding Georgia 24
  - The Charter of 1732 24
- Savannah, Tomochichi, and Mary Musgrove 25
  - Savannah 25

2.2 The Trustee Period 26
- New Immigrants Arrive 26
- Oglethorpe's Trip to England 27
- The "Malcontents" 27
- Conflict with Spain 28
- Farewell to Oglethorpe and the Trustee Period....29

2.3 Georgia as a Royal Colony 30
- Colonial Government 30
- Henry Ellis and James Wright 31

Chapter 2 Review....32

Chapter 3 The American Revolution and Georgia 35

3.1 Causes of the Revolution 35
- The French and Indian War 35
  - Effects of the War on Georgia 35
- Tensions Rise Between Great Britain and the Colonies 35

The Proclamation of 1763 36
The Stamp Act 36
The Intolerable Acts 37
Georgia's Discontent 37
Independence Declared 38
3.2 The Revolution in Georgia 39
In the Wake of Independence 40
Georgia's Constitution of 1777 40
Georgia's Battles 40
Button Gwinnett and the Florida Campaigns 40
Savannah and Kettle Creek 41
Austin Dabney and Nancy Hart 41
The Siege of Savannah 42
British Aggression and Surrender 42
3.3 Georgia and the Birth of a Nation 43
The Constitutional Convention 44
The "Great Compromise" and Slavery 44
Georgia's Reasons for Ratifying the Constitution 45
Chapter 3 Review 47

Chapter 4 Antebellum Georgia **49**

4.1 Education, Religion, and the Quest for Land 49
The University of Georgia and a New Capital 49
Louisville and Milledgeville 49
The Methodists and Baptists 50
Headrights, Lotteries, and Fraud 50
The Yazoo Land Fraud 51
4.2 New Technologies and Economic Growth 52
The "Cotton Kingdom" of the South 52
The Rise of "King Cotton" 52
Railroads 53
The Creeks and Cherokee 54
Georgia and the Creeks 54
Chief William McIntosh and the Treaty of Indian Springs 54
The Plight of the Cherokee 55
The Dahlonega Gold Rush 55
Worcester v. Georgia and the Trail of Tears 56
4.4 Slavery, States' Rights, and Secession 57
States' Rights and the Doctrine of Nullification 57
Slavery 58
The Missouri Compromise and the Compromise of 1850 58
The Georgia Platform 58
The Kansas-Nebraska Act 59
The Dred Scott Case 59
The Election of 1860 and Southern Secession 59
Georgia's Decision to Secede 60
Alexander Stephens 60
Chapter 4 Review 61

Chapter 5 Civil War and Reconstruction 63

5.1 The War and its Impact on Georgia 63
The War Begins 63
Fort Sumter 63
Union Blockade 64
Eastern Theater 64
Antietam and the Emancipation Proclamation 65
Gettysburg 65
Western Theater 66
Chickamauga 66
The Atlanta Campaign 66
Sherman's March to the Sea 67
Surrender and Aftermath 67
5.2 Reconstruction 68
The Radical Republicans 69
The Freedmen's Bureau and Federal Legislation 69
Reconstruction in Georgia 70
Sharecropping and Tenant Farming 70
Georgia's Reconstruction Government 70
Unrest During Reconstruction in Georgia 71
Chapter 5 Review 72

Chapter 6 From Reconstruction to WWI 75

6.1 Politics and the Economy in Post War Georgia 75
The Bourbon Triumvirate and the "New South" 75
The Bourbon Triumvirate 75
Henry W. Grady and the "New South" 76
The International Cotton Exposition and New Industry 76
Tom Watson and the Populists 77
The Election of 1896 and the Decline of Populism 77
The County Unit System 78
6.2 Race Relations and Reform 79
Rebecca Latimer Felton 79
Segregation in the South 79
Key African-American Figures 80
The "Atlanta Compromise" 81
Niagara and the NAACP 81
Ethnic Violence and Disfranchisement in Georgia 81
Voting Restrictions on Blacks 81
The 1906 Atlanta Race Riot 82
The Leo Frank Case 82
6.3 Georgia and World War I 83
The US Enters the War 83
Georgia's Contributions to the War 84
Fighting Georgians and the Selective Service Act 84
Military Bases 85
War Time Production 85
The War Ends 85
Chapter 6 Review 87

Chapter 7 Georgia Between the Wars 89

7.1 The Boll Weevil and Depression 89
The Wrath of the Boll Weevil 89
The Great Depression 90
Consumerism and Prosperity 90
........90
Farmers and Overproduction 90
Black Tuesday 91
Depression in Georgia 91
7.2 Eugene Talmadge, FDR, and the New Deal 92
Franklin Delano Roosevelt and the New Deal 92
The Agricultural Adjustment Act 92
The Civilian Conservation Corps 93
Social Security 93
Rural Electrification Administration 93
Governor Eugene Talmadge 94
Chapter 7 Review........95

Chapter 8 World War II 97

8.1 The World Goes to War........97
Fighting Begins 97
Totalitarian Dictators in Europe 97
Japan's Aggression 97
Europe Goes to War........98
Roosevelt Confronts Isolationism 98
Lend-Lease 98
Pearl Harbor 99
8.2 Georgia and the War 100
On Land, Air, and Sea 100
Citizen Sacrifice and Military Bases 100
Bell Aircraft 100
Shipyards 101
Farming and Industry 101
Carl Vinson and Richard Russell 101
8.3 Victory and Aftermath 102
Victory in Europe and Japan 102
The Holocaust 102
The Effects of the Holocaust in Georgia 103
Farewell to FDR 103
Chapter 8 Review........105

Chapter 9 Postwar Economic, Political, and Social Change 107

9.1 Postwar Economics and Growth 107
Industry, Agriculture, and the Growth of Atlanta 107
Economic Changes 107
Changes in Agriculture 108
The National Highway Act 108

Influential Atlanta Mayors 109
William Hartsfield 109
Ivan Allen, Jr. 110
Professional Sports 110
9.2 Postwar State Politics 111
Ellis Arnall 111
The Gubernatorial Election of 1946 111
The 1956 Georgia State Flag 112
Death of the White Primary and the County-unit System 112
9.3 Georgia and the Civil Rights Movement 113
The Movement Takes Off 113
Benjamin Mays 113
Dr. Martin Luther King, Jr. 113
The Albany Movement 114
Integration and Backlash 115
Brown v. Board of Education (1954) 115
Integration at UGA 115
Integration in Elementary and Secondary Schools 115
The Sibley Commission 116
The Axe Handle Governor 117
Chapter 9 Review 119

Chapter 10 Georgia's Modern Age **121**

10.1 Shifts in Political Power 121
Reapportionment 121
Atlanta's First African-American Mayors 122
Maynard Jackson 122
Andrew Young 122
Rise of the Two-party System in Georgia 123
Important Georgia Republicans in the Modern Age 123
10.2 Jimmy Carter 124
From Governor to President 124
Victory and Crisis 125
The Camp David Accords 126
Farewell to Washington 126
10.3 Image, Growth, and Industry 127
Georgia's Transportation Systems 127
The Busiest Airport in the World 127
Interstate Highways 127
Deepwater Ports 128
Railroads 128
Georgia's Modern Economy 128
Trade: Past and Present 128
Key Industries and International Business 129
Special Events and Facilities 130
Major Businesses and Entrepreneurs 130
Coca-Cola 131
The Home Depot 131
Georgia Pacific 131

Delta Airlines 132
Chick-fil-A 132
AFLAC 132
Impact of Immigration 133
A Multicultural State 133
Illegal Immigration 133
Chapter 10 Review....................135

Chapter 11 Georgia's Geography 137

11.1 Georgia's Place in the World 137
Georgia as a World and National Region 137
Georgia's Location on the Globe....................137
Georgia as Part of a National Region 138
Georgia's Climate 139
Climate and Economic Development 139
Hurricanes, Tornadoes, and Droughts 140
11.2 Regions Within Georgia 141
The Appalachian Plateau....................141
Ridge and Valley 141
Blue Ridge 141
The Piedmont 142
The Coastal Plain 142
11.3 Other Geographic Features 143
The Fall Line 143
Barrier Islands 143
Georgia's Rivers 144
The Okefenokee Swamp 144
Chapter 11 Review....................146

Chapter 12 Georgia's Government 149

12.1 Georgia's Constitution....................149
Principles on Which Georgia's Constitution is Founded....................149
Structure of the Georgia Constitution 150
Georgia's Bill of Rights and the Amendment Process 150
12.2 Branches of State Government 151
The Legislative Branch 151
Duties, Powers, and the Legislative Process 152
Organization of the General Assembly....................153
The Executive Branch 153
Governor and Lieutenant Governor....................153
Powers and Duties of the Governor....................154
Other Elected Executive Officials 154
Appointed Officials, Boards, and Agencies 154
The Judicial Branch....................155
12.3 Georgia's County and City Governments....................157
County Governments....................157
Municipal and Special Purpose Government....................158
Different Models of Municipal Government....................158
Special-Purpose Governments....................159

12.4 Spending and Revenue 159
State and Local Spending 159
Spending Choices 160
Government Revenue 161
Fees, Fines, and Grants 161
Taxes 161
Chapter 12 Review 163

Chapter 13 Georgia's Judicial System 165

13.1 Criminal Law 165
Criminal Courts and Cases 165
Criminal Court Proceedings 165
The Defendant and Attorneys 165
Pretrial Procedures 166
Criminal Trials 167
Criminal Court Appeals 168
State Criminal Cases in Federal Courts 168
13.2 Civil Law 169
Civil Cases 169
Civil Courts and Trials 170
Civil Jurisdictions 170
Civil Trials 170
Civil Appeals 170
State Civil Cases in Federal Courts 171
13.3 Georgia's Juvenile Justice System 172
Juvenile Courts 172
Jurisdiction 172
The Juvenile Court Process 172
Formal Hearings 173
Georgia's Seven Deadly Sins 173
Juveniles' Rights 174
Chapter 13 Review 175

Chapter 14 Responsible Citizenship and Political Process 177

14.1 Rights and Responsibilities of Citizens 177
Elections and Political Involvement 177
Secretary of State 178
The Role of Political Parties in Georgia's State Government 178
How Georgia Conducts Elections 179
14.2 Citizens and Financial Responsibility 180
Personal Money-Management Choices 180
Bankruptcy 181
Budgets 181
Saving and Spending 182
Savings Accounts and Investing 182
Reasons to Save 183
Chapter 14 Review 184

Practice Test 1 187

Practice Test 2 197

Index 209

PREFACE

Passing the 8th Grade CRCT in Georgia Studies will help students who are learning or reviewing material for the EOC Test. The materials in this book are based on the testing standards as published by the Georgia Department of Education.

This book contains several sections. These sections are as follows: 1) General information about the book; 2) A Diagnostic Test; 3) An Evaluation Chart; 4) Chapters that teach the concepts and skills that improve graduation readiness; 5) Two Practice Tests. Answers to the tests and exercises are in a separate manual. The answer manual also contains a Chart of Standards for teachers to make a more precise diagnosis of student needs and assignments.

We welcome comments and suggestions about the book. Please contact the author at

American Book Company
PO Box 2638
Woodstock, GA 30188-1383

Toll Free: 1 (888) 264-5877
Phone: (770) 928-2834
Fax: (770) 928-7483
web site: www.americanbookcompany.com

ABOUT THE AUTHORS

Lead Author:

Kindred Howard is a 1991 alumnus of the University of North Carolina at Chapel Hill, where he graduated with a B.S. in Criminal Justice and national honors in Political Science. In addition to two years as a probation & parole officer in North Carolina, he has served for over twelve years as a teacher and writer in the fields of religion and social studies. His experience includes teaching students at both the college and high school level, as well as speaking at numerous seminars and authoring several books on US history, American government, and economics. Mr. Howard is currently completing both a M.A. in history from Georgia State University and a M.A. in biblical studies from Asbury Theological Seminary. In addition to serving as Social Studies Coordinator for American Book Company, Mr. Howard is the president/CEO of KB Howard Writing, Consulting, and Administrative Services and lives in Kennesaw, Georgia, with his wife and three children.

Contributing Authors:

Ernest Everett Blevins earned a B.S. in Anthropology from the College of Charleston in 1993 and an MFA in Historic Preservation from Savannah College of Art & Design in 2001. Currently he is completing a thesis for a MA in Public History from the State University of West Georgia and has taken doctoral courses at Georgia State University in history and archaeology. His experience includes teaching at Georgia Highlands College and authoring several published articles on history, historic preservation, and genealogy. Mr. Blevins lives in Villa Rica, Georgia with his wife and three children.

Sandra Bassett is a 1979 graduate of West Georgia College where she graduated with a B.A. degree in History and a minor in Secondary Education. She received both a M.Ed. (1981) and an Ed.S.(1987) in Broad Field Social Studies from Georgia State University, and is currently working toward completion of an Ed.D. in Instructional Leadership from Argosy University. For over twelve years she has trained prospective teachers and taught middle school social studies in Georgia. Currently, she teaches at Rockdale Career Academy in Conyers. Mrs. Bassett is married, has three children, and lives in Stockbridge, Georgia.

Meredith Barr attended the University of West Georgia and graduated in 2002 with a B.A. in history and a minor in English. As a freelance writer, she has authored materials for several educational publications and has taught high school English for three years. Ms. Barr is currently enrolled in West Georgia's Graduate School of Education.

Joshua Williams is a 2006 alumnus of Georgia State University, where he graduated magna cum laude with B.A. in History with a minor in Political Science. He is currently completing a M.A. in Social Studies Education at Georgia State University.

Jeffery Wells graduated *cum laude* from the University of Georgia in 1996 with a B.A. in history. He later received his M.A. in history from Georgia College & State University in 2006. He has taught for over 10 years and is an assistant professor of history and coordinator of the history and education departments at Georgia Military College's Atlanta campus. His current responsibilities include teaching several courses in history and world civilizations. Mr. Wells has served on his county's Board of Education and is the author of a number of articles on Georgia history and society.

Michael B. Cassidy serves as assistant counsel at the New York State Governor's Office of Regulatory Reform. Before his appointment he served as a graduate fellow in government law and policy at the Government Law Center of Albany Law School. He is the author of several law journal articles on constitutional law, and serves as Editor-in-Chief of *Perspective*, a journal published by the New York State Bar Association. Mr. Cassidy graduated with a B.S. in Political Science from the State University of New York at Plattsburgh and a J.D. from Albany Law School, where he served as an Article Editor on the Albany Law Journal of Science and Technology.

Susan J.E. Illis graduated from Westminster College with an undergraduate degree in history and has an M.A. in history from the University of Pittsburgh. She has worked as an archivist for various universities, libraries, museums, and historical societies. In addition, she is the author of several published articles.

8th Grade Georgia Studies Diagnostic Test

The purpose of this diagnostic test is to measure your knowledge of Georgia social studies. This diagnostic test is based on the revised Social Studies Georgia Performance Standards and adheres to the sample question format provided by the Georgia Department of Education.

General Directions:

1 Read all directions carefully.

2 Read each question or sample. Then choose the best answer.

3 After taking the test, you or your instructor should score it using the evaluation chart following the test. This will enable you to determine your strengths and weaknesses.

1. W.E.B. DuBois' reaction to Booker T. Washington's "Atlanta Compromise" speech was SS8H7

   A. supportive because he viewed it as helpful to African-Americans.

   B. disturbed because he felt that Washington wanted to end segregation too soon.

   C. irritation because he believed Washington's views supported whites and segregation rather than blacks.

   D. confusion because Washington would not clearly state how he felt about segregation.

2. Who would have been most opposed to slavery? SS8H2

   A. Alexander Stephens

   B. John C. Calhoun

   C. James Oglethorpe

   D. A leader of the "malcontents"

3. The most common way governments raise revenue is through SS8E4

   A. fees. C. fines.

   B. grants. D. taxes.

4. A cotton farmer in Georgia just after World War Iwould have been most concerned about SS8H8

   A. Black Tuesday

   B. Populism

   C. the boll weevil

   D. the Cold War

There are four candidates who wish to run for governor of Georgia:

- Emily is an immigrant who has lived in Georgia for 16 years, is a member of the Democratic Party, and is 39 years old
- Paul is a native Georgian, is not a member of a political party, and is 52 years old.
- Sam is a registered Republican from Savannah who is 28 years old.
- Miguel was born in Macon, but his parents were illegal immigrants. He is a member of a third party and is 31 years old

5. Which of these candidates is ineligible to run for governor? SS8CG3

   A. Emily C. Sam

   B. Paul D. Miguel

6. What role has trade played in Georgia's history? SS8E2

   A. It has been important since the colony's founding.

   B. It did not become important until cotton became a profitable cash crop.

   C. It became important once farmers diversified crops during the Great Depression.

   D. It has become important in recent years as Georgia's business and industries have grown

7. Which of the following statements best describes the "Bourbon Triumvirate"? SS8H7

   A. Southern leaders who wanted to see the South's culture and economy return to the way they were before the Civil War.

   B. Republicans who governed in the South during Reconstruction

   C. Former slaves who served in the state legislature during Reconstruction

   D. Southern Democrats who dominated Georgia politics during the late 1800s

8. How did the county-unit system limit the political influence of African-American voters? SS8H12

   A. It made it illegal for blacks to vote.

   B. It granted blacks the right to vote without allowing them to run for office.

   C. It kept political power in the hands of heavily white rural areas rather than urban areas populated by African-Americans.

   D. It restricted blacks from voting in the Democratic primary.

9. What was significant about the gubernatorial election of 1946? SS8H11

   A. It resulted in a brief period in which two men claimed to be governor of Georgia at the same time.

   B. It marked the first time blacks could vote in a state election.

   C. It was the first time a governor was elected to a term of four years

   D. It marked the end of Herman Talmadge's political career.

10. The highest court in Georgia is the SS8CG4

    A. Georgia Supreme Court

    B. Georgia Court of Appeals

    C. Georgia Superior Court

    D. Georgia Probate Court

11. The first inhabitants of Georgia who lived between 10,000 and 13,000 years ago were known as what? SS8H1

    A. Colonists

    B. Paleo Indians

    C. Woodland peoples

    D. Mississippians

12. In what way did the French and Indian War most impact Georgia? SS8H3

    A. It added territory to the colony and increased security once Britain took control of Florida.

    B. It devastated much of the colony because of the fierce battles that took place.

    C. Many Georgians starved because both British and French troops took their crops to feed their armies.

    D. It had no effects on Georgia because all of the fighting took place in the North.

13. Georgia's current state constitution consists of SS8CG1

    A. twenty-two articles describing how county governments function.

    B. a declaration of state sovereignty and by-laws defining freedom.

    C. a preamble, state bill of rights, and articles defining the state's highest laws.

    D. articles establishing a governor, a unicameral legislature, and a superior court.

14. David wants to buy a new car. Since the car costs more than the amount of money he has, David pays for half the car out of his savings account and borrows the rest. David now has SS8E5

    A. budget. C. debt.

    B. constituency. D. bankruptcy.

15. The University of Georgia was SS8H5

    A. the first state-supported university chartered in the United States.

    B. founded prior to the American Revolution.

    C. based on other state-supported universities that were founded earlier.

    D. re-named Franklin College for a brief time during the Civil War.

16. Which of the following actions by farmers contributed to the Great Depression? SS8H8
   - A. overproduction
   - B. underproduction
   - C. crop diversification
   - D. segregation

17. Members of the General Assembly must follow the guidelines in the state constitution that govern the SS8CG2
   - A. legislative branch.
   - B. executive branch.
   - C. judicial branch.
   - D. municipal executives.

18. Philip believes that Gavin violated the conditions of their contract when he failed to finish painting Philip's house. If Philip takes Gavin to court it will be in SS8CG4
   - A. criminal court
   - B. civil court.
   - C. appeals court.
   - D. juvenile court.

19. Entrepreneurs start businesses in hopes of receiving more money for their goods or services than they spend to produce their goods/services. The extra money they make that is greater than the money they had to spend is called SS8E3
   - A. taxes.
   - B. expenditures.
   - C. profit.
   - D. credit.

20. During the trustee period, Georgians were most concerned about SS8H2
   - A. acts passed by Parliament that interfered with colonists' liberties.
   - B. slaves escaping to northern states.
   - C. the Spanish threat in Florida.
   - D. the effects of the Yazoo Land Fraud.

21. President Roosevelt promoted a policy of Lend-Lease prior to Pearl Harbor because SS8H9
   - A. he did not trust either side fighting in Europe.
   - B. he wanted to help those fighting German aggression despite public opposition to the war.
   - C. he still believed Germany could become a US ally.
   - D. he feared most US citizens wanted a war.

22. Georgia was one of the first states to ratify the US Constitution because SS8H4
   - A. most Georgians did not want a strong central government.
   - B. Georgia merchants in Savannah did not want to establish overseas trade too quickly.
   - C. it was one of the last colonies to support the Continental Congress and needed to show the rest of the states that it was devoted to the new government.
   - D. it needed a central government that could provide military protection and establish trade.

23. How did African-Americans and many progressive whites react to the adoption of the above flag in 1956? SS8H11
    A. They were offended by it and saw it as an attempt to maintain Georgia's segregated past.
    B. They were not pleased but did not see it as important in light of other matters.
    C. They supported it as a positive change.
    D. They were indifferent because they saw it as having little to do with race.

24. The effect of Georgia's climate on the state's development can BEST be described as SS8G1
    A. positive because of its mild temperatures and distinctive seasons.
    B. negative because of the harsh winters and unpredictable summers.
    C. limited because modern technology makes climate unimportant.
    D. positive because it discourages population increase.

25. What role do committees play in the legislative process? SS8CG2
    A. They directly decide what bills become laws.
    B. They decide what bills passed by the General Assembly actually go to the governor.
    C. They elect leaders like the house speaker and the lieutenant governor.
    D. They review proposed bills and make recommendations to the General Assembly.

26. Georgia's position on slavery in new territories during the mid-1800s was clearly stated in the SS8H6
    - A. Dred Scott decision.
    - B. New South.
    - C. Atlanta Compromise.
    - D. Georgia Platform.

27. Which of the following was LEAST impacted by William Hartsfield? SS8H10
    - A. Atlanta's politics
    - B. Atlanta's race relations
    - C. Atlanta's airport
    - D. Atlanta's professional sports teams

28. In what ways do Hartsfield-Jackson International Airport, I-85, and the port at Savannah impact Georgia's economy? SS8G2
    - A. They allow imports to arrive and reach Georgians while keeping domestic products at home.
    - B. They make Georgia accessible to people from all over the world, help provide jobs for state citizens, and allow the state to import and export products efficiently.
    - C. They provide jobs for Georgians while discouraging foreign economic competition
    - D. They have very little impact because they simply provide modes of transportation.

29. Their willingness to use new methods in order to spread their faith and establish churches throughout the Georgia frontier enabled which of the following groups to impact Georgia after the revolutionary war? SS8H5
    - A. Mormons and Catholics
    - B. Presbyterians and Anglicans
    - C. Jews and Salzburgers
    - D. Baptists and Methodists

30. How many county governments are there in Georgia, and how are they usually governed? SS8CG5
    - A. 10 – governed by district mayors
    - B. 150 – governed by appointed commissioners
    - C. 159 – governed by elected commissioners
    - D. 180 – governed by elected boards

31. A fifteen-year-old caught stealing beer from a convenience store is likely to have his/her case heard in SS8CG6
    - A. juvenile court.
    - B. superior court.
    - C. civil court.
    - D. probate court.

32. Georgia was SS8H3
    - A. the first colony to call for rebellion against the British.
    - B. one of the first colonies to send delegates to the Continental Congress.
    - C. the only colony not to sign the Declaration of Independence.
    - D. slower than most colonies to break with England.

33. During the Great Depression, the federal government paid farmers subsidies in an effort to SS8H8
    - A. end overproduction.
    - B. increase cotton production.
    - C. exterminate the boll weevil.
    - D. buy out farms.

34. Which of the following individuals would have been LEAST likely to support Mayor William Hartsfield? SS8H10
    - A. an African-American business leader
    - B. a white business leader
    - C. a segregationist
    - D. an advocate of air travel

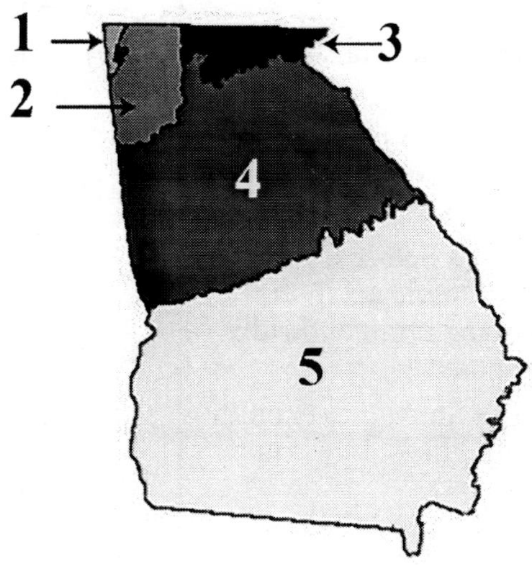

35. Look at the map above. What number corresponds to the most populated region in Georgia? SS8G1

A. 1
B. 2
C. 3
D. 4

36. Which of the following accurately describes Benjamin Mays? SS8H11

A. He was a strong influence on Martin Luther King, Jr.
B. He was the first black mayor of Atlanta.
C. He organized the first student sit-ins of the civil rights movement.
D. He played a major role in bringing the 1996 Olympics to Atlanta.

37. Which of the following MOST accurately describes Jimmy Carter? SS8H12

A. He was the first Republican in Georgia to be elected governor after Reconstruction.
B. He is remembered by many as a progressive governor and unsuccessful president.
C. He was often criticized for being too militaristic with the Soviets and for missing opportunities for peace in the Middle East.
D. He served two terms as president before retiring to Georgia.

38. Hernando de Soto's expedition into Georgia had what effect on Native Americans? SS8H1
    A. none because Native Americans had already left the region
    B. very little because de Soto feared the natives and stuck to routes away from Native American lands.
    C. devestating because de Soto's forces often killed Native Americans in violent confrontations and brought deadly diseases like smallpox
    D. beneficial because de Soto quickly built lasting alliances with the Native Americans he encountered.

39. Which of the following crops was MOST profitable for Georgia in the 1700s? SS8E1
    A. peanuts
    B. silk
    C. rice
    D. cotton

40. An offense that falls under Georgia's "Seven Deadly Sins" is any crime for which a juvenile may be SS8CG4
    A. executed.
    B. deported.
    C. confined in a Youth Detention Center.
    D. tried in the adult judicial system.

41. What impact did the 1996 Olympic Games have on Georgia? SS8E2
    A. They made the region world-known and boosted economic development.
    B. They left the city in financial distress after having to pay for a huge event.
    C. They helped the economy only for a short time.
    D. They benefited Atlanta but did little to help the rest of the state.

42. Which of the following was an effect of the Great Depression in Georgia? SS8H8
    A. More state citizens moved to the cities.
    B. More people left the cities for rural areas.
    C. Cotton prices rose.
    D. Public education thrived as people left the farms to get an education.

43. African-Americans were MOST inspired to fight in the Civil War after SS8H6
    A. the South fired on Fort Sumter.
    B. Confederate leaders adopted the Georgia Platform.
    C. the passage of the Kansas –Nebraska Act.
    D. Lincoln issued the Emancipation Proclamation.

44. The Sibley Commission was formed for the purpose of SS8H11
    A. protecting private property rights.
    B. preventing school desegregation.
    C. studying the effects of integration on the University of Georgia.
    D. implementing school desegregation as peacefully as possible.

45. Which of the following is a responsibility of the executive branch of state government? SS8CG3
    A. introducing bills to raise revenue
    B. declaring laws passed by the General Assembly unconstitutional
    C. establishing new towns and cities in Georgia
    D. overseeing the enforcement of state agricultural policies

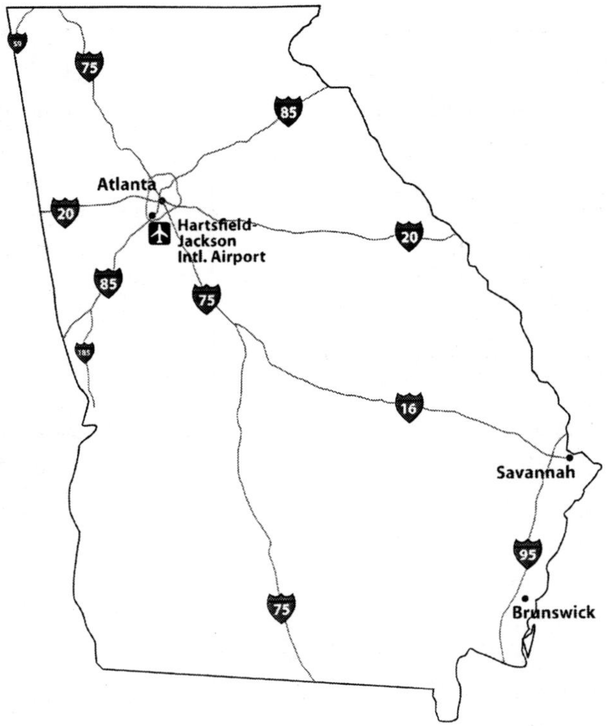

46. Look at the map above. Someone wishing to ship pick-up trucks and farm equipment across the Atlantic to Africa would MOST LIKELY ship the cargo from SS8G2
    A. Hartsfield-Jackson International Airport.
    B. North I-75.
    C. Atlanta.
    D. Brunswick.

47. A naval officer commanding a ship at war with the Japanese during World War II would have been MOST indebted to SS8H9
    A. Carl Vinson.
    B. Tom Watson.
    C. Eugene Talmadge.
    D. William Hartsfield.

48. A progressive Georgian in the 1940s who wanted to end the poll tax and see African-Americans treated equally would have supported which governor? SS8H10
    A. Eugene Talmadge
    B. Ellis Arnall
    C. Herman Talmadge
    D. Lester Maddox

49. How did Georgia's representatives to the Constitutional Convention feel about the slave trade? SS8H4
   A. They hated it because it violated people's freedom.
   B. They supported it because Georgia's plantation economy needed slaves.
   C. They did not care either way because they were not slave owners.
   D. They were upset that there was no slave trade and passed an amendment requiring one to start shortly after the convention.

50. The Yazoo Act upset many Georgians because it resulted in SS8H5
   A. the unfair treatment of Native Americans in northern Georgia.
   B. a scandalous land deal involving much of western Georgia.
   C. interference from the federal government during the Great Depression.
   D. restrictions on slavery in new territories out west.

51. Which of the following is an example of a state expenditure? SS8E4
   A. new highways
   B. taxes
   C. tolls
   D. court ordered fines

52. Who were the Highland Scots? SS8H2
   A. hired soldiers fought for the British during the Revolutionary War
   B. Europeans who fought for the colonies during the Revolutionary War
   C. Scot settlers who opposed Oglethorpe and formed a band known as the "malcontents"
   D. Scotsmen who settled in Georgia during the colonial period

53. Which of the following is true regarding Georgia's role during World War I? SS8H7
   A. Very few Georgians volunteered to fight in the war.
   B. Georgia contributed textiles and agricultural products that helped the war effort.
   C. The war ended before Georgians could get involved.
   D. Most Georgians who fought had to be trained elsewhere due to Georgia's lack of military facilities.

54. Which two men made history by becoming the first African-Americans to succeed one another as mayor of a major US city? SS8H11
   A. Alonzo Herndon and Maynard Jackson
   B. Maynard Jackson and Andrew Young
   C. Andrew Young and Shirley Franklin
   D. William Hartsfield and Maynard Jackson

55. Which of the following MOST affects your ability to borrow money and get a good interest rate on loans? SS8E5
   A. your political party
   B. whether or not you are an entrepreneur
   C. how often you vote
   D. your credit score

56. Georgia was more hesitant than the other colonies to break with Great Britain because SS8H3
   A. Georgians liked King George and thought Parliament's laws were fair.
   B. it was one of the few colonies where most people supported the Stamp Act.
   C. the colony was very dependent on Great Britain for protection and trade.
   D. Georgia had been attacked by other British colonies and did not yet trust them.

57. The success of people like "Bo" Callaway, Newt Gingrich, and Sonny Perdue is evidence of SS8H12
    A. the rise of the two-party system in Georgia.
    B. the survival of the "solid South."
    C. the role played by entrepreneurs in Georgia.
    D. aAdvantages of the white primary.

58. Which of the following resulted from Georgia's "cotton kingdom"? SS8H5
    A. textiles grew in importance
    B. trade decreased
    C. slavery became less important to the state
    D. the number of plantation owners decreased

59. What was the impact of Sherman's "march to the sea"? SS8H6
    A. It convinced the South that they could win the war.
    B. It convinced President Lincoln to issue the Emancipation Proclamation.
    C. It left a path of destruction from Atlanta to Savannah that crippled the Confederacy.
    D. It forced Robert E. Lee to evacuate Georgia

60. The Paleos, Woodland Peoples, and Mississippians were
    A. Southerners who fought for the Confederacy.
    B. Southerners who supported the Union.
    C. Native Americans who lived in Georgia before Europeans arrived.
    D. settlers who lived in the Yazoo territory.

Evaluation Chart for Georgia Studies Diagnostic Test

Directions: On the following chart, circle the question numbers that you answered incorrectly, and evaluate the results. These questions are based on the *standards and benchmarks published by the Georgia Department of Education.* Then turn to the appropriate chapters, read the explanations, and complete the exercises. Review other chapters as needed. Finally, complete the Practice test(s) to assess your progress and further prepare you for the **Georgia 8th Grade CRCT in Georgia Studies**.

Note: Some question numbers will appear under multiple chapters because those questions require demonstration of multiple skills.

Chapter	Diagnostic Test Question(s)
Chapter 1: Native American Cultures and Europeans	38, 60
Chapter 2: Great Britain and Colonial Georgia	2, 20, 39, 52
Chapter 3: The American Revolution and Georgia	12, 22, 32, 49, 56
Chapter 4: Antebellum Georgia	15, 26, 29, 50, 58
Chapter 5: Civil War and Reconstruction	43, 59
Chapter 6: From Reconstruction to WWI	1, 7, 53
Chapter 7: Georgia Between the Wars	4, 8, 33, 42
Chapter 8: World War II	21, 47
Chapter 9: Postwar Economic, Political, and Social Change	9, 23, 27, 34, 36, 44, 48
Chapter 10: Georgia's Modern Age	6, 8, 19, 28, 37, 41, 46, 54, 57
Chapter 11: Georgia's Geography	24, 35
Chapter 12: Georgia's Government	3, 5, 10, 13, 17, 25, 30, 45, 51
Chapter 13: Georgia's Judicial System	10, 18, 31, 40
Chapter 14: Responsible Citizenship and Political Process	14, 55

Chapter 1
Native American Cultures and the First Europeans

This chapter covers the following Georgia standard(s).

SS8H1	The student will evaluate the development of Native American cultures and the impact of European exploration and settlement on the Native American cultures in Georgia.

1.1 Native American Cultures

Paleo Indians

The first people to live in what is today Georgia were **Native Americans** (original inhabitants of the Americas and their ancestors) known as the **Paleo Indians**. *Paleo* means "ancient" or "very old." These people lived some 10,000 to 13,000 years ago during the period 11,000 – 8,000 BC. Archaeologists (scientists who study the remains of past civilizations) have found artifacts that suggest the Paleo Indians relied heavily on the Savannah, Ocmulgee, and Flint rivers for survival. In addition to being a source of food and nourishment, these rivers were also an important means of travel. The Paleo Indians were a *migratory* people, meaning that they moved often. Migration was necessary because the Paleo Indians depended on hunting and gathering for food. Living in groups of roughly 25 to 50 people, these communities would move to gather nuts and berries, as well as to hunt large game like bison, mastodons, and mammoths (mastodons and mammoths are extinct today). Their weapons included spears with stone points and something known as the *atlatl.* The atlatl was basically a "dart thrower" which allowed hunters to kill their prey from a safe distance rather than getting too close and risking injury or death. Since farming was not yet developed, Paleo Indians had to follow the animals they hunted in order to survive. Once a community used up its food supply and the game moved on, the group packed up and moved as well.

Archaic Peoples

Next came the **Archaic peoples**. The Archaic Period lasted from roughly 8,000 – 1,000 BC and is divided into three subperiods (the early, middle, and late Archaic Periods), each defined by significant developments in the Archaic peoples' way of life. The *early Archaic peoples* were also hunters and gatherers, although they tended to hunt smaller game because many of the larger animals had become extinct. They developed more advanced stone knives and scrapers for cutting and carving, better spears with smaller points for hunting, and stone tools. They began using fire to cook food and stay warm and lived in small, simple houses. In addition, evidence suggests that people of this period also traded such things as tools, food, rocks, and other supplies. Although they likely moved less than the Paleo Indians, early Archaic peoples were still migratory, moving from time to time to find the food they needed.

The *middle Archaic Period* featured a significant change in *climate* (the kind of weather an area tends to have over a long period of time). Temperatures became warmer and the air drier. As a result, seasonal changes were not as harsh and middle Archaic peoples could stay in one place for longer periods of time. The change in climate also meant that water levels went down, allowing middle Archaic peoples to rely more on shellfish, like mussels and clams, as a source of food. In addition, Archaic hunters developed special weights for their spears which allowed them to throw their weapons farther and kill game more easily. Since hunters could now kill more kinds of game, people could remain in areas for longer periods and did not have to move as much to find food.

Evidence suggests that by the *late Archaic Period*, people began settling down in more permanent communities. These communities grew over time and introduced new social standards. Archaic peoples established most of these settlements close to water sources such as the Savannah River because they offered fresh water for drinking and hygiene, as well as abundant food sources like fish and shellfish (shellfish actually served as the Archaic peoples' main source of food during this time). Late Archaic peoples developed **horticulture** (the science of growing plants and trees) and began growing their own food. They also used pottery and soapstone vessels to store and cook food and more advanced weapons and tools such as the stone *grooved axe* (a stone axe head mounted on a wooden handle).

THE WOODLAND PEOPLES

Village layout

The **Woodland peoples** lived from 1000 BC – 1000 AD and developed more advanced villages built in circular arrangements of up to twenty houses. These houses surrounded an open plaza where people of the village often gathered. It was during this period that communities began banding together to form **tribes** (a group of people who share a common identity due to their culture, ancestry, etc.) Woodland peoples developed more advanced and decorative ceramic cooking vessels and pottery as well. A mixture of sand and grit made pottery sturdier and meant it lasted longer. Woodland peoples also formed a trading network that stretched from the Gulf Coast to what is today the Midwest United States. They traded things like shells for exotic stones, minerals, and copper. Horticulture improved, allowing the Woodland peoples to introduce corn, squash, and wild greens as important crops. Meanwhile, fishing and gathering nuts and berries remained important sources of food, while hunting became easier thanks to a new weapon: the *bow and arrow.*

Woodland peoples also practiced rituals and ceremonies. They constructed small, dome-shaped earthen **mounds** which functioned as stages for ceremonies and burial sites. Archaeologists have found pipes, tools, and jewelry made of copper and stone at such sites, suggesting that these people believed in an afterlife where the dead would still need their possessions.

Mound

The development of fortified settlements during the Woodland period suggests that different tribes went to war with each other from time to time and felt the need to protect themselves from enemy attacks. In addition, relationships with outsiders seemed to drop off during this period. Many archaeologists believe that trade decreased because there is less evidence of contact between Woodland peoples and communities outside of Georgia from this time period.

Rocks laid in eagle shape

THE MISSISSIPPIANS

Mississippian village

The **Mississippian Period** lasted from 800 –1600 AD and was the last period in Native American history before European explorers arrived. Like their predecessors, the Mississippians tended to rely on and live near rivers. Their houses were often rectangular or circular pole structures made of woven saplings and cane. The rooftops were often covered with sun-baked clay, daub, or thatch, with a hole left in the middle of each hut to allow smoke from indoor fireplaces to escape. Smaller Mississippian villages consisted of only 100 or so people, but some settlements grew to include thousands! Villages were usually divided into three sections: The *central plaza*, which served as the main meeting place and center for religious ceremonies; the *residential zone* where people lived; and the *defensive zone*, which was surrounded by a palisade (defensive wall) and was designed to keep out enemies and dangerous animals. The Mississippians also developed a *class structure.* In other words, some people were identified as "elites" (chiefs/upper class) and were given larger houses, special clothes and jewelry, and finer foods than everyone else. Others were viewed as members of a lower class made up of farmers, craftsmen, warriors and laborers. As Mississippian farmers came to better understand horticulture, they grew a large variety of crops. Corn, beans, squash, and pumpkins all became more common as Mississippians tended to grow most of their own food. With the exception of deer, any game they hunted tended to be small (rabbits, squirrels, reptiles, etc.) Meanwhile, the Mississippians also developed artistic costumes, copper jewelry, blades, pipes, stone axes, digging sticks, bone hoes, and even tattoos.

Etowah Indian Mounds

Mississippians continued the practice of constructing **mounds**—some of which were as tall as 100 feet high! They served as bases of chieftains' houses, stages for ceremonies, and/or burial sites. *Etowah Indian Mounds* in Cartersville, Georgia is an example of just such a site.

The end of the Mississippian period came between 1350 and 1600 AD, when many of the Mississippians mysteriously left their villages. Why did they leave? Historians are not exactly sure. It remains one of history's unanswered questions. What is certain is that the arrival of Europeans greatly changed the course of Native Americans in the region that later became Georgia.

Practice 1.1 Native American Cultures

1. Who were the earliest known people to live in what is today Georgia?

   A. Paleo Indians
   B. Archaic peoples
   C. Woodland peoples
   D. Mississippians

2. What impact did the development of *horticulture* have on pre-European Native American peoples?

   A. It allowed them to hunt more easily.
   B. It made shellfish their most important source of food.
   C. It led to better farming so that they did not have to move around so much.
   D. It made pottery more durable and useful.

3. How were *mounds* important to early Native American peoples in what is today Georgia? What kind of evidence has been found to support this conclusion?

1.2 The Europeans Arrive

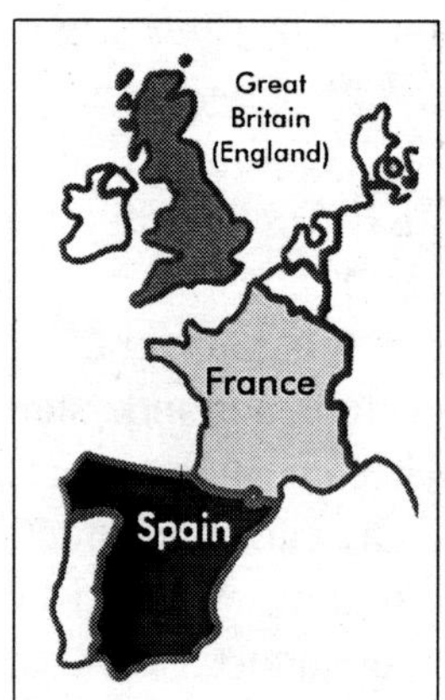

European explorers came to the "New World" of the Americas for several reasons. Mostly, they came for **gold, glory, and God**! In other words, some came to get rich, believing the Americas to have abundant resources, including gold. Some came to win glory and honor back home as courageous explorers and national heroes. Still others came as missionaries to spread the Christian religion to Native Americans. Of all the European nations that set up colonies in the Americas, Spain, England, and France were the most powerful. Of these three, **Spain** was the first to set foot in modern day Georgia.

SPANISH EXPLORATION OF GEORGIA

HERNANDO DE SOTO

Hernando de Soto

During the first half of the sixteenth century, Spanish *conquistadors* (conquerors) like Hernando Cortes and Francisco Pizzaro successfully conquered the Aztecs of modern-day Mexico and the Incas of modern-day Peru. (The Aztecs and Incas were powerful Native American tribes that ruled these regions before the Spanish arrived.) In the process, these European conquerors won glory, fame, and great riches. Their accomplishments inspired other Spanish explorers to seek such glory and wealth as well. In 1539, **Hernando de Soto** landed in North America. After spending the winter in what is now Florida, he and his party of more than 600 men crossed over into what we know as Georgia. De Soto hoped to gain glory and riches for both himself and his country. More specifically, he hoped to find lots of gold! He and his men entered Georgia near what is today Albany in 1540 and journeyed northward. Eventually, de Soto's party made its way into the Carolinas, Tennessee, and Alabama. Their interactions with Native Americans marked the first time that these native peoples had ever seen white men or horses.

Some of the encounters between de Soto and the Native Americans were peaceful. Others, however, were violent. Although the Spaniards were often outnumbered, they had more advanced weapons, like guns and crossbows. During one battle between the Spanish and Native Americans in Alabama, over 11,000 Native Americans and 70 Spaniards were killed. More deadly for the Native Americans, however, were **diseases** like smallpox, measles, and influenza that the Europeans brought with them. Since Native Americans had never been exposed to these diseases before, their immune systems had no resistance. As a result, large numbers of Native Americans (some historians estimate almost half the population) died of diseases in addition to the thousands killed by de Soto's soldiers.

DeSoto meets Native Americans

In the end, de Soto's expedition failed. He died somewhere along the Mississippi River in 1542, never having found his abundant gold. He did, however, leave a harsh mark on the Native American inhabitants he came in contact with and opened the door for future explorers who set their sights on Georgia.

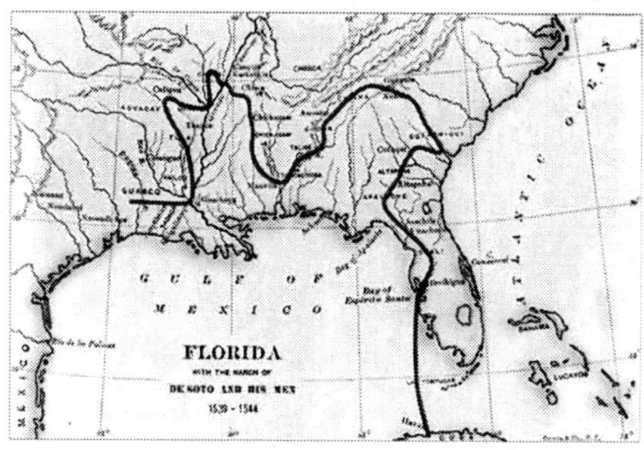

Map of DeSoto's Travels

Spanish Missions

In 1564, news reached Spain that the French were trying to colonize areas in modern-day South Carolina and Florida. Spain considered this a threat and sent Pedro Menendez de Avilles, an outstanding soldier and sailor, to claim and hold "Spanish territory." After establishing a **colony** in St. Augustine, Menendez and other settlers traveled to St. Catherines Island off of the coast of Georgia in 1566. A *colony* is simply a settlement that, although in a new land, is still considered part of the country that established it.

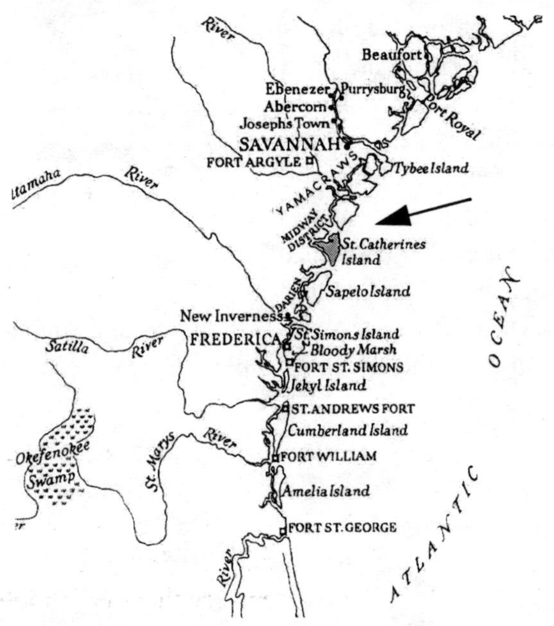

Once on St. Catherines, the Spansh named the area **Guale** after the local Native American chief with whom Menendez struck up a friendship. There, the Spanish established their first **mission**, known as *Santa Catalina*. Spanish missions were settlements established to convert Native Americans to Christianity through the Catholic church. Unfortunately for Spain, however, their earliest efforts to establish successful missions did not go well. One priest, Pedro Martinez, was even killed by hostile Native Americans. However, with backing from King Philip II, Spain eventually set up additional missions along Georgia's barrier islands.

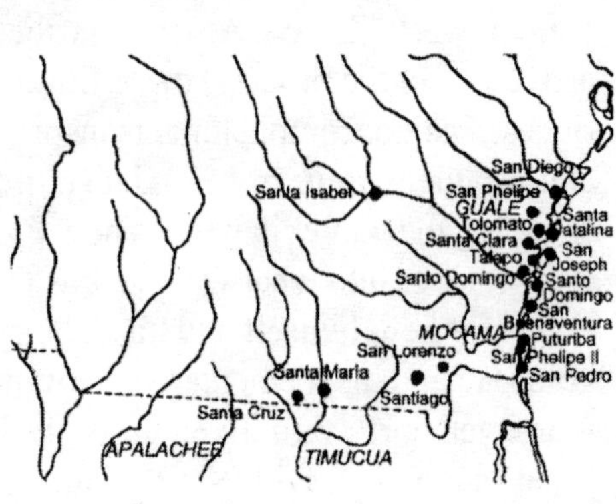

Spanish names for Settlements

The missions were run by *friars* (Catholic priests dedicated to lives of poverty, service, and hard work) who labored to "civilize" and educate Native Americans in the ways of Spain, as well as to convert them to Christianity. Technically, local chiefs ruled over the friars. In reality, however, the friars usually acted like they were in charge. Still, some Native American chiefs gladly welcomed the Spanish missionaries because they often showered the chiefs with expensive gifts from Europe.

Ruins of Spanish Mission, St. Mary's, GA
Library of Congress

Finally, however, a violent conflict known as the **Juanillo Revolt** did occur in 1597. A Native American named Juanillo was greatly angered when a Spanish priest appointed another man to be the local chief. As a result, Juanillo and his band of supporters attacked the Spanish in Guale, killing a number of friars. The Spanish then killed Juanillo and many of his followers. After the rebellion, the Spanish abandoned the missions for a time. By 1603, however, they had restored them and the missions flourished once again. Guale continued to be important to the Spanish because it provided food for Florida and Native American labor for farming, building roads, and constructing military defenses in St. Augustine. By 1667, Spain had established 70 missions and 40 missionaries in Georgia.

THE END OF THE SPANISH MISSIONS

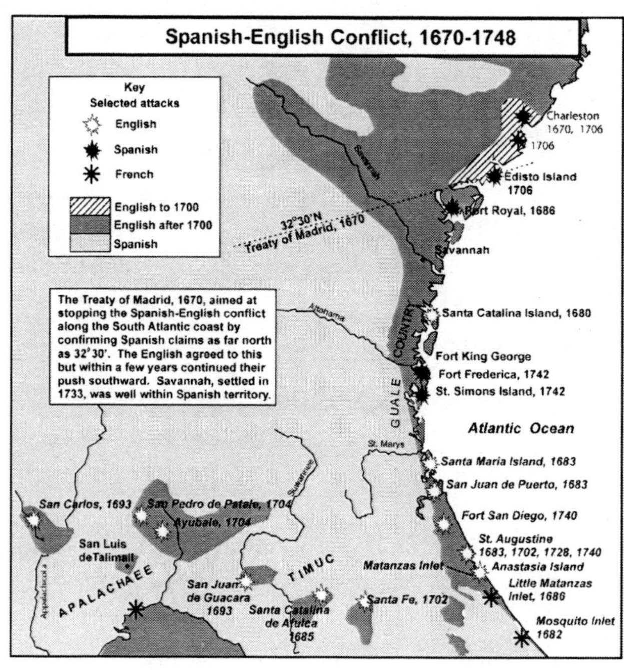

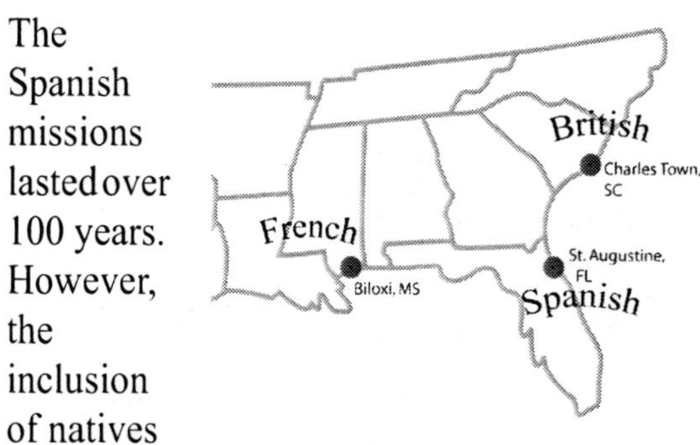

The Spanish missions lasted over 100 years. However, the inclusion of natives into Spanish colonial society harmed the Native American population. War and diseases introduced by the Europeans killed many. Also, both **France** and **Great Britain** became more threatening to the Spanish in Georgia during this time. In 1607, Britain established a colony at Jamestown, Virginia which occasionally aided English seaman who launched raids against Spanish ships. In 1670, the British moved even closer when they founded Charles Town (today Charles Town is called Charleston) on the coast of what is today South Carolina. Meanwhile, the French moved further east into what is modern-day Alabama and began to push their way into territory the Spanish felt belonged to them. Finally, in 1686, following attacks by Native Americans and pirate raids along the shores of Guale (both of which the British encouraged), the Spanish abandoned the missions along the Georgia coast for safer territory farther south. Although the Spanish and other European powers continued to have military skirmishes in the area for years to come, the age of the Spanish missions and Spain's strongest period of influence in Georgia was over. It wasn't long, however, before other European settlers made their presence felt in the region.

Practice 1.2 The Europeans Arrive

1. Who was the first Spanish explorer to enter Georgia in search of gold and glory?

   A. Juanillio
   B. Hernando de Soto
   C. Pedro Martinez
   D. Santa Catalina

2. What purpose were the Spanish missions supposed to fulfill?

   A. look for gold
   B. launch military raids against other colonies
   C. fight Native Americans
   D. civilize Native Americans and convert them to Christianity

3. How did the presence of British and French colonies affect the Spanish missions in Georgia?

Chapter 1 Review

Key People, Terms, and Concepts

Native Americans
Paleo Indians
Archaic peoples
horticulture
Woodland peoples
tribes
mounds
Mississippian Period
gold, glory, and God
Spain
Hernando de Soto
diseases
colony
Guale
mission
Juanillio Revolt
France and Great Britain

Multiple Choice

1. Which statement **best** describes the *Paleo Indians*?
   A. They were farmers.
   B. They hunted mostly small game, like rabbits.
   C. They built lots of mounds.
   D. They were a migratory people.

2. Which period in Native American history included a significant change in climate and the development of *horticulture*?
   A. Paleo Period
   B. Archaic Period
   C. Woodland Period
   D. Mississippian Period

3. The last Native Americans to live in what is today Georgia before the arrival of any European explorers were
   A. the Paleo Indians.
   B. the Archaic peoples.
   C. the Mississippians.
   D. the Woodland peoples.

4. Which of the following have contributed a great deal to what we know about pre-European Native American cultures?
   A. conquistadores B. friars C. archaeologists D. atlatls

5. The first Europeans to explore Georgia were from which country?
   A. Spain B. Great Britain C. France D. Mexico

6. Hernando de Soto can **best** be described by which of the following statements?
   A. He was a Spanish missionary who established missions along Georgia's barrier islands.
   B. He was the first Spanish explorer to enter Georgia in search of gold and glory.
   C. He was a conquistador who defeated the Aztecs in Mexico and inspired future Spaniards to explore places like Georgia.
   D. He established a Spanish colony on St. Catherines island that he named "Guale."

7. Which of the following statements **best** describes how Spain felt about French and British colonies in the southeast?
   A. They were glad to have other Europeans in the area to help them fight the Native Americans.
   B. They were nervous but cooperated with the British and French to try and convert the natives to Christianity.
   C. They were angry and felt defensive because the British and French were seen as a threat.
   D. They didn't care because they were too busy taking care of their missions.

8. Which of the following statements **best** describes the Spanish presence in Georgia after 1686?
   A. It grew in order to resist the French and British.
   B. For the most part, there wasn't one because the Spanish had abandoned their missions and moved farther south.
   C. It was stable for another 100 years.
   D. The Spanish remained but fell under the authority of British rule.

Chapter 2
Great Britain and Colonial Georgia

This chapter covers the following Georgia standard(s).

SS8H2	The student will analyze the colonial period of Georgia's history.

2.1 THE FOUNDING OF BRITISH GEORGIA

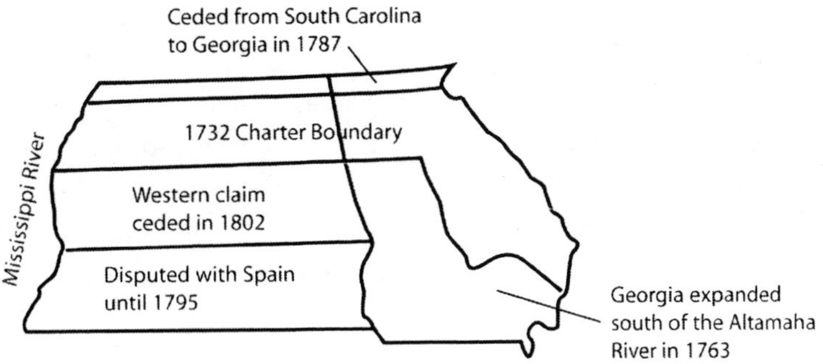

Great Britain claimed the territory we know as Georgia as early as the 1660s. However, it was not until 1717 that it approved its first colony in the region. As it turned out, the original colony never came to pass because it lacked support. Eventually, however, the British did establish a permanent settlement thanks mostly to the vision and leadership of one man.

JAMES OGLETHORPE AND THE CHARTER OF 1732

James Oglethorpe

James Oglethorpe was born in 1695 in England. In 1722, voters elected him to Parliament (England's legislative body) and he eventually became chairman of a committee examining conditions in British jails. Oglethorpe was greatly disturbed that the jails were dirty, full of disease, and prisoners were usually treated harshly. He was also concerned that many of the prisoners were **debtors**. In other words, they were in jail only because they owed people money. Since one of his friends had also died while imprisoned as a debtor, Oglethorpe felt compelled to fight for the release of such prisoners.

Debtor's prison

REASONS FOR FOUNDING GEORGIA

King George II

Oglethorpe came up with a plan he was sure would benefit both Great Britain and English debtors. He asked the British crown to award a *charter* that would allow his group of 21 men to set up a colony south of the Carolinas. (A charter was a written document signed by the king that granted certain rights. In this case, it allowed Oglethorpe's group to establish a colony). Oglethorpe and his associates envisioned this colony serving several purposes. For one, they saw it helping Great Britain **economically**. They convinced King George II that the colony could produce goods like silk, cotton dyes, and wine that England normally had to import from other countries. Second, Oglethorpe believed the colony would provide **protection** against the Spanish. Great Britain already had colonies in Virginia and the Carolinas, but it had no line of defense between these territories and their Spanish rivals in Florida. Since Spain still claimed much of the southern coast as its own, the threat of attack was always a concern in places like Charles Town. Oglethorpe argued convincingly that a colony between the Carolinas and Florida would help ensure the safety of British colonists and economic interests. Third, Oglethorpe wanted the new colony to serve a **charitable** purpose. He knew that it would be easier to win the release of debtors in England if they had somewhere to go to find work and land after gaining their freedom. Oglethorpe hoped his colony would provide such a place. Many people in England supported the idea of a colony for the very reasons Oglethorpe's group proposed. Some also supported it because of **religious** reasons. They saw it as a great opportunity to send Protestant missionaries to the region to convert the Native Americans. Although Spanish missionaries had converted many Native Americans to Catholicism, most people in England were Protestant and believed that the Native Americans needed to learn and follow Protestant teachings about Christianity.

THE CHARTER OF 1732

Finally, King George II awarded Oglethorpe and his associates their charter. The **Charter of 1732** officially sanctioned the founding of *Georgia* (named in honor of the king). It also established the conditions under which the colony would be established. Under this charter, Georgia would be ruled by a group of **trustees** for 21 years. (Trustees are people who have a responsibility on behalf of others.) After that, it would be ruled directly by the King through a royal governor. Under the charter:

- ***No trustee could own land or hold office.*** Such limitations prevented leadership from becoming corrupt and kept the colony from becoming a region of large plantations. Oglethorpe and his associates wanted the colony to be mostly for small farmers and to provide a settlement for debtors who otherwise would not have land or work in England.
- ***No Catholics***. In the 1700s, nations identified religion with nationality as much as faith. Protestant nations and Catholic nations seldom got along. Since England was Protestant, it did not want Catholics in Georgia who might cooperate with Catholic Spain.
- ***No Lawyers***. The leaders wanted the colonists to learn to settle disputes among themselves rather than in court. They reasoned that if there were no lawyers, people would have to work things out amongst themselves.
- ***A Common Council***. The council consisted of 15 men, at least eight of which had to be present for decisions to be made. In reality, though, Oglethorpe was seen as the true leader of the colony.

Savannah, Tomochichi, and Mary Musgrove

After interviewing applicants for the trip, the trustees chose people to settle Georgia. Those who were selected were promised 50 acres of land, tools to work the land, and enough food to get them through the first year. Settlers also had to agree to abide by certain rules.

- Each man had to promise to defend the colony against hostile enemies.
- Settlers could not sell the land awarded them by the charter, nor could they borrow money against it. They could, however, pass it on to a male heir.
- Colonists had to use a certain portion of their land to grow mulberry trees. The trustees believed that silkworms would eat the leaves of these trees and that their cocoons could be used to produce silk.
- Each colonist had to agree to obey all regulations put in place by the trustees.

Mary Musgrove

Tomochichi

Despite Oglethorpe's original intentions, no debtors were chosen for the trip. In fact, very few people who had been in prison ever made it to Georgia. Finally, on November 17, 1732, those who were chosen departed from England aboard the ship *Ann.* On January 13, 1733, they arrived in South Carolina. While the others stayed in port, Oglethorpe searched for a place to settle. The land he chose was seventeen miles south of the Savannah River at a place called *Yamacraw Bluff.* Oglethorpe chose it because there was access to fresh water and because its high ground made it easy to defend from potential enemies. It was also close to South Carolina and a relatively safe distance from Spanish settlements further south. Oglethorpe was able to gain this territory peacefully in large thanks to John and **Mary Musgrove**. The Musgroves acted as interpreters and mediators between Oglethorpe and the chief of the Yamacraw tribe, **Tomochichi**. Mary's role was particularly important because she was part Native American and she alone served as the colony's interpreter after John died in 1735. Meanwhile, Tomochichi and Oglethorpe quickly developed a friendship. In fact, the chief even accompanied Oglethorpe on one of his trips to England. Thanks to the trust between these two men, Great Britain secured the site at Yamacraw Bluff and named it **Savannah**.

Savannah

Layout of early Savannah

Oglethorpe and his associates based the blueprints for Savannah (blueprints are plans of how to design a building, town, etc.) on plans designed by Oglethorpe's friend who had died in prison, Robert Castell. They centered the town around a series of squares (many of which remain today). On the north and south sides of each square were twenty lots. Each square was divided into blocks, or *tithings*, measuring 60 × 90 feet. Each male settler received five acres of land as a garden plot on the edge of town and another 45 acres of land in the country for farming. The settlers also built Fort Argyle on the Ogeeche River and Fort Thunderbolt along Augustine Creek to protect the colony from attacks by hostile natives and/or the Spanish.

Practice 2.1 The Founding of British Georgia

1. Which of the following men wanted to establish a colony for debtors and became the first leader of Georgia?
   A. Robert Castell
   B. King George II
   C. James Oglethorpe
   D. John Musgrove

2. Which of the following is a reason why the British wanted to establish the colony of Georgia?
   A. to sell slaves to the Spanish
   B. to have a place from which to attack the Spanish in South Carolina
   C. to provide a safe place for Catholics
   D. to produce silk and other products they normally had to import

3. What was the name of the first settlement founded by British settlers in Georgia?
   A. Atlanta B. Savannah C. Macon D. Augusta

4. Who were Mary Musgrove and Tomochichi? What role did they each play in Georgia's history?

2.2 THE TRUSTEE PERIOD

NEW IMMIGRANTS ARRIVE

Jewish Immigrant

The trustees governed Georgia from 1733 – 1752. During the first year, forty settlers died due to illnesses that Oglethorpe thought were caused by drinking rum, but in reality resulted from the lack of a healthy diet, poor sanitation, and a climate the settlers were not used to. Fortunately for the sick colonists, a second group of settlers arrived in July 1733. The group consisted of 42 **Jewish immigrants**. (Jewish people believe in the Old Testament of the Bible but, unlike Protestant and Catholic Christians, do not believe in the New Testament.) Although Georgia's charter did not prohibit Jewish settlers, many of the trustees in England objected to their presence in the colony. Oglethorpe, however, welcomed them because the colony was struggling and needed more able-bodied men. Among these new arrivals was a doctor named Samuel Nunis. Oglethorpe was especially excited about Nunis' arrival because the colony's first doctor had died. Thanks to Dr. Nunis, the colony ended up making it through the first year's medical crisis.

J. M. Boltzius
German Lutheran

A Salzburger Church
Rincon, GA

In 1734, more settlers arrived. The **Salzburgers** (named after the town they came from) were German Lutherans who came to Georgia to escape Catholic persecution in their home country. Upon their arrival, Oglethorpe awarded them land 25 miles from Savannah where they established the new settlement of *Ebenezer*, which means "Rock of Help." Eventually, because the land was close to a swamp and not well suited for farming, they moved to another site and established another settlement called *New Ebenezer.* Since they spoke German, the Salzburgers stayed somewhat separated from settlers in Savannah. However, their strong work ethic made them some of the most productive citizens in the early colony.

Meanwhile, another group of settlers established themselves in Georgia as well. The **Highland Scots** were Scotsmen who came to Georgia in the mid 1730s and settled in modern-day Darien. These settlers spoke Gaelic rather than English, wore kilts (skirt-like traditional Scottish garb) rather than pants, and enjoyed good relations with the local Native Americans. Part of the reason the Highland Scots and Native Americans got along so well may have been because they organized their families and societies in much the same way. The Scots identified themselves by *clans*, which were very similar to Native American tribes. The Scots were also skilled and fearless fighters who saw it as their role to help protect the colony from the French to the west and the Spanish to the south. The Highland Scots even made sure their women were well trained in the use of muskets and knew how to load and fire cannons.

Highland Scots

Oglethorpe's Trip to England

Once Oglethorpe was sure the Salzburgers were secure in Ebenezer, he left on a trip to England. He took with him his good friend Tomochichi and even presented him to King George II and the Archbishop of Canterbury (highest ranking minister in the Church of England). The trustees in England and others were thrilled to meet Oglethorpe's Native American friends and hear his stories of the new colony. The trip strengthened relations between the British and Native Americans, renewed support in London, and resulted in more financial support for the colony. Oglethorpe also won the approval of new regulations that he wanted. These new regulations came to be known as the **Rules of 1735**. Under these rules, rum and other strong drink could not be bought or sold in the colony, trade with Native Americans was more strictly regulated, and slavery was strictly forbidden. Although the original charter had stated similar restrictions as well, influences like slavery and rum had drifted into Georgia from other colonies. Oglethorpe was very much opposed to both slavery and liquor because he believed they caused much of the colony's problems. He blamed rum for much of the colony's health problems and he believed that slavery would lead to idleness on the part of Georgia landowners. He also feared that slavery would turn Georgia into a land of large plantation owners who raised cash crops, rather than allowing it to remain a place where even small farmers could make a living.

Oglethorpe returned to Georgia in 1736, accompanied by more Salzburgers, another group of German Protestants known as *Moravians*, and a couple of young Anglican missionaries (Anglican means they were part of the Church of England) named John and Charles Wesley. John Wesley later returned to England and became the leader of a movement that eventually became the Methodist church.

John Wesley

The "Malcontents"

When Oglethorpe arrived back in Georgia, he returned to find that many of the colonists were unhappy. Oglethorpe's new regulations, as well as many old ones, were not popular. They didn't appreciate being told that they couldn't drink and sell rum, nor did they like having their trade with the Native Americans restricted. The most divisive issue, however, was over **slavery** (slavery is a system in which people are "owned" like property. In the 1700s, many colonies already allowed Africans and some Native Americans to be owned as slaves). Neighboring South Carolina allowed slavery, which enabled its farmers to grow large amounts of rice, cotton, and tobacco. As a result, South Carolina's economy thrived much more than Georgia's. Georgians also suffered financially because the mulberry trees they grew were the wrong kind for producing silk. The other crops they had hoped to grow for economic gain did not do well either. In short, many of the colonists were mad, blamed Oglethorpe and the trustees for the colony's failures, and wanted more freedom to pursue economic gain.

Oglethorpe and the trustees did not want slaves in Georgia, however, for several reasons. For one, they wanted the colony to be a settlement of yeoman farmers (small land owners growing crops mostly to feed themselves and the colony rather than for trade). They also feared that slavery might lead to a violent uprising. Slaves might fight for the Spanish or hostile Native Americans, hoping to be awarded their freedom once the British were defeated. Finally, the trustees believed that slavery would lead farmers to demand more land, thereby dispersing settlers further apart and making the colony harder to defend.

As time went on, the colonists became more and more divided. The Salzburgers and Highland Scots wanted to keep slavery out of Georgia and supported the leaders. Those who wanted slavery and resented the leaders' rules became known as the **Malcontents**. The Malcontents also wanted the colony to change its rules regarding **land ownership**. They wanted to be able to own more than 50 acres, sell their land if they wished, and did not want to be limited to passing land on only to male heirs. While Oglethorpe was on one of his trips to England, these malcontents held a meeting that resulted in a petition signed by 117 settlers. In the petition, they demanded the right to own slaves and manage their land as they saw fit. Ultimately, many of the Malcontents moved either to South Carolina or to regions of Georgia where the trustees' regulations were not strictly enforced. Oglethorpe and other leaders would not have long to worry about the grumblings of the Malcontents, however, thanks to the Spanish threat in Florida.

CONFLICT WITH SPAIN

Fort Frederica

Spanish Florida became upset after the British built a fort on St. John's Island (an island claimed by the Spanish) to protect their new settlement of *Frederica.* After refusing to withdraw his forces, Oglethorpe requested a garrison of soldiers from England to defend the colony. Great Britain granted his request and also bestowed on him the title, *General and Commander in Chief of the Forces of South Carolina and Georgia.* In 1740, Oglethorpe used his new title to assemble a military force that he hoped would invade Florida. He raised an army of about 2000 men, comprised of Georgians, South Carolinians, and Native Americans friendly to the British. The war that followed lasted until 1742 and came to be called the **War of Jenkin's Ear**, after a British ship captain who had supposedly had his ear cut off by the Spanish years before. On June 15, 1740, Spanish forces hit Oglethorpe with a surprise attack and forced him to retreat to St. Simon's Island. For the next two years, smaller skirmishes went on between the two sides, with neither gaining any real advantage.

Finally, in 1742, Oglethorpe tasted victory. He caught invading Spanish troops by surprise on St. Simon's Island in what became known as the *"Battle of Bloody Marsh."* The battle was not that big, but it was important because it stopped the Spanish advance. Oglethorpe then sent a fake letter that he knew would be intercepted by the Spanish. The letter said that British naval ships were on their way to St. Simons. Even though this was not true, the Spanish believed it and retreated back to Florida. By tricking the Spanish back across the Florida border, Oglethorpe greatly secured southern Georgia for the British. The Spanish never again posed a serious threat to Georgia.

Farewell to Oglethorpe and the Trustee Period

General Oglethorpe

In the late 1730s, the trustees in England believed Oglethorpe was not doing a good job of keeping them informed about what was happening in Georgia. They sent a man named *William Stephens* to act as the colony's secretary and communicate with the trustees. In 1741, the trustees divided Georgia into two counties. Stephens became the leader of the northern county and governed from Savannah. Meanwhile, Oglethorpe led the southern county from Frederica, a settlement in south Georgia. Oglethorpe resented Stephens to some degree because, not only did he challenge Oglethorpe for authority in the colony, but he also failed to strictly enforce the colony's regulations. For this reason, Stephens was popular with many colonists and a number of people who had left under Oglethorpe now returned to the northern county. Finally, in 1743, Oglethorpe went to England to give account for his failure to take St. Augustine during the war with Spanish Florida. He never saw Georgia again! Although the British government found him innocent of any charges, he elected not to return to America.

Rice Farming on a Plantation

William Stephens then became president of the entire colony. More and more, colonists ignored the trustees' regulations until they were eventually done away with. Colonists could sell and buy rum, own more land, females could be heirs, and landowners could sell or borrow against their land if they wished. Most notably, by 1750, slavery was officially allowed. As a result, the colony's economy grew and the population increased. Settlers learned to grow rice as a cash crop (crop raised in large amounts that brings in lots of money for a farmer and region) and the **plantation system** began. Plantations were large farms on which cash crops were grown and which relied on lots of slave labor. Over time, the plantation system would become the foundation of Georgia and the South's economy.

In the end, the trustees failed in many ways. Their regulations were never very popular, often ignored, and ultimately done away with. In addition, their vision of producing silk and other products to benefit England turned out to be a flop. Finally, Georgia never became the home for debtors that Oglethorpe originally hoped for. The trustees did, however, successfully establish Britain's final colony in what would become the United States and kept it going until the crown could establish a stronger government. In 1752, after nearly two decades, the trustees surrendered their charter a year early. The Trustee Period was over.

Practice 2.2 The Trustee

1. Which statement is **true**?
   A. The Georgia colony allowed Jews and Protestants but not Catholics.
   B. People who lived in Georgia had to be members of the Church of England.
   C. Malcontents were people who supported Oglethorpe against William Stephens.
   D. Oglethorpe had to return to England after he lost the southern county of Georgia to the Spanish.

2. How did the "Malcontents" feel about slavery?
   A. They were angry that the trustees went back on their word and allowed slavery.
   B. They wanted slavery because it would help the economy thrive like in other colonies.
   C. They hated slavery but were willing to allow it in exchange for maintaining restrictions on land ownership.
   D. They didn't care if the colony had slavery or not so long as Georgia kept its policy against the sale of rum.

3. How did life in Georgia change under William Stephens?
   A. Slavery was abolished for good.
   B. More people left the colony because he enforced regulations too strictly.
   C. Landowners eventually had more freedom to do what they wanted with their land.
   D. Women finally got the right to vote.

4. In what ways did the trustees fail? How was the Trustee Period in some ways a success?

2.3 Georgia as a Royal Colony

Colonial Government

John Reynolds

Georgia became a **royal colony** in 1752. In other words, it was under the direct rule of King George II rather than a group of trustees. In October 1754, **John Reynolds** arrived as the colony's first royal governor. He established a representative government, meaning that the colonists themselves would have a voice in running their colony. As **governor**, Reynolds served as the king's direct representative and had the most power in Georgia. He could decide when the assembly met and when it adjourned (ended its session), had say over land grants, negotiated with Native Americans, and was the commander of the colony's militia (military force).

The colony also had a **bicameral assembly**. (*Bicameral* simply means that it had two houses.) The lower house was called the *Commons House of Assembly*. It had the power to introduce legislation (laws) and decide issues involving money. Members of this house were elected by the landowners of the colony. Members of the upper house were appointed by the governor. It was called the *Governor's Council* and could introduce legislation (so long as it did not deal with money), grant rights to land, make appointments, and hear appeals from lower courts. The purpose of having two houses was to make sure that neither one got too powerful. Only white males who owned land could vote or hold office in the assembly

Governor Reynolds also established a **court system** for the colony. It was responsible for settling legal disputes and consisted of several levels so that cases could be appealed. Some appeals and more serious cases were settled by the Governor's Council.

HENRY ELLIS AND JAMES WRIGHT

Although Reynolds successfully established a new government in Georgia, he was not very popular with colonists. He did not take advice well, often appointed unqualified people, spent money carelessly, and was sometimes perceived as abusing his position. In 1757, **Henry Ellis** arrived and replaced Reynolds. Ellis was a much more tactful leader, which means that he knew how to do his job and keep people happy at the same time. He learned from Reynold's mistakes, replacing many of the men he appointed and listening to public opinion. During his brief three years as governor, Ellis tried to abolish slavery (he failed) and established good relations with the **Creeks** (an influential Native American tribe in Georgia). He also gained popularity when he stood up to South Carolina and refused to grant it any authority over Georgia's militia. Although the people liked him, Ellis became ill and had to leave in 1760.

A Creek, Drawn by Frederick Remington

Tah-chee, a Cherokee

James Wright replaced Ellis and became Georgia's longest ruling royal governor. Born in Charles Town and educated in England, Wright was attorney general of South Carolina before becoming governor of Georgia. Like Ellis, he believed that Georgia needed more wealth, more land, more people, and better defenses. Following the French and Indian War (we will discuss this war in chapter 3), Wright acquired new lands for Georgia that stretched all the way to the Mississippi River. He also acquired additional land through peaceful negotiations with the **Cherokee** (another important Native American tribe) and Creeks. During his time as governor, Wright added over 6 million total acres of land to Georgia! He also granted colonists the right to own more land. The plantation system produced lots of rice and Georgia's economy grew. His policies and accomplishments attracted more settlers to the region and increased Georgia's population. Wright remained governor until Georgia eventually decided to join the other twelve colonies in a war for independence.

James Wright

Practice 2.1 Georgia as a Royal Colony

1. Which of the following statements is **true**?

   A. John Reynolds was extremely popular among the colonists and only left because he got ill.

   B. Although the governor was appointed by the king, the assembly had most of the power in Georgia.

   C. James Wright was governor of Georgia longer than anyone else.

   D. Since they would not negotiate, Governor Wright had to take land from the Cherokee by violent force.

2. How were the Commons House of Assembly and the Governor's Council different?

3. What were some of James Wright's accomplishments as governor?

CHAPTER 2 REVIEW

Key People, Terms, and Concepts

James Oglethorpe
debtors
reasons for founding Georgia
Charter of 1732
trustees
Mary Musgrove
Tomochichi
Savannah
Jewish immigrants
Salzburgers
Highland Scots
Rules of 1735
slavery
malcontents
land ownership
War of Jenkin's Ear
plantation system
royal colony
John Reynolds
governor
bicameral assembly
court system
Henry Ellis
James Wright
Creeks and Cherokees

Multiple Choice

1. Which of the following best describes James Oglethorpe?
   A. He was a supporter of slavery.
   B. He did not believe in relying on women for help.
   C. He was a strong leader.
   D. He acquired a great deal of land after the French and Indian War.

2. Which Georgia governor won popularity by listening to public opinion, establishing good relations with Native Americans, and standing up to South Carolina when it came to Georgia's militia?
   A. James Oglethorpe
   B. Henry Ellis
   C. John Reynolds
   D. James Wright

3. John Reynolds established which of the following in Georgia?
   A. slavery
   B. regulations against rum
   C. a representative government
   D. restrictions against Catholics

4. Which of the following best describes Tomochichi?
   A. He was a Native American whom Oglethorpe enslaved and took to England as a prisoner.
   B. He was a Native American chief who befriended Oglethorpe and allowed him to settle Savannah in peace.
   C. He was the husband of Mary Musgrove.
   D. He was a Native American chief who helped James Wright acquire land.

5. What effect did slavery have on Georgia?
   A. It hurt the colony's economy.
   B. It led to the plantation system.
   C. It increased the rights of blacks because they were finally welcome in the colony.
   D. It caused a drop in the colony's population.

6. How did the founding of Georgia affect debtors in England?
   A. It affected them very little because hardly any debtors ever came to Georgia.
   B. It improved their lives greatly because it was a colony specifically for debtors.
   C. It helped some, but since most debtors became slaves once they reached Georgia their lives were still hard.
   D. It was great for the hundreds of Protestant debtors who came, but Catholic debtors had to go to South Carolina.

7. Which of the following statements would have most likely been made by a "Malcontent"?
   A. "Slavery is wrong and we cannot have it in Georgia."
   B. "God bless Oglethorpe and our trustees!"
   C. "Catholics should be allowed in Georgia."
   D. "It's my land! I should have a right to sell it or to have slaves who work it!"

Chapter 3
The American Revolution and Georgia

This chapter covers the following Georgia standard(s).

SS8H3	The student will analyze the role of Georgia in the American Revolution.
SS8H4	The student will describe the impact of events that led to the ratification of the United States Constitution and the Bill of Rights.

3.1 Causes of the Revolution

The French and Indian War

By 1750, Great Britain and France were the two most powerful nations with colonies east of the Mississippi River. Unfortunately, these two nations also hated each other and had a long history of fighting. This caused serious problems as British colonists moved west and came into contact with more and more Native Americans and French settlers. Finally, in 1754, these tensions resulted in the **French and Indian War**. The war was so named because British colonists—along with the help of British troops—fought against the French and their Native American allies (some Native Americans helped the British, too). After nine years of fighting in North America, France finally surrendered and gave up all its lands in Canada and east of the Mississippi. In addition, the British also gained Florida from Spain. Great Britain now stood alone as the one, true colonial power in eastern North America.

Effects of the War on Georgia

Although no actual fighting took place in Georgia, the French and Indian War initially had beneficial effects on the colony. For starters, the **territory grew**. With the French gone, the Mississippi River now became Georgia's western border (back then, the states of Alabama and Mississippi did not yet exist). Also, since Great Britain now owned Florida, Georgia was much **more secure**. Georgians no longer had to worry about a Spanish threat from the south.

Georgia, 1763

Tensions Rise Between Great Britain and the Colonies

Soon after the French and Indian War, the colonies and Great Britain began having a hard time getting along. The colonies did not like that Great Britain tried to exercise greater control over the colonies after years of **salutary neglect**. *Salutary neglect* simply means that, in a lot of ways, England allowed the colonies to govern themselves. This made a lot of sense because the American colonies were a long way from England and communication between the two took a lot of time. After victory over the French, however, Britain had lots of new land in North America and was in debt from the war. As a result, the king and Parliament felt they needed more say over things in America. They ended up taking several steps that offended the colonists and led them to eventually declare independence.

THE PROCLAMATION OF 1763

King George III

In an effort to manage Britain's new territories, King George III issued the **Proclamation of 1763**. This proclamation created four new colonies (Quebec in Canada, Granada in the Caribbean, East Florida, and West Florida). It also expanded Georgia's borders. However, the proclamation also upset many in the middle and northern colonies because it stated that colonists could not move into previously French territory west of the Appalachian Mountains. King George III felt that this was necessary to maintain peace with the Native Americans living in this region. Many colonists resented this regulation, however, because they saw it as limiting their personal freedom and economic opportunities.

THE STAMP ACT

Colonists Read about the Stamp Act

While the Proclamation of 1763 addressed the problem of land, it did little to deal with the war debt. Britain needed money. Since the war had been fought largely to protect the British colonists, the crown and Parliament reasoned that the colonies should help cover the costs. As a result, Parliament passed a series of acts (laws) meant to ensure that the American colonists paid their fair share. One of the laws that made colonists the angriest was the **Stamp Act** in 1765. Although it was not the first tax passed, it was one of the most offensive because it affected nearly anyone trying to conduct business. The Stamp Act created a tax on all legal documents, licenses, newspapers, etc. (A *tax* is money that citizens must pay the government.) It required that all such documents have a government stamp. Before you could get the stamp, you had to pay the tax.

Samuel Adams
Sons of Liberty

People were so angry that many of the colonies sent delegates to the *Stamp Act Congress* that met in New York City that same year. (Georgia did not send representatives because its assembly was not in session at the time to pick delegates.) One of the Congress' leaders, James Otis of Massachusetts, summed up the discontent of the colonists when he proclaimed, "No taxation without representation!" In other words, since the colonists had no one representing them in Parliament when it passed new taxes, they believed they should not have to pay them. Soon, protests against the Stamp Act spread throughout the colonies. Colonists engaged in *boycotts* (refusal to buy British products in hopes that British businesses would get tired of losing money and pressure Parliament to change the law). Meanwhile, groups like the **Sons of Liberty** formed in several colonies (including Georgia) and used violence and threats to make sure no stamps were sold and that everyone stuck to the boycotts.

The day before the Stamp Act was to go into effect in Georgia, protestors in Savannah burned an effigy of the stamp master. (An effigy is a dummy made to represent someone.) The event was the first example of mob protest against a British law in Savannah and it greatly alarmed Governor Wright. It was almost a month after the act went into effect before Georgia received any stamps. Even then, however, thanks to violent threats from the **Liberty Boys** (part of Georgia's chapter of the Sons of Liberty), no stamp master was present in Georgia to administer them. Finally, a month later, a new stamp master arrived and a few stamps were issued. Georgia was the only colony to ever sell any of the stamps. Most colonies simply refused. South Carolinians from Charles Town actually threatened to invade Savannah when they heard that stamps had been sold. Governor Wright called in troops to protect the city, however, and no successful invasion occurred. Eventually, Parliament had no choice but to repeal (cancel) the Stamp Act.

THE INTOLERABLE ACTS

Boston Tea Party

Although the Stamp Act was repealed, other offensive acts followed. One of these involved prices on British tea. In December 1773, one group of colonists in Boston, Massachusetts decided they'd had enough. They dressed as Mohawk Indians, marched to Boston Harbor, boarded British ships hauling tea, and began dumping the crates overboard. The episode became known as the *Boston Tea Party* and it made Parliament so mad that it passed a series of laws the colonists called the **Intolerable Acts**. These acts placed a military governor over Massachusetts, closed Boston Harbor, and expanded the border of English Canada so as to take land away from several colonies. To deal with the crisis, representatives from nearly every colony gathered in Philadelphia for the *First Continental Congress* in the fall of 1774. Only Georgia did not send delegates. In a statement to the king, the First Continental Congress wrote that the colonies had a right to be represented in their government and, since they were not represented in England, should be allowed to live by their own laws instead of Parliament's. The king and Parliament, however, disagreed with the Congress. By early 1775, it was clear that tensions between the Crown and the colonies were reaching a breaking point!

GEORGIA'S DISCONTENT

Patriots Tar and Feather Tories

As Parliament continued to pass laws taxing the colonies, discontent grew in Georgia. Within the colonial assembly, legislators began to openly complain about Britain's policies. This often put leaders in the Assembly at odds with Governor Wright, who was loyal to the crown. Businessmen and those who lived in cities like Savannah grew impatient and resentful of British taxes because they affected their ability to do business and freely go about their daily lives. However, in the country, where most Georgian's lived, people did not feel the direct effects of British taxes as easily. As a result, the colony became divided. Many Georgians who owed their positions and/or wealth to England remained **Tories** (colonists loyal to the king). Many others became **Patriots** (colonists who favored independence from England) because they felt oppressed by Parliament's taxes and believed that their rights and freedoms were being trampled on. Meanwhile, many rural Georgians simply didn't care because they lived fairly isolated lives, did not feel directly affected by England's new laws, and were not witnesses to much of the protest and debate that took place in the cities.

As mentioned earlier, Georgia did not send delegates to the First Continental Congress. Georgia still preferred to focus on its own relationship with England rather than join a united effort against the "mother country." This was in part because Georgia was the youngest of the 13 colonies and still had strong ties to Great Britain. Many Georgians still had relatives in England and depended on Great Britain economically for survival. In addition, because much of Georgia's territory was still frontier land occupied by Native American tribes, the colony needed the military protection and security that Britain offered. As a result, Georgians feared going too far in offending the royal government.

Like other colonists, however, Georgians were upset about the Intolerable Acts. Leaders called a meeting in 1774 to discuss the problem and issued a statement to Parliament. In their statement, the Georgians insisted that the British government recognize the rights of colonists as Englishmen and stated their belief that the Intolerable Acts violated these rights. Although more cautious than its fellow colonies, Georgia was also growing unhappy with British rule.

INDEPENDENCE DECLARED

Lyman Hall

Continental Congress

In April 1775, colonists and "red coats" (British soldiers) fired the first shots of the American Revolution at Lexington and Concord in Massachusetts. Less than a month later, the *Second Continental Congress* met to decide what to do. This time, **Lyman Hall** made his way to Philadelphia as Georgia's *unofficial* representative. The fact that he was unofficial, however, left the other colonies very angry with Georgia. They felt that the youngest colony was not doing enough to support their cause. Finally, however, in July 1775, Georgia elected to send additional delegates to join Hall as Georgia's *official* delegation to the Continental Congress.

Button Gwinnett

George Walton

At first the Congress tried to find a peaceful solution to its differences with the king. When the king refused to compromise, however, it became clear that this would not work. The Congress voted to form the first Continental Army and elected George Washington of Virginia to be its commander. It then chose to officially declare independence. The Congress appointed a young delegate, also from Virginia, named Thomas Jefferson to pen a statement outlining the reasons for the colonies' separation from Great Britain. On July 4, 1776, the delegates to the Second Continental Congress adopted the **Declaration of Independence**, proclaiming that the American colonies were forevermore a united and free nation. Three Georgians signed the document: **Lyman Hall**, **Button Gwinnett,** and **George Walton** (at only 26 years old, Walton was the youngest signer of the document). When the Declaration of Independence was finally read publicly in Savannah in August 1776, Patriots rejoiced, fired cannons in celebration, and even held a mock funeral for King George. By contrast, more than a thousand Tories left Georgia. Many of them fled to other British colonies in Canada or the Caribbean. Others went to England. Most Tories, however, stayed. They remained both to protect their property and because they believed it would only be a short while before Great Britain crushed the revolution.

Practice 3.1 The American Revolution and Georgia

1. Which two colonial powers fought one another for control of North America during the French and Indian War?

   A. Great Britain and Native Americans
   B. France and Native Americans
   C. Great Britain and France
   D. Georgia and Great Britain

2. For many years, Great Britain basically let the colonies govern themselves. This practice was known as what?

   A. salutary neglect
   B. colonial legislation
   C. independence
   D. royal proclamation

3. What was significant about Lyman Hall, Button Gwinnett, and George Walton?

   A. They each represented Georgia at the Stamp Act Congress.
   B. They each represented Georgia at the First Continental Congress.
   C. They each signed the Declaration of Independence on behalf of Georgia.
   D. They each went to Philadelphia as unofficial representatives to the Second Continental Congress.

4. What were the Stamp Act and the Intolerable Acts, and why did they make so many colonists mad?

5. Explain the difference between *Tories* and *Patriots*.

3.2 The Revolution in Georgia

Colonists in Savannah responded to the news of Lexington and Concord by raiding British storehouses and stealing arms and gunpowder. Soon, other protests and acts of defiance followed. As it became clear a war was coming, towns, churches, and even families began to divide into Tories (the British called them "loyalists") and Patriots. In July 1775, a group of Patriots from towns throughout Georgia met in Savannah to set up a Patriot government called the **Provincial Congress**. The creation of the Provincial Congress gave Georgia two governments; one, a patriot government that sent official delegates to the Continental Congress, and the other, a loyalist government under Governor James Wright. Eventually, the Patriots proved too strong. In January 1776, Governor Wright barely escaped and fled aboard a British ship, leaving Georgia under patriot rule.

In the Wake of Independence

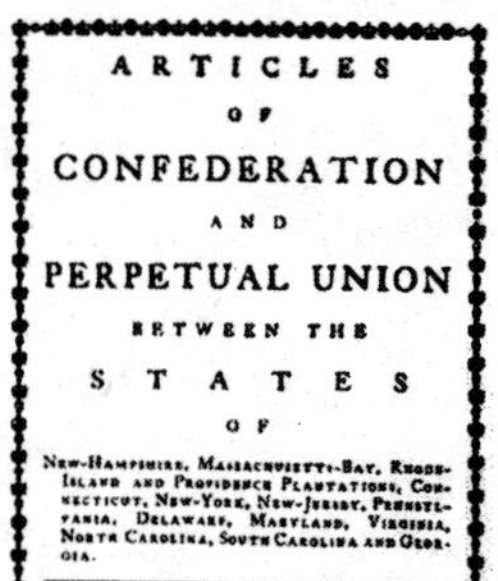
ARTICLES
OF
CONFEDERATION
AND
PERPETUAL UNION
BETWEEN THE
STATES
OF
New-Hampshire, Massachusetts-Bay, Rhode-Island and Providence Plantations, Connecticut, New-York, New-Jersey, Pennsylvania, Delaware, Maryland, Virginia, North Carolina, South Carolina and Georgia.

With independence, Congress' responsibilities increased. It now made decisions for a nation. It established a committee to draft a new national set of laws. **Button Gwinnett** of Georgia was part of this committee. He and his colleagues came up with a body of laws known as the **Articles of Confederation**. The Articles served as the United States' first constitution until 1788. In addition, the former colonies were now independent *states* and set up their own new governments as well.

Georgia's Constitution of 1777

In May 1777, Georgia formed its government under a new state constitution: the **Constitution of 1777**. This document lasted until 1789 and, like the Declaration of Independence, supported the ideas of "natural rights" and governments ruling by the "consent of the governed." In other words, all human beings are born with rights that no ruler may rightfully take away, and governments only have a right to rule so long as they serve the people and uphold their rights. The constitution also divided power among three separate branches of government: the executive branch (the governor), the legislative branch (the Georgia Assembly), and the judicial branch (state courts). Georgians made sure power was divided in order to prevent any person or body of government from becoming too powerful and abusing its authority. The constitution also divided Georgia into eight counties: Burke, Chatham, Effingham, Camden, Wilkes, Glynn, Richmond, and Liberty.

Although many Georgians were excited about their new government, there were problems as well. Since Georgians did not trust a strong governor, it placed most of the power in its assembly. The Assembly got to appoint the judges and the governor. It could also reject any of the governor's proposals it didn't like. As a result, power wasn't really divided evenly. Also, the Assembly was *unicameral* (one house) instead of *bicameral* (two houses). This also meant that the legislature could pass and enforce decisions without any second house to check its authority.

Georgia's Battles

Button Gwinnett and the Florida Campaigns

In July 1776, the 13 original British colonies declared independence from Great Britain. However, **British Florida** was not one of these colonies. This meant the region was once again a threat to Georgia. Soon after the Declaration of Independence, Georgia Patriots attempted to invade Florida. They failed, however, and were forced to retreat. After Georgians ratified the Constitution of 1777, **Button Gwinnett** became chief executive of the General Assembly and authorized another invasion of Florida. This invasion also failed and, once again, Georgia's troops had no choice but to return home defeated.

Lachlan McIntosh

A Duel

A short time later, one of Gwinnett's political rivals, Lachlan McIntosh, publicly insulted him, proclaiming he was a, "…lying rascal!" Gwinnett got so mad that he challenged McIntosh to a duel. A duel was a one-on-one battle to the death that was usually fought with pistols. In colonial times, if an aristocrat (member of the upper class) felt someone had insulted his honor, he often challenged that person to a duel. McIntosh survived the duel, but Gwinnett was seriously wounded and died a few days later. Since both men were greatly respected, their feud caused division. Many patriots, including Lyman Hall, supported Gwinnett. Others, however, including George Walton, supported McIntosh.

SAVANNAH AND KETTLE CREEK

For the first couple of years, the British tried to end the war by defeating Washington's army up north. However, Washington proved harder to defeat than they had planned. Therefore, in 1778, Great Britain decided to focus more of its efforts in the South. Many people in the South were still Tories and the British hoped it could count on their help to defeat the revolution. In December 1778, the British attacked and captured **Savannah**. The patriot government was forced to flee and an "old friend," Governor Wright, returned to serve as royal governor. Ebenezer and Augusta fell a month later. Meanwhile, British troops from Florida invaded from the South. The patriot cause seemed in trouble in Georgia.

Elijah Clarke

Andrew Pickens

In February 1779, Georgia's patriot militia (armed force made up of civilians rather than professional soldiers) finally won a key victory at the battle of **Kettle Creek**. Colonel **Elijah Clarke**, a North Carolinian who'd moved south some years earlier, led a force with Andrew Pickens that defeated roughly 700 British troops, many of whom were Tories, and stopped the British attempt to round up loyalist support in the Georgia upcountry. The victory allowed the Georgians to capture badly needed weapons and supplies and made Clarke an instant hero. Although it was a relatively small battle compared to those fought in other states, the victory at Kettle Creek greatly lifted the morale of Georgia's Patriots and gave them hope that they could defeat the powerful British army. Eventually, the British pulled back to Savannah, allowing the Patriots to re-establish their own government in Augusta for a time.

AUSTIN DABNEY AND NANCY HART

Another hero at Kettle Creek was **Austin Dabney**. Dabney was a slave who fought in the war in place of his white master. He was severely wounded at the Battle of Kettle Creek and walked with a limp for the rest of his life. Georgia's government rewarded Dabney for his brave service with his freedom and a plot of land after the war. He allotted part of the land to the Harris family which had cared for him and nursed him back to health after his wounds at Kettle Creek. He eventually even helped send their son to college and left his property to the Harris family after his death. Historians estimate that roughly 5,000 African-Americans (some free but most slaves) served in the Continental Army during the Revolutionary War. Some, like Dabney, were granted their freedom after the war (we only know of two besides Dabney who were granted their freedom in Georgia). Many other blacks fought for the British, hoping to be rewarded once "His Majesty's forces" won the war. Of course, the British lost, leaving most blacks still living in slavery after the revolution.

Nancy Hart holds British soldiers captive

Women also played an important role in Georgia's revolutionary cause. One of the most interesting was **Nancy Hart**. Hart was a feisty frontier woman who cared for her family alone while her husband was off fighting the British. She stood nearly six feet tall, had a face scarred by smallpox, and was reportedly cross-eyed. As one historical account put it, "She had no share of beauty." Although most historians are not entirely sure how many of the stories about Hart are true rather than just legends, she is generally remembered as a spy and a faithful Patriot. Most of her efforts were against Tories. From time to time she would disguise herself as a man and wander into loyalist camps to get information. On one occasion, Hart is reported to have held a group of Tories at musket point until help arrived. Not only did these officers have to deal with the humiliation of being held at bay by a cross-eyed, gun toting woman, but they ended up being hanged as well. Regardless of how many stories about Hart may be exaggerated, she will forever live in history as the most colorful example of how women in Georgia served and supported the patriot cause during the Revolutionary War.

The Siege of Savannah

In the fall of 1779, Patriot troops under the command of Benjamin Lincoln tried to take back Savannah after the French navy arrived off the coast of Georgia. (As you probably remember from what we read earlier, the French had a long history of fighting the British, so they helped the Americans during the Revolutionary War). Lincoln's 1,500 patriots now joined 4,000 French troops in a *siege* of the city. A siege is when a military force surrounds a city and doesn't let anyone in or out. Eventually, the people in the city have to surrender to avoid starving. Finally, on October 9, the French and American forces attacked. Despite a long bombardment against the city (a bombardment is when naval ships continually fire on a target), the attack failed. The **Siege of Savannah** ended with the French navy sailing away and Lincoln's troops withdrawing in defeat.

Benjamin Lincoln

British Aggression and Surrender

Following his defeat at Savannah, Lincoln marched north to Charles Town. There, in May 1780, British troops under the command of General Lord Cornwallis captured both the city and Lincoln's army. Soon, the British recaptured Augusta and most of upcountry Georgia as well. After defeating patriot forces at Camden, SC, Cornwallis then made plans to invade North Carolina. However, surprise patriot victories at Kings Mountain and Cowpens delayed his advance and revealed that things would not be so simple for Cornwallis after all.

General Cornwallis

In May 1781, patriot troops under the command of **Elijah Clarke**, Andrew Pickens, and Colonel "Light Horse" Harry Lee, attacked and successfully retook Augusta. The 300 surviving loyalists surrendered on June 6, 1781, as the British again pulled back to Savannah. This time, Augusta remained in Patriot hands for good. For the remainder of the war, Clarke and his Georgia militia fought only small skirmishes and occasionally engaged in battles against Native Americans who launched raids against settlements along the Georgia frontier.

Eventually, Cornwallis advanced into North Carolina and Virginia. In October 1781, however, he made a crucial mistake at Yorktown. Hoping to be re-supplied by British ships, Cornwallis encamped his army with its back to the Atlantic Ocean. George Washington then marched south and trapped the British general between himself and the French navy floating off shore. Realizing there was no escape, Cornwallis surrendered on October 19, 1781. Although negotiations went on for two more years before the *Treaty of Paris* officially ended the war, Washington's victory at Yorktown effectively brought the revolution to a close.

Cornwallis surrenders to Washington

Practice 3.2 The Revolution in Georgia

1. What Georgian helped write the Articles of Confederation, was elected chief executive of Georgia's patriot assembly, and eventually died as the result of a duel with a political rival?

   A. Lyman Hall
   B. Button Gwinnett
   C. Elijah Clarke
   D. George Washington

2. What was special about Austin Dabney?

   A. He was a slave who won his freedom for brave service during the war.
   B. He captured several British leaders despite being wounded and cross-eyed.
   C. He commanded the patriot troops who won a key victory at Kettle Creek.
   D. He led a heroic attack during the Siege of Savannah.

3. Why was the victory at Kettle Creek important even though it was smaller than most Revolutionary War battles?

3.3 Georgia and the Birth of a Nation

As mentioned earlier, the United States' first national body of laws was called the *Articles of Confederation.* The Articles turned out to be a disappointment, however, because they gave too much power to the states and not nearly enough to the national (federal) government. For instance, the national government could not collect taxes; it had to ask the states for money. As you might guess, this did not work very well and the government could not afford to organize an army or carry out the duties of government. In addition, the national government could not pass laws without at least nine of the thirteen colonies agreeing. Since states often wanted different things, such cooperation didn't happen often. In short, the national government simply did not have enough authority to rule effectively. Things were a mess! Although they'd won independence, the states were not united as a country. Something had to change.

The Constitutional Convention

Constitutional Convention

Finally, in 1787, a delegation of representatives from every state but Rhode Island met in Philadelphia to fix the problem. They ended up throwing out the Articles altogether and writing a new document: the **United States Constitution**. The Constitution was a huge improvement over the Articles of Confederation. Since many of the delegates had different ideas, the document they wrote was the result of a number of important *compromises*. A compromise is when people with different opinions each give up a little of what they want in order to come to an agreement everyone can live with.

William Few

Abraham Baldwin

Although Georgia originally sent several delegates to the convention, only two—**William Few** and **Abraham Baldwin**—actually signed the Constitution. Baldwin was a chaplain (minister to soldiers) during the Revolutionary War and moved to Georgia afterwards. He practiced law in Augusta and helped establish the University of Georgia. Meanwhile, Few moved to Georgia in the mid 1770s and also served in the Revolutionary War. He was elected to the Georgia Assembly and helped establish Georgia's Constitution in 1777. In 1780 he was elected to the Continental Congress before eventually representing Georgia at the Constitutional Convention in 1787.

The "Great Compromise" and Slavery

Most of the delegates at the convention agreed that it would be good to separate the powers of government between three branches: 1) a legislative branch to make the laws, 2) an executive branch to enforce the laws, and 3) a judicial branch to make sure the laws are fairly applied. They disagreed, however, on how these branches should be set up and how much power they should have. Large states liked the *Virginia Plan* because it called for a bicameral legislature with representation based on population in both houses. In other words, the more people a state had, the more representation it would get in the legislature. Smaller states, however, hated this idea because they did not have as many people. They liked the *New Jersey Plan* because it called for only one house that gave each state just one vote. When the convention voted on which plan to accept, **Abraham Baldwin** of Georgia voted last. The Virginia Plan led by one vote when Baldwin's turn came. Baldwin, however, voted for the New Jersey Plan, making it a tie. As a result, the convention ended up approving what became known as the **Great Compromise**. The compromise created a bicameral house with one house giving each state a number of representatives based on population (the House of Representatives) and the other house giving each state the same number of representatives: two per state (the US Senate). Together, the two houses form the *US Congress*. The delegates also approved an executive branch headed by a new *President of the United States* and a judicial branch of federal courts, with the *US Supreme Court* acting as the highest court in the land.

A Plantation

Slave Trade

Meanwhile, **slavery** was another important issue at the Constitutional Convention. Slavery was an institution in which white citizens owned blacks as "property." Although some blacks were free, most were slaves. When the United States won its independence, many felt that slavery should be done away with because it contradicted the principles of freedom expressed in the Declaration of Independence. Many others, however, wanted to keep slavery. Southerners especially wanted to continue slavery because it provided free labor that their economy greatly depended on. Not only that, but they wanted to count slaves as part of the population so that they could get more representatives in Congress. Northern states, however, did not depend on slavery as much. Even if slavery continued, they did not want slaves counted as part of the population. This debate resulted in the **Three-fifths Compromise** and a **slave trade compromise**. The Three-fifths Compromise stated that slaves would count as "three-fifths of a person." In other words, for every five slaves a state had, it would be given credit for having three people. Meanwhile, the slave trade compromise assured states in the Deep South that the slave trade (business of bringing slaves into the country to buy and sell them) would be allowed to continue for at least twenty more years. Georgia's representatives to the convention helped ensure that both slavery and the slave trade survived under the Constitution.

Georgia's Reasons for Ratifying the Constitution

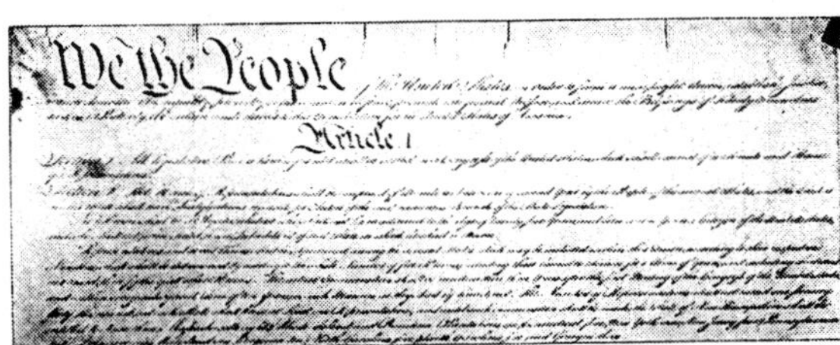
U. S. Constitution

After approving the Constitution, the delegates sent it to the states for ratification (in order to become law, it had to be approved by at least nine of the 13 states). Even though the document was much better than the Articles of Confederation, many citizens and leaders did not like it. They felt that it gave too much power to the national government and, in particular, to the president. In addition, they also felt that the document needed a section guaranteeing the rights of citizens. Eventually, the Constitution was ratified, but not until Congress agreed to consider amendments (additions) to the document limiting the powers of government and protecting the rights of the people. One of Congress' first acts was to approve twelve amendments to the Constitution. The states ratified ten of them that became known as the **Bill of Rights**. These amendments ensure that the government does not violate the rights of its citizens and are meant to protect the freedoms fought for during the Revolutionary War.

Georgia became the fourth state to ratify the United States Constitution in December 1787. The state had several **reasons for being one of the first to ratify** the new document. For one, Georgia was still very much a frontier region. Florida was once again foreign territory just to the south and Georgians were waging an "on again, off again" war with the Creek Indians. As a result, the state wanted a strong central government that could provide military help if necessary. Also, Savannah and those who depended on good trade relations in order to make money liked the idea of a strong central government that could negotiate profitable trade agreements. As a result, nearly all of Georgia liked the Constitution.

Practice 3.3 Georgia and the Birth of a Nation

1. There was much debate at the Constitutional Convention over which of the following issues?
   A. whether or not to declare independence
   B. how to change state governments
   C. the best way to end slavery
   D. how many representatives each state should have in the new Congress

2. Which of the following is a reason why Georgia ratified the US Constitution so quickly?
   A. It wanted help fighting Tories.
   B. It wanted to know it could count on a national government for protection.
   C. It was afraid Savannah would remain under British control if the country did not have a national constitution.
   D. It felt like Georgia's Constitution of 1777 was a failure and wanted a new one.

3. What was the "Great Compromise," and how did Abraham Baldwin's actions contribute to it?

Chapter 3 Review

Key Terms, People, and Concepts

French and Indian War
effects of French and Indian War on Georgia
salutary neglect
Proclamation of 1763
Stamp Act
Sons of Liberty
Liberty Boys
Intolerable Acts
Tories
Patriots
Lyman Hall
Button Gwinnett
George Walton
Declaration of Independence
Provincial Congress
Articles of Confederation
Constitution of 1777
British Florida
capture of Savannah
Kettle Creek
Elijah Clarke
Austin Dabney
Nancy Hart
siege of Savannah
United States Constitution
William Few
Abraham Baldwin
Great Compromise
slavery
Three-fifths Compromise
Slave Trade Compromise
Bill of Rights
Georgia's reasons for ratifying the US Constitution

Multiple Choice

1. What effect did the end of the French and Indian War initially have on Georgia?
   A. It enraged Georgians because it made the colony smaller.
   B. It benefited the colony because it gave it more territory and made the colony more secure.
   C. It endangered the colony because Florida was now a British colony.
   D. It had little effect because no fighting ever occurred in Georgia.

2. Tories can **best** be described as which of the following?
   A. Colonists who supported independence.
   B. Colonists who supported the king.
   C. Colonists who didn't really care because British laws did little to affect their lives.
   D. Patriots who used violence and threats to keep people from buying British stamps.

3. How did Patriots in Georgia respond to the Stamp Act and Intolerable Acts?
   A. They were angered by them and made their protests known.
   B. They supported them because, as the youngest colony, they had strong ties to England.
   C. They were upset and immediately chose delegates to the Continental Congress.
   D. They were concerned and refused to ratify the Constitution until these acts were removed and replaced with the Bill of Rights.

4. Why were the other twelve colonies upset with Georgia before July 1775?
   - A. They thought Georgia was responsible for the Intolerable Acts.
   - B. Georgia was the only colony supporting slavery and the slave trade.
   - C. No Georgian would sign the Declaration of Independence.
   - D. Up until that time, Georgia did not seem very supportive of the revolutionary cause.

5. What was distinctive about Lyman Hall?
   - A. He went to Philadelphia to protest against the revolution on behalf of Tories in Georgia.
   - B. He was the youngest signer of the Declaration of Independence.
   - C. He initially went to Philadelphia as an unofficial representative of Georgia to the Second Continental Congress.
   - D. He was one of only three slaves in Georgia to win his freedom as a reward for how he served during the war.

6. Who is the quote below **most likely** talking about?

   > "Black skin or not... free or not...he's one heck of a soldier. It's men like him what allowed us to whoop them Tories at Kettle Creek."

   - A. Button Gwinnett
   - B. George Washington
   - C. Austin Dabney
   - D. Austin Powers

7. Which of the following is **true** regarding Georgia's Constitution of 1777?
   - A. It made many colonists nervous because it gave too much power to the governor.
   - B. Because people didn't trust a strong governor, it gave the assembly most of the power.
   - C. It did away with counties and combined Georgia into just one state.
   - D. It was repealed once the Declaration of Independence was signed.

8. Who led Georgian Patriots to victory at Kettle Creek, retook Augusta in 1781, and fought numerous skirmishes against Native Americans along the Georgia frontier?
   - A. Elijah Clarke
   - B. Lachlan McIntosh
   - C. Nancy Hart
   - D. Austin Dabney

9. Which of the following **best** describes Nancy Hart?
   - A. She often used her beauty to get close to Tory officers and get information.
   - B. She was a little, timid woman, but she still managed to help the revolution.
   - C. She was considered ugly, feisty, and a brave Patriot.
   - D. She was a Tory and eventually had to leave Georgia after the war.

10. How did Georgians feel about the Constitution?
    - A. Most were against it because they felt it gave too much power to the president.
    - B. It worried them because they did not want a strong central government.
    - C. They supported it because they thought Georgia needed the national government to be strong.
    - D. Georgians did not care because they were too focused on fighting the Creeks.

Chapter 4
Antebellum Georgia

This chapter covers the following Georgia standard(s).

SS8H5	The student will explain significant factors that affected the development of Georgia as part of the growth of the United States between 1789 and 1840.
SS8H6	The student will analyze the impact of the Civil War and Reconstruction on Georgia.

4.1 Education, Religion, and the Quest for Land

The University of Georgia and a New Capital

Early view of the University of Georgia

Following the revolution, Georgia's leaders wanted to make sure that their new state promoted education. In February 1784, the General Assembly set aside 40,000 acres of land to establish a state "college or seminary of learning." Abraham Baldwin wrote the charter, and the state legislature approved it in 1785. Several years went by, however, before the General Assembly took action to build such a college. Finally, in 1799, the trustees for the school met and laid plans to open the university. They named Abraham Baldwin the first president and allotted 633 acres along the banks of the Oconee River for the school. Built in Athens, the new institution was originally called Franklin College, in honor of Benjamin Franklin. However, it ultimately became known as the **University of Georgia** and held its first classes in 1801. As the first state-supported college in the nation, the University of Georgia became a model for other state university systems in the US. Interestingly, *both* the University of Georgia and the University of North Carolina claim to be the oldest state-supported university in the United States. Georgians argue that Georgia is clearly the oldest because it was founded first. North Carolinians, however, point out that, while Georgia was the first chartered, the University of North Carolina was the first to actually open its doors to students in 1795.

Louisville and Milledgeville

The General Assembly made **Louisville** the new capital of Georgia in 1786. Modeled after Philadelphia, the town was named in honor of King Louis XVI of France for his country's help during the revolution. It was located midway between the two previous capitals (Savannah and Augusta) because the site served as a good compromise between western settlers and coastal planters. In 1796, the new government buildings were finally ready and the government moved from Augusta to Louisville. Eventually, western expansion and an outbreak of malaria in Louisville caused state officials to move the capital again in 1804. **Milledgeville** remained the capital from 1804 to 1868.

THE METHODISTS AND BAPTISTS

The Constitution of 1777 had a great impact on religion in Georgia. Since the Anglican Church was the official church of England and the king was its recognized head, independence from Great Britain meant that many US citizens now stood separated from the only church they'd ever known. Many of these citizens started setting up American versions of the Anglican Church, while others sought new churches in which to express their faith. Catholics established themselves in Savannah and upcountry Georgia, while Congregationalists (Presbyterians who believed each congregation should exercise its own, independent church governance), Lutherans, and Jewish citizens all continued to practice their faith.

First African Baptist Church, Savannah, GA

By far, however, the two religious groups that impacted Georgia the most towards the end of the 1700s were the **Baptist** and **Methodist**. Both of these churches grew rapidly because of their willingness to use new methods to reach people along the frontier. This was especially important in Georgia where so many settlers still lived in fairly isolated, rural areas. Unlike Presbyterians and other Christian denominations that required specially trained, ordained ministers to conduct religious ceremonies, the Baptists and Methodists were willing to allow more freedom to local congregations and non-ordained leaders. The Baptists were known for the independence of their congregations and their emotional preaching. In 1788, they even established the first all African-American Baptist church in Savannah. It was controlled and led entirely by its black members (an incredible feat considering that most of its congregation were slaves).

The Methodists, on the other hand, were a group that effectively used what they called *circuit riders*. These were specially trained ministers who traveled the countryside on horseback, preaching passionate sermons and performing sacraments (communions and baptisms). Meanwhile, they allowed much of the daily church government to be led by local leaders. Together, the Baptists and Methodists came to be the most dominant Christian denominations in Georgia and eventually founded universities as well. In 1834, the Methodists founded what became Emory University. A few years later, in 1839, the Baptist founded what became Mercer University.

HEADRIGHTS, LOTTERIES, AND FRAUD

With independence came disputes about land. During the war, the same land often switched back and forth between Tory and Patriot owners, depending on who was winning. After the war was over, the state had to settle on who owned what land. In addition, many Georgians set their minds on acquiring new lands to the west. Many received land by means of the **headright system**. Under the headright system, white males who were considered to be the "heads" of families were granted the right to a certain amount of land. The state expected these people to settle the land within a few months of taking ownership and make it productive (for example, farming the land, building mills, etc.) The headright system continued until 1803.

Georgia also conducted several **land lotteries** between 1803 and 1833. Land lotteries allowed eligible Georgians to "gamble" for land. Most white males, heads of households, war veterans, and widows could purchase chances to win the opportunity to buy land in the lotteries. How many opportunities you had to win depended on your place in society (for example, war veterans and widows usually got more chances). Those who did win could then purchase acres of land from the government. Georgia dispersed thousands of acres of land through the land lotteries.

The Yazoo Land Fraud

After the Revolutionary War, Georgia's western territory stretched far into present-day Alabama and Mississippi. This territory was called the *Yazoo lands*, after the Yazoo River that flows through the region. Because the territory was so large, Georgia knew that it would be difficult to defend it against hostile Native Americans and foreign threats, especially since the British still had a presence in North America, and the Spanish possessed Florida and New Orleans. As a result, Governor George Matthews and various other leaders looked for a way to get rid of the excess land.

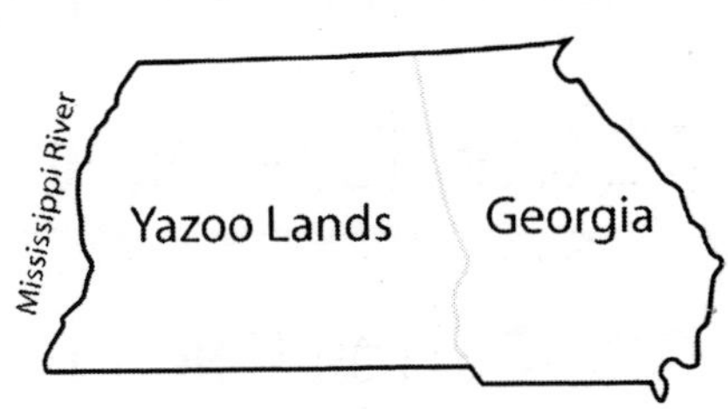

Governor Matthews decided to transfer the land to the federal government in the late 1780s. After his attempt failed, however, a group of land speculators who wanted to purchase the land at a ridiculously low price and then resell it at a profit offered to buy the territory. Meanwhile, state Senator James Gunn, a major stockholder in one of the companies (this means he owned part of one of the companies and stood to make a lot of money if the land was sold) bribed a number of his fellow legislators so that they would support the plan. Under the *Yazoo Act of 1795*, the state of Georgia sold between 35 and 50 million acres of land to these speculators for roughly one cent per acre.

When word got out about what had taken place, Georgians were furious and voted many of the officials who had supported the deal out of office. The General Assembly then passed the *Rescinding Act*. The act reversed the Yazoo sale, and the state eventually ceded ownership of the western territory to the federal government. However, by that time, many of the land speculators had already sold much of the Yazoo territory to people who wanted to keep their land. These new landowners now sued, and the case went all the way to the Supreme Court. The Court ruled that, even though the Yazoo deal was corrupt, it was still a legal contract. It struck down the Rescinding Act as unconstitutional and the federal government eventually settled with the landowners by paying them roughly $5 million. Not only was the **Yazoo Land Fraud** a notorious scandal, but it also created bitterness against the federal government on the part of many Georgians because they resented the Supreme Court striking down a state law. Eventually, the Yazoo territory became two new states: Alabama and Mississippi.

Practice 4.1 Antebellum Georgia

1. What was the first state-supported university ever chartered in the United States?

   A. The University of Georgia
   B. Emory University
   C. The University of North Carolina
   D. Mercer University

2. The Baptists and Methodists became the two most influential religious groups in Georgia due to which of the following reasons?
   A. They were the only denominations proclaiming to believe in the Bible.
   B. Only Baptists and Methodists had formally trained ministers.
   C. They were willing to use new methods to reach people along the frontier.
   D. They were the first churches to think of using colleges to train preachers.

3. What was the Yazoo Land Fraud, why did it upset Georgians, and how did it affect relations between state leaders and the Supreme Court?

4.2 New Technologies and Economic Growth

The "Cotton Kingdom" of the South

Cotton gin

As Georgia entered the 1800s, its economy relied heavily on agriculture (farming). In particular, it relied on several important *cash crops* (crops that provide a large amount of income for a region): rice, indigo, tobacco, and cotton. Of these, **cotton** eventually became the main cash crop, not only in Georgia, but throughout the South. This was in large part due to the invention of the **cotton gin** in 1793. The cotton gin enabled people to separate seeds from cotton much faster than before and increased the rate at which cotton could be produced and sold. It also increased the demand for slavery because plantation owners had lots of land and needed slaves to harvest all their cotton. As a result, both cotton and slavery became increasingly important to the South's economy.

The Rise of "King Cotton"

Cotton

Several factors contributed to the South becoming a **Cotton Kingdom**. For starters, in 1812, the US declared war on Great Britain (this conflict became known as the *War of 1812*). The war greatly reduced the amount of cotton that could be imported from other countries, so US farmers began producing more of it themselves. In addition, northeastern textile mills and manufacturers began producing more domestic products as well (domestic products are products produced in the US). As a result, the demand for cotton was high even though imports of cotton were unavailable. By the time the fighting ended in 1815, southern farmers had become much more efficient at producing large amounts of cotton and the nation had truly developed its own economy independent of having to rely on Great Britain for help.

In Georgia, the railroads also helped the cotton industry because they allowed agricultural goods to be transported more easily and efficiently. Southern businessmen also established a number of **textile mills** (factories where cotton is used to produce finished products) in Georgia. Eventually, the growth of textile mills, agricultural industries, and railroads led to other new industries as well, such as banking and insurance.

RAILROADS

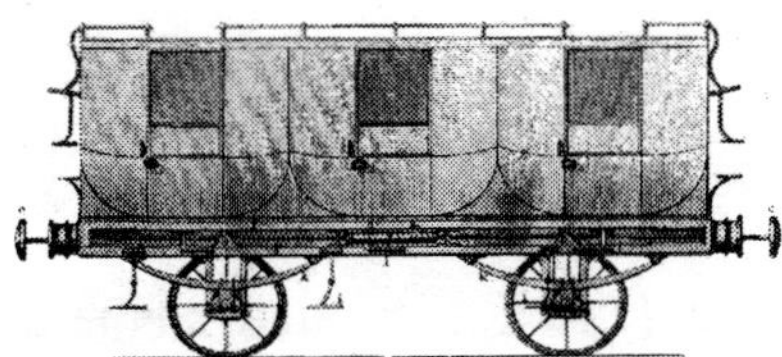

Another key invention was **railroads**. Georgia constructed its first railroads during the 1830s after Savannah businessmen learned that South Carolina was building a rail line from Charleston to Hamburg. This greatly concerned leaders in Georgia because Charleston and Hamburg competed with Savannah and Augusta for business.

Railroads meant that farmers and businessmen could transport their products much faster and easier. Therefore, any port city accessible by railway was easier to ship goods out of than one that wasn't. Georgia had to develop a rail line as well or risk losing tons of money to South Carolina. The General Assembly chartered three rail lines in 1833: The Georgia Railroad Co. (an Athens-Augusta line), the Central of Georgia Railroad Co. (a Savannah-Macon line), and the Monroe Railroad Co. (a Macon-Forsyth line). Eventually, the state also chartered the Western and Atlantic Railroad in 1836 that linked central Georgia with Chattanooga, Tennessee.

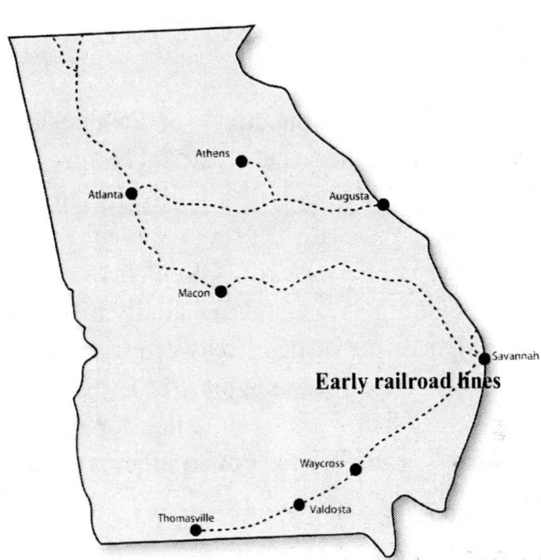

Early railroad lines

Despite a nationwide depression from 1837 to 1844, the "railroad boom" continued in Georgia. In the 1850s, various independent railroads in Georgia began to combine their lines. By 1861, the state had the most sophisticated railway system in the Deep South and one of the best in the nation. Not only did the railroad industry give Georgians access to both eastern and western markets, it also gave rise to a new, bustling town that served as a major connector between the main lines. Originally named *Terminus*, then *Marthasville,* this railroad hub finally came to be called **Atlanta**.

Practice 4.2 New Technologies and Economic Growth

1. The cotton gin had which of the following effects on Georgia?

   A. It made harvesting cotton easier so that slaves were no longer needed.

   B. It made harvesting cotton more efficient and increased the state's dependence on the crop.

   C. It caused many mills to close and go out of business.

   D. It made it harder for large plantation owners to make money.

2. Why were railroads so important to antebellum Georgia and how did they impact the state?

THE CREEKS AND CHEROKEE

GEORGIA AND THE CREEKS

During the Revolutionary War, many Native Americans in Georgia fought as allies of the British. In exchange for their help, the British promised to return land taken by white settlers once Britain won the war. Unfortunately for these Native Americans, however, they chose the wrong side. Once the war was over and Georgia was a state, white Georgians once again turned their eyes towards taking even more Native American land.

The first tribe to feel the effects of such desires was the **Creeks**. The Creeks were prominent in southern and western Georgia and did not want to give up their land. Initially, **Chief Alexander McGillivray** led the Creeks in resisting white expansion. He supported the British during the revolution and continued to have harsh feelings towards the US because of its policies towards Native Americans after the war. President George Washington actually met with McGillivray in 1790 in hopes of peacefully settling disputes between the Creeks and white Georgians. They signed the *Treaty of New York*, in which the Creeks gave up some of their land in exchange for a promise that whites would not move west beyond a certain point. It wasn't long, however, before the government started breaking its promises to the Creeks.

Chief McGillivray

Of course, the Creeks did not like being pushed off their land. However, due to the popularity of **Indian removal** (a policy that sought to remove Native Americans from their land to make room for white settlers), the federal government's support of Georgia's efforts to take land from Native Americans, and Florida's new status as a US territory, the Creeks felt pressured to make a deal. In 1821, they signed a treaty that gave away all Creek land between the Ocmulgee and Flint rivers. Governor John Clark then called the General Assembly into session and called for a land lottery to distribute the new territory.

CHIEF WILLIAM MCINTOSH AND THE TREATY OF INDIAN SPRINGS

Chief McIntosh

After winning a close election in 1823, Governor George Troup sought to increase his popularity by attempting to drive the Creeks from their remaining land. Fortunately for Troup, his first cousin was a Creek chief named **William McIntosh** (McIntosh was part Native American and part Scot). With the help of the federal government, Troup got McIntosh and a few other Creek leaders to sign the **Treaty of Indian Springs** in 1825. The treaty gave up all Creek lands to the state of Georgia and greatly angered many of the Creek people. In fact, some were so furious that they dragged McIntosh from his home not long after the treaty, stabbed him to death, and took his scalp.

Governor Troup

President John Q. Adams

Meanwhile, a new president, John Quincy Adams, took office in Washington in 1824. Adams thought that the Treaty of Indian Springs was corrupt because he knew that most Creeks did not support it. This made Governor Troup and other Georgia leaders furious and created great tension between Washington and Milledgeville (Georgia's capital). Finally, despite a separate treaty between the federal government and the Creeks, Troup insisted that the land obtained through the Treaty of Indian Springs be allotted to white Georgians. He even threatened to fight the US Army if it tried to interfere and told the Georgia militia to be prepared. In the end, the federal government did not think it was worth the risk of provoking armed conflict in Georgia. By 1827, the state had taken possession of all Creek lands and the Treaty of Indian Springs was in full force.

The Plight of the Cherokee

Sequoyah

The **Cherokee** were the other main Native American tribe in Georgia. They lived mostly in northern Georgia and parts of the western Carolinas. Of all the Native American tribes in the US, the Cherokee adapted the most to white culture. They lived in houses, farmed, owned property, and some even owned slaves. One of the Cherokee's most noted figures was **Sequoyah**. Also known as George Gist (his father was a Virginian and his mother a Cherokee), Sequoyah was fascinated by how whites were able to communicate through writing. He decided to create a written language for the Cherokee as well. Between 1809 and 1821, Sequoyah created a *syllabary*. Unlike an alphabet that consists of symbols for each letter, a syllabary contains symbols for syllables. The syllabary not only made the Cherokee the first Native American tribe to have a written language, but it also allowed them to communicate with one another through letters, newspapers, etc.

Chief John Ross

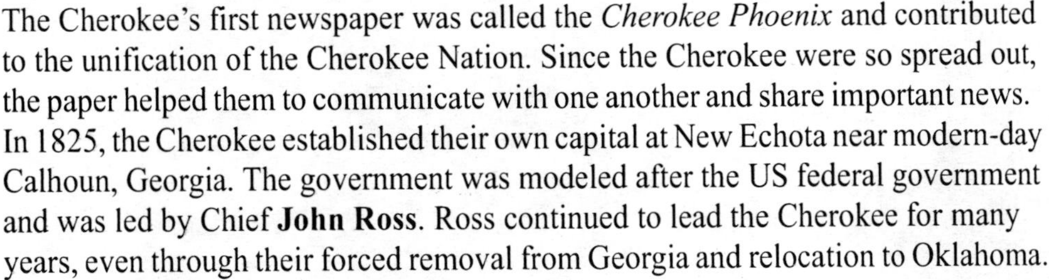
The Cherokee's first newspaper was called the *Cherokee Phoenix* and contributed to the unification of the Cherokee Nation. Since the Cherokee were so spread out, the paper helped them to communicate with one another and share important news. In 1825, the Cherokee established their own capital at New Echota near modern-day Calhoun, Georgia. The government was modeled after the US federal government and was led by Chief **John Ross**. Ross continued to lead the Cherokee for many years, even through their forced removal from Georgia and relocation to Oklahoma.

The Dahlonega Gold Rush

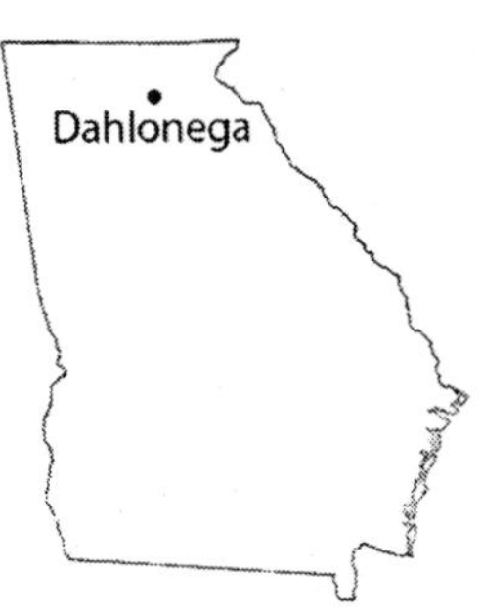

The new tribal government encouraged the Cherokee people, but it also increased tensions between Native Americans and Georgians who wanted their land. Finally, in 1829, settlers discovered gold in Cherokee territory, setting off the **gold rush of 1829**. Almost immediately, white settlers flooded into northern Georgia to get rich. A number of new towns sprung up as a result. One of them was Dahlonega, taken from the Cherokee word for "golden." Meanwhile, the Georgia Assembly began passing laws denying the Cherokee rights to both their land and the gold. There was little the Cherokee could do.

Worcester v. Georgia and the Trail of Tears

Samuel Worcester

One law passed by the Georgia Assembly was meant to keep whites from helping the Cherokee. It stated that whites could not live in Cherokee territory without swearing an oath of allegiance to the governor. In 1832, a Christian missionary named Samuel Worcester refused to swear such an oath because he saw it as his sacred duty to help the oppressed tribe. He and another missionary were sentenced to prison but appealed their case all the way to the Supreme Court. Under the leadership of Chief Justice **John Marshall**, the Court ruled in ***Worcester v. Georgia (1832)*** that Georgia must set Worchester and his colleague free because the laws of the state were invalid (did not count) in Cherokee territory. This enraged Georgia's governor, Wilson Lumpkin, and frustrated President **Andrew Jackson**. Jackson believed firmly in Indian removal, and he wanted to get the Cherokee out of Georgia. When the state refused to release the missionaries, President Jackson made his famous statement: "John Marshall has made his decision, now let him enforce it." Eventually, Georgia released the missionaries as part of a compromise, but the case once again created bitterness between the state's government and the nation's highest court.

John Marshall

Governor Lumpkin

Initially, the Cherokee celebrated the *Worcester* decision because they thought it meant they could keep their land. The state's defiance of the Court, however, combined with Jackson's refusal to come to the Cherokee's aid, resulted in the tribe continuing to lose more and more of its territory. Finally, in 1835, the US government forced the Cherokee to sign a treaty giving up all of their lands in Georgia. In 1838, the United States Army rounded up the last of the Cherokee and forced them to march 800 miles west to the Oklahoma territory. Many members of the tribe died from disease, starvation, and exposure to the cold weather along the way. Today, the Cherokee remember this journey as the **Trail of Tears**.

Andrew Jackson

Trail of Tears

Practice 4.3 The Creeks and Cherokee

1. Who were the Creeks and Cherokee?
   A. the two main Native American tribes in Georgia
   B. the two last Native American tribes in the United States
   C. the only Native American tribes not to have a written language
   D. two of the Native American tribes that supported Indian removal

2. What did Alexander McGillivray and William McIntosh have in common?
   A. They were both Cherokee chiefs who resisted white expansion.
   B. They were both Creek chiefs who played major roles in the tribes relations with the state of Georgia.
   C. They both refused to give up Native American lands.
   D. They both were Georgia legislators who wanted to take Native American territory.

3. Who was Sequoyah and what significant contribution did he make to Cherokee history?

4. What was the "Trail of Tears" and why did it come to be known by that name?

4.4 Slavery, States' Rights, and Secession

States' Rights and the Doctrine of Nullification

John C. Calhoun

Georgia was not the only southern state to get upset with the federal government prior to the Civil War. Many southerners were angry because they believed the national government was intruding more and more on **states' rights** (the authority states have to govern what goes on inside their own borders). Under the Tenth Amendment, any powers not specifically prohibited by the Constitution or delegated to the national government are "reserved for the states." Many southern states understood this to mean that they could ignore federal laws which they believed violated the Constitution. Such a view was known as the **doctrine of nullification** because it claimed that state authority could "nullify" (cancel) national laws. In 1832, South Carolina invoked the doctrine of nullification when it threatened to secede (leave the union) over the issue of tariffs. Tariffs are taxes placed on goods imported from other countries in order to protect manufacturers in the US. Southerners often opposed tariffs because they were meant to help northern businessmen compete with foreign manufacturers, rather than southern plantation owners who often imported foreign goods. Southerners also hated tariffs because foreign countries often retaliated with tariffs of their own. Such tariffs hurt the South because it sold a lot of cotton overseas. President Jackson got so mad over South Carolina's stubborness that he threatened to find the nearest tree and hang South Carolina Senator John C. Calhoun. The two sides eventually compromised, but the dispute over states' rights continued up until the Civil War.

Slavery

The Missouri Compromise and the Compromise of 1850

In the 1800s, **slavery** continued to be a heated issue. The North relied mostly on factories, manufacturing, and business rather than agriculture. Therefore, it did not need slavery in order to maintain its economy. However, since the South still relied on cash crops like cotton, it depended heavily on slave labor to work its large plantations. As a result, friction continued to build between those in the North who wanted to end slavery and those in the South who wanted to protect it. The debate became even more intense as the nation expanded west. As new territories and states joined the union, they had to decide whether or not to allow slavery (many northern states began abolishing slavery in the 1800s). Both southerners and northerners were concerned about slavery in new territories because, as these areas became states, they sent representatives to Congress. Whichever side had the most members in Congress would have the advantage when it came time to make laws about slavery and other key issues. In 1820, Congress approved the **Missouri Compromise** in an effort to please both those who opposed slavery and those who favored it. The agreement admitted Missouri as a slave state and Maine as a free state. It also stated that all new states north of a certain point would be free, and all states south of that point would allow slavery. Congress hoped that by guaranteeing certain states would be free and others slave, it could help maintain peace between the North and South.

Fugitive Slaves Captured
Library of Congress

As the country continued to gain new territories, however, the issue of slavery only continued to cause division. Many wanted to forbid slavery in new territories. Others wanted to guarantee that states could decide the issue for themselves. Still others wanted to guarantee the right to own slaves in any new territory or state. Once again, an important compromise helped settle the issue temporarily. The **Compromise of 1850** admitted California to the Union as a free state while allowing the rest of the western territories to decide the issue by *popular sovereignty*. In other words, the people who lived there would vote on whether or not to have slavery. It also established the *Fugitive Slave Law*, which required northern states to return runaway slaves to the South. Since many Northerners were against slavery, they just ignored the law.

The Georgia Platform

Robert Toombs

Alexander Stephens

The Compromise of 1850 caused division in the South. Radical supporters of states' rights opposed the compromise and advocated resistance—even if it meant secession. Meanwhile, "unionists" (southerners who wanted the South to remain part of the union) supported the compromise. Two Georgia Congressmen who played key roles in securing support for the compromise among southerners were Robert Toombs and **Alexander Stephens**. After helping to win its passage in Congress, the two men returned to Georgia to gather support for the compromise there as well. South Carolina appeared ready to secede, but other southern states were undecided. Whatever Georgia decided would likely influence the entire South. The state called a special convention where it voted to accept the compromise and remain part of the Union. It also issued the **Georgia Platform**, which stated that, although the state accepted the Compromise of 1850, it would not hesitate to resist any effort by Congress to outlaw slavery in the new territories.

The Kansas-Nebraska Act

Clash Between Pro-slavery and Anti-slavery Forces

Kansas and Nebraska were originally free territories. Congress, however, changed this when it passed the **Kansas-Nebraska Act** in 1854. The new law said that these areas could vote on whether or not to have slaves (popular sovereignty). The law basically repealed (cancelled) the Missouri Compromise and led to a civil war in Kansas between pro-slavery and anti-slavery forces. As more and more people poured into Kansas to support both sides, the fighting became so violent that the territory became known as "Bleeding Kansas." Kansas finally became a free state in 1861.

The Dred Scott Case

Another event sparking anger was the **Dred Scott case** that went before the Supreme Court in 1857. The case involved a slave named Dred Scott who sued for his freedom after his master died. The Court ruled that Scott had no right to sue since he was not a citizen and that states could not deprive slave owners of their "property" without due process (a right guaranteed under the Fifth Amendment of the Constitution). This made abolitionists (people wanting to outlaw slavery) and people who favored popular sovereignty (letting each state decide for themselves) furious because it meant that slave owners could keep their slaves in any state. Southern slaveholders, however, were pleased with the decision.

Dred Scott

The Election of 1860 and Southern Secession

In 1854, a number of Free Soilers, anti-slavery Democrats, and Whigs (these were political parties that existed at the time) united and formed the *Republican Party.* Although the party had a lot of abolitionists, it officially only sought to restrict slavery in new states and territories, not outlaw it where it already existed. In 1860, the Republicans nominated **Abraham Lincoln** for president of the United States. When Lincoln won the election, many Southerners were concerned. They did not trust that Lincoln only wanted to limit slavery; they were sure he wanted to end it. As a result, South Carolina decided to secede from the Union in December 1860. By February, six other states, including Georgia, seceded as well. Eventually, even more followed. The southern states set up a new government and called themselves the **Confederate States of America**.

Abraham Lincoln

Georgia's Decision to Secede

Georgians were up in arms over Lincoln's election. They quickly divided into two major groups: radical secessionists, who wanted to leave the Union right away, and "cooperationists," who wanted the southern states to get together and come up with an organized plan before seceding. Governor Joseph E. Brown called a legislative session to determine if the state would have a convention to vote on secession. The session was full of passionate debate as leaders on both sides argued for and against secession. In the end, the legislature voted in favor of a convention. At the convention, Georgians elected to leave the Union, and on January 19, 1861, the state officially seceded.

Governor Brown

Alexander Stephens

Alexander Stephens played a key role both in Georgia's debate over secession and the new southern government. Stephens was a lawyer from Crawfordville and served in the United States Congress from 1843 to 1859. He was a sickly man and never weighed over 100 pounds. Still, one northern politician described him as, "the strongest man in the South." Although he supported states' rights, he was a cooperationist who voted against secession at the state convention. However, once Georgia made its decision to leave the Union, he quickly became a key figure in the South's new government. He was elected vice president of the Confederacy and served in that office throughout the war

Alexander Stephens

Practice 4.4 Slavery, States' Rights and Secession

1. Someone who believes in states' rights would most likely support which of the following statements?

   A. US citizens should always obey federal laws.
   B. National laws are more important than state laws.
   C. The national government has no right to tell states how to handle their own business.
   D. There is no need for a national government.

2. What was the purpose of both the Missouri Compromise and the Compromise of 1850?

   A. They were meant to peacefully resolve disputes over slavery in US territories.
   B. They were passed by the General Assembly to settle the issue of whether or not Georgia should secede from the Union.
   C. They were adopted to proclaim that states had the right to "nullify" laws they believed were unconstitutional.
   D. They formally established the Confederate States of America.

3. Who was Alexander Stephens and what role did he play in both Georgia's decision to secede and the new confederate government?

Chapter 4 Review

Key Terms, People, and Concepts

University of Georgia
Louisville and Milledgeville
Methodists and Baptists
headright system
land lotteries
Yazoo Land Fraud
cotton
cotton gin
"King Cotton"
textile mills
railroads
Atlanta
Creeks
Chief Alexander McGillivray
Indian removal
William McIntosh
Treaty of Indian Springs
Cherokee
Sequoyah
John Ross
Gold rush of 1829
John Marshall
Worchester v. Georgia
Andrew Jackson
Trail of Tears
states' rights
Doctrine of nullification
slavery
Missouri Compromise
Compromise of 1850
Alexander Stephens
Georgia Platform
Kansas-Nebraska Act
Dred Scott case
Abraham Lincoln
Confederate States of America
Georgia's decision to secede

Multiple Choice Questions

1. *Circuit riders* were associated with which of the following?
   A. The University of Georgia
   B. Baptists
   C. Methodists
   D. Cooperationists

2. Events in which Georgians had the chance to win the right to buy land from the state were known as
   A. headright systems.
   B. land lotteries.
   C. circuit riders.
   D. Yazoo deals.

3. Atlanta formed mainly as
   A. a railroad hub.
   B. a center for textile mills.
   C. part of the Yazoo Land Fraud.
   D. part of the Gold Rush of 1829

4. With which of the following statements would a secessionist most agree?
   A. "We should not be too hasty to leave the Union."
   B. "Let's give Lincoln a chance, perhaps he will be a good president."
   C. "The South must break away from the Union before the federal government rips away all our rights."
   D. "States' rights is a dangerous principle."

5. What did President Andrew Jackson mean when he said: "John Marshall has made his decision, now let him enforce it."?
   A. He would not support the South's decision to secede.
   B. He would not stop the hanging of South Carolina Senator John C. Calhoun.
   C. He would not support Marshall's attempts to take Native American lands.
   D. He would not act to ensure Georgia respected the decision of the Supreme Court.

6. The Georgia Platform was important because it did which of the following?
   A. stated that Georgia would support the Compromise of 1850 so long as the federal government did not outlaw slavery in the western territories
   B. announced Georgia would not support the Missouri Compromise
   C. announced Georgia would not support slavery in western territories
   D. proclaimed that Georgia had seceded and was no longer part of the Union

7. Which of the following most upset Georgians?
   A. the Supreme Court's decision in the Dred Scott case
   B. the Kansas-Nebraska Act
   C. the election of Abraham Lincoln
   D. South Carolina's decision to secede

8. Which of the following is true regarding Alexander Stephens?
   A. He was a cooperationist who opposed secession at the Georgia convention.
   B. He was a secessionist who always wanted to leave the Union.
   C. He opposed the Compromise of 1850 because he thought it violated states' rights.
   D. He was elected president of the new Confederate States of America in 1860.

Chapter 5
Civil War and Reconstruction

This chapter covers the following standard(s).

SS8H6	The student will analyze the impact of the Civil War and Reconstruction on Georgia.

5.1 The War and its Impact on Georgia

The War Begins

Once they seceded, the southern states set up their own *confederacy*. A confederacy is a system of government in which the states have more power than the national government. In other words, while the states depend on the national government for unity, they still have the right to do what they want in most matters (don't forget, states rights was a big reason the South seceded). The Confederates elected former Mississippi senator, *Jefferson Davis*, to be their president and former Georgia congressman, Alexander Stephens, to be their vice president. They made Montgomery, Alabama their first capital.

Jefferson Davis

Fort Sumter

President Abraham Lincoln knew he could not let the South secede. However, he also knew that US citizens had different opinions about going to war. Many in the North were sick of the slavery debate. They wanted Lincoln to let the South leave and take their disgusting slavery with them. Others wanted to preserve the Union but favored negotiating (talking to work out a peaceful solution) with the South. Only a few favored force. As a result, Lincoln did not have enough support to launch any military action against the Confederacy even if he wanted to. If there was going to be a war, the South would have to start it.

In April, 1861, Union troops located at Fort Sumter, South Carolina, were running low on supplies. Lincoln sent word to the governor of South Carolina that he was sending ships with food for the soldiers but no weapons. South Carolina would not tolerate Union troops so close to home any longer, however, and on April 12, Confederate forces opened fire. The South's attack forced the Union troops to leave the fort, but it also gave Lincoln the support he needed. Many northerners who at first opposed the war now felt the Union had been attacked. They were ready to support their president if he decided war was necessary.

Attack on Fort Sumter

Meanwhile, in the South, more states decided to secede. Virginia left the Union on April 17, and the Confederacy soon decided to move its capital from Montgomery to Richmond. Eventually, North Carolina, Tennessee, and Arkansas left as well.

Union Blockade

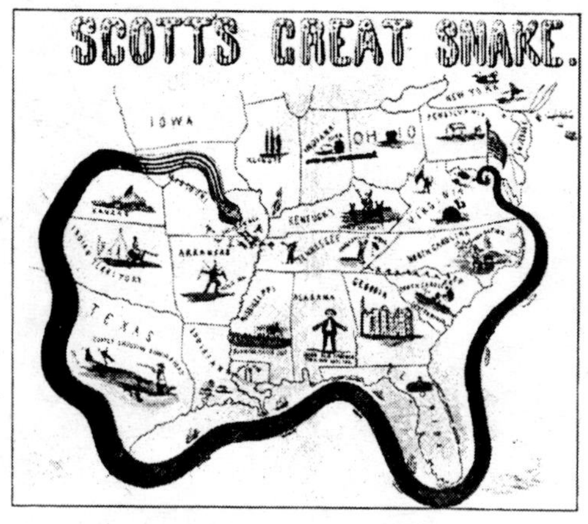

Winfield Scott's Blockade Line

Most people thought that any war between the Union and Confederacy would not last long. Northerners especially thought it would be no time before their military beat the South into submission. After all, the North had more men, more labor, more railroads, and more supplies. Northerners underestimated, however, the South's determination. Southerners believed they were fighting for their homeland and their way of life. When Confederate forces defeated Union troops at the First Battle of Bull Run in July 1861, it became clear the war would not be over so quickly. President Lincoln then adopted Union General Winfield Scott's *Anaconda Plan*. It called for a **naval blockade** of the southern coast. A blockade means that the Union's ships lined the coast and would not let any Confederate ships in or out. The Union hoped this would cause the South to run out of supplies and prevent it from trading its cotton overseas. As a result, the South would have no choice but to surrender. It was called the "Anaconda Plan" because, like an anaconda (a giant snake that squeezes its prey to death), it would encircle the Confederacy and slowly squeeze the life out of it.

Blockade runner

Since Georgia greatly depended on its coastal ports, the blockade had a huge impact on the state. After Union forces established a base off the coast of South Carolina at Hilton Head Island, President Jefferson Davis sent General **Robert E. Lee** to Savannah to take charge of defending the Georgia and Florida coasts. Lee could do little to stop the blockade, however. By spring 1862,Union Admiral Samuel DuPont made good on his vow to "cork up Savannah like a bottle." Hardly any ship could make it in or out of Georgia. Only the occasional **blockade runner** made it through. Blockade runners were ships that tried to slip through the blockades with supplies and goods Southerners needed or with shipments of cotton bound for overseas.

Eastern Theater

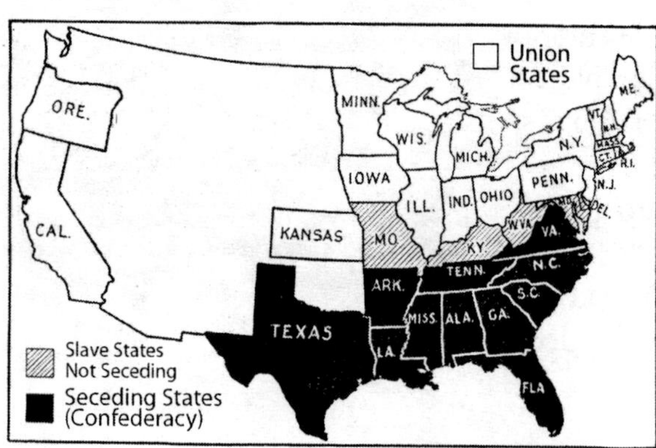

On land, the Confederacy and Union armies fought in two *theaters*. Part of the war was fought in the East (known as the **Eastern Theater**), and part of the war was fought in the West (the **Western Theater**). The Eastern Theater consisted of battles fought in Virginia, Maryland, West Virginia, and Pennsylvania. The majority of Georgians who fought in the war fought in the Eastern Theater as part of General Robert E. Lee's Army of Northern Virginia. The Western Theater, on the other hand, involved battles fought in Tennessee, Kentucky, Mississippi, Alabama, and eventually, Georgia, as the war entered its final stages.

ANTIETAM AND THE EMANCIPATION PROCLAMATION

Robert E. Lee

After taking over as the commander of the Army of Northern Virginia, Robert E. Lee quickly proved that he was a great military leader. He consistently defeated the Union army even though he was always outnumbered. In September 1862, Lee made a bold move. Confident from his successes, he decided to invade the North! The plan almost worked because the Union army had no idea where Lee's army was or what its next move might be. Then, as luck would have it, some Union soldiers found a copy of Lee's plans for the invasion wrapped around some cigars in an abandoned Confederate camp. Now aware of what Lee was doing, the Union army met Lee at Antietam Creek in Maryland. The battle of **Antietam** was the bloodiest one-day battle of the war and stopped the Confederate invasion.

Emancipation Proclamation

Antietam also gave Lincoln a much needed victory. Up until that point, things had not been going well for the Union and many people blamed the president. Antietam won Lincoln enough support to issue the **Emancipation Proclamation** on January 1, 1863. The proclamation was an executive order that freed the slaves in the Confederate states. It did not free slaves in slave states loyal to the Union because President Lincoln could not afford to lose these states' support. Still, Lincoln's proclamation made it clear that the war was now a fight for freedom as well as for the Union. Many African-Americans enlisted in the army and fought bravely, aware that they were fighting for the liberation of their own people. Perhaps the most celebrated African-American unit, the *54th Massachusetts*, actually saw its first combat in Georgia. (The movie *Glory* tells the story of the 54th Massachusetts.)

GETTYSBURG

Pickett's Charge, Gettysburg

Lee did not give up on his plans to invade the North. In 1863, he tried again. This time the main battle occurred when the two armies met by accident outside the little town of Gettysburg, Pennsylvania. The three day battle of **Gettysburg** was the bloodiest battle of the entire war. More than 51,000 soldiers died on the battlefield. It was also a huge turning point. As the battle was raging, Confederate Vice President Alexander Stephens attempted to win safe passage to Washington to meet with President Lincoln and discuss terms of peace. He and Jefferson Davis hoped that Lee would win at Gettysburg and that Lincoln would feel pressured to end the war. Once Lincoln learned the Union had won, however, he refused to allow Stephens through the Union lines.

All the South could do after Gettysburg was try to hold on long enough for the North to get tired of fighting. Unfortunately for the Confederacy, however, President Lincoln eventually gave command of his army to a "no nonsense" warrior named **Ulysses S. Grant**. Although his tactics resulted in the deaths of thousands of his own men, Grant eventually crushed the southern resistance and forced Lee's final surrender in April 1865.

Ulysses S. Grant

Western Theater

Chickamauga

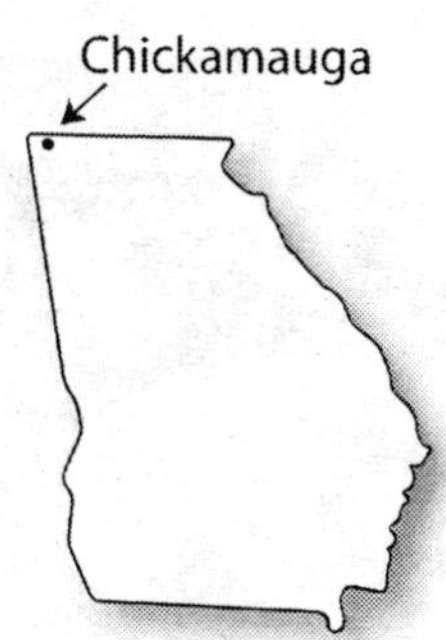

While the war raged on in the East, fierce fighting took place in the West as well. In September 1863, the Union army captured Chattanooga, Tennessee, just north of the Georgia border. Union forces then moved into northwest Georgia where they met Confederate troops under the command of General Braxton Bragg at the battle of **Chickamauga**. The battle resulted in both sides losing more than 16,000 men and forced the Union army to retreat back to Tennessee. Despite the victory, President Davis was upset with Bragg for not pursuing his enemy in an attempt to drive its forces out of the Confederacy. He replaced Bragg with General Joseph Johnston. Meanwhile, Lincoln was also displeased. He gave command of all Union forces in the West to General Ulysses S. Grant, who had just conducted a successful siege of Vicksburg, Mississippi. (A siege is like a blockade on land; it is when an army surrounds a town or fort and doesn't let anything in or out. Eventually, the town has to surrender or starve.)

Braxton Bragg

Joseph E. Johnston

The Atlanta Campaign

William T. Sherman

In 1864, Lincoln appointed Grant to be overall commander of the entire Union army. Grant decided to take command of the eastern forces and put his most trusted general, **William T. Sherman**, in charge of his western forces. In May 1864, Sherman began an invasion of Georgia. He wanted to reach Atlanta because of its importance as a railway hub. If Sherman took Atlanta, he could seriously hurt the South by disrupting its major rail lines. As Sherman advanced south, General Johnston's confederate forces tried to delay his march with several small attacks. Johnston did not want to meet Sherman in a full-scale battle because Sherman had more men and Johnston feared that a defeat would mean the end of his army. Finally, after a series of bloody

Battle of Kennesaw Mountain

fights, Johnston's forces prepared to make their stand just north of Atlanta at **Kennesaw Mountain**. When a direct assault on Kennesaw Mountain failed, Sherman decided to flank (move around) Johnston's army to reach Atlanta. The move worked and, on July 8, the first Union forces crossed the Chattahoochee River to reach the outskirts of Atlanta.

Jefferson Davis was furious with Johnston for not engaging Sherman in a full-scale battle and replaced him with General John Bell Hood. By then, however, it was too late. Hood evacuated the city on September 1, 1864, and Sherman's army moved into Atlanta the very next day. Sherman's successful **Atlanta campaign** not only placed the city under Union control, it also reignited support for President Lincoln in the North. Before Atlanta, many Northerners wanted to negotiate with the South and end the war. After Sherman's success, however, people in the Union believed victory was in sight and re-elected Lincoln to a second term.

Confederate Defenses in Battle of Atlanta

Sherman's March to the Sea

After taking Atlanta, Sherman ordered much of the city burned. He then began a march from Atlanta to Savannah that became known as his **march to the sea**. On its way to the coast, Sherman's army burned buildings, destroyed rail lines, set fire to factories, and demolished bridges. Sherman hoped to cripple the South's ability to make and ship supplies so that it could not keep fighting. People in Savannah were so terrified by news of the destruction that when Sherman finally reached the city they surrendered without a fight. Sherman then turned north into the Carolinas. All the while, General Joseph Johnston continued trying to resist Sherman as best he could.

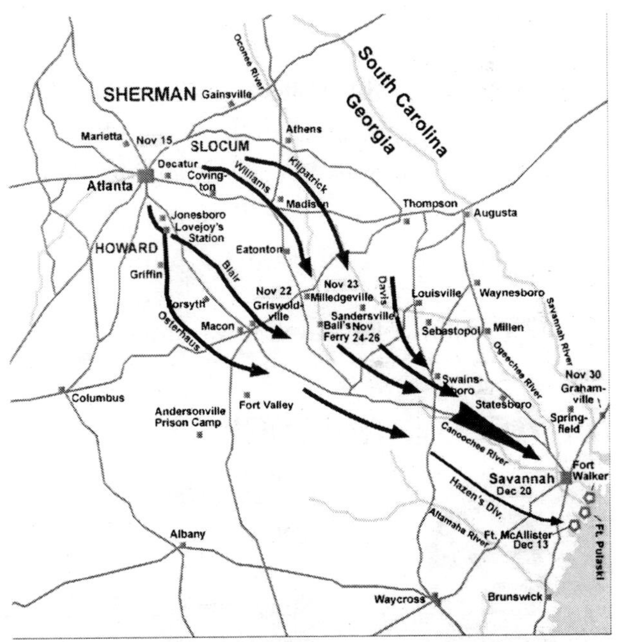

March to the Sea

Surrender and Aftermath

On April 9, 1865, General Robert E. Lee finally surrendered to Ulysses S. Grant at Appomattox Courthouse in Virginia. Two weeks later, the largest and last major surrender of the war took place when General Joseph Johnston surrendered to General William Sherman in North Carolina. After four years, the long, bloody war was over. Roughly 25,000 of the 125,000 Georgians who fought for the Confederacy died during the war. In addition, Sherman's ruthless march left much of the state devastated and in ruins.

Lee surrenders to Grant

Andersonville prison

One of the most notorious sites in all of the Civil War was the Confederate prison at **Andersonville**, Georgia. By the summer of 1864, Andersonville had so many union prisoners that its population was greater than all but four Confederate cities. Because the prison was so overcrowded and unsanitary, nearly 13,000 of its prisoners died of disease and starvation. The suffering at Andersonville was so horrible that the Union executed the prison's commander, Major Henry Wirz, for war crimes after he was captured.

Practice 5.1 The War and its Impact on Georgia

1. What was the purpose of the Union's blockade?
   A. to destroy rail lines
   B. to keep the South from trading goods by ship
   C. to force Lee's surrender at Gettysburg
   D. to take Atlanta

2. What did the Emancipation Proclamation do?
   A. It freed all slaves in the United States.
   B. It put Ulysses S. Grant in charge of all Union forces.
   C. It allowed slaves to fight in the Confederate army
   D. It freed the slaves in the Confederate states.

3. Why did Sherman think it was important to conquer Atlanta and what was his "march to the sea"?

5.2 Reconstruction

Andrew Johnson

Once the war was over, the federal government had to decide what to do about the states that seceded. Lincoln wanted to rebuild rather than punish the South. He felt all US citizens, including Southerners (Lincoln never acknowledged that Southerners had left the Union), had suffered enough. Sadly, he never got the chance to see the nation healed. An actor named John Wilkes Booth assassinated Lincoln while he attended a play at Ford's Theatre on April 14, 1865. **Andrew Johnson** succeeded Lincoln as the nation's seventeenth president and took on the burden of reuniting the country.

The Radical Republicans

Thaddeus Stevens
Radical Republican

The process of rebuilding the South was known as **Reconstruction.** President Johnson was a southern Democrat who remained loyal to the Union during the war. Therefore, he favored a form of reconstruction that was less harsh and did very little to guarantee the rights of freed slaves. Opposing President Johnson was a group of leaders in Congress known as the **Radical Republicans**. They were Republicans who believed in a more radical form of reconstruction. They felt the South should be punished for causing the war, and support for their views grew after Lincoln's assassination. They also believed that the majority of a state's voting population should have to swear allegiance to the United States before it could be re-admitted to the Union and that the civil rights of freed slaves should be protected. The Radical Republicans also felt strongly that Congress, rather than the president, should be in charge of Reconstruction. The conflict over Reconstruction grew so heated between the president and the Radical Republicans that Congress eventually impeached Johnson. Impeachment is when the Congress charges the president with wrongdoing in hopes of removing him/her from office. If the House impeaches the president and two-thirds of the Senate finds him/her guilty, then the president is removed from office. One vote in the Senate saved Johnson, however, and he remained in office until the end of his term.

The Freedmen's Bureau and Federal Legislation

In 1865, Congress created the **Freedmen's Bureau** in order to help freed slaves. It was the first federal relief agency in US history. The Freedmen's Bureau provided clothes, medical attention, food, education, and even land to African-Americans coming out of slavery. Lacking support, it eventually ended in 1869. However, during its brief time, it helped many slaves transition to freedom in Georgia and throughout the South.

Ex-slave Enjoys Freedom

Under the Radical Republicans, Congress also passed major legislation to help African-Americans after the war. Prior to Lincoln's death, the **Thirteenth Amendment** to the Constitution ended slavery throughout the country. States, however, often still refused to count blacks as citizens. Therefore, in 1866, Congress passed a civil rights act to guarantee citizenship rights to African-Americans. Since many Republicans feared that the Supreme Court might rule the law unconstitutional, Congress also passed a new amendment to the Constitution that was ratified in 1868. The **Fourteenth Amendment** granted citizenship to African-Americans and guaranteed them all the rights protected by the Bill of Rights. Finally, Congress passed yet another amendment that was ratified during the presidency of Ulysses S. Grant in 1870. The **Fifteenth Amendment** guaranteed that no citizen could be denied the right to vote by either the federal government or a state because of the color of their skin or because they used to be a slave. As a result, black men could vote in state and national elections (women could not because, back then, women were not allowed to vote, regardless of their race).

Reconstruction in Georgia

Sharecropping and Tenant Farming

Sharecropper

Although African-Americans were happy to see slavery end, they still had to adjust to a new way of life. Most southern blacks had been slaves all their lives; only a few had gained their freedom prior to the war or been born free. In most cases, they had no money, no land, and no property. In order to survive, many blacks in Georgia and the South turned to **sharecropping** and **tenant farming**. Sharecroppers agreed to farm a portion of a white landowner's land in return for housing and a share of the crop. Some landowners were dishonest, however, and often cheated their black tenants. As a result, sharecropping became almost like slavery for some African-Americans. Tenant farming, on the other hand, was when a family rented a portion of land and owned the crops they grew. While tenant farmers were less at the mercy of landowners than sharecroppers, both systems served to keep blacks working on land owned by whites.

Georgia's Reconstruction Government

Henry M. Turner

Rufus Bullock

Georgia had to have some form of government after the war. For a while, the federal government took over and appointed a provisional governor. A new state convention officially abolished slavery in 1866. A year later a new state legislature ratified the Thirteenth Amendment. The US army then ruled Georgia for a time until Washington set up a stable state government. In 1867, a convention made up mostly of "*scalawags*" (white southerners who supported the Republican Party) adopted a new state constitution that lasted until 1877. A year later, Radical Republican, Rufus Bullock, became governor and Georgia ratified the Fourteenth Amendment. Something else amazing happened in Georgia too: 32 African-Americans were elected to the state House and Senate! One of these black legislators was **Henry McNeal Turner**. Turner was a bishop in the African Methodist Episcopal Church and, unlike many black leaders, doubted that whites and blacks could live peacefully together after slavery. He complained about the way blacks were treated in the South and urged them to move to Africa rather than stay in the US. Few blacks followed Turner's directions, but he helped draw attention to the plight of African-Americans in the post-civil war South.

Unrest During Reconstruction in Georgia

Ku Klux Klan Members

Many Georgians did not welcome such drastic changes to state politics. A faction of conservative Democrats successfully plotted and expelled 28 African-American representatives from the Georgia legislature not long after their election. They based their actions on the argument that blacks' right to vote in the South did not give them the right to hold political office. Some groups also used violence to frighten African-Americans and keep them from exercising their civil rights. One of the most infamous groups was the **Ku Klux Klan**. Klansmen would dress up in white sheets and hooded masks, then go out at night terrorizing blacks and whites who tried to help them. They often lynched those they targeted (lynching is when a group kidnaps someone and kills them, usually claiming that the person did something offensive). Both during and after Reconstruction, the Klan grew in Georgia and the southern United States.

Rutherford B. Hayes

Republican governor Rufus Bullock was concerned about the unrest in Georgia and outraged that the black legislators had been expelled. He asked the federal government to bring back military rule and Georgia ended up reorganizing its government again in 1869. The new legislature returned many of the expelled African-Americans to office and ratified the Fifteenth Amendment in January 1870. Six months later, the federal government readmitted Georgia to the Union.

In 1876, both the Republicans and the Democrats claimed that their candidates had won the presidential election. After months of arguing, Republican Rutherford B. Hayes finally became president due to a compromise. The **Compromise of 1877** made Hayes the winner in exchange for the Republicans agreeing to end Reconstruction. After over a decade of being told what to do by Washington, southern states could again run their own governments. Because they were bitter against the Republicans both in Washington and at home, Georgia and its southern neighbors entered a century long period known as the *"solid South."* The term means that, for roughly a hundred years, only Democrats won elections for high offices; they had a "solid" grip on southern political power.

Practice 5.2 Reconstruction

1. The process of rebuilding the South after the Civil War was known as
   - A. radical republicanism.
   - B. solid South.
   - C. Reconstruction.
   - D. the Compromise of 1877.

2. Which of the following statements is **true** concerning African-Americans in Georgia after the war?
   - A. Some won election to political office.
   - B. They were not allowed to run anymore for public office after the Supreme Court ruled that the right to vote did not give them the right to hold office.
   - C. Most of them owned their first land as sharecroppers or tenant farmers.
   - D. Radical Republicans tried to limit the rights of African-Americans with laws that kept them from voting.

3. What was important about the 13th, 14th, and 15th Amendments to the Constitution? Explain how each affected African-Americans in the United States after the Civil War.

CHAPTER 5 REVIEW

Key Terms, People, and Concepts

naval blockade
Robert E. Lee
blockade runner
Eastern Theater
Western Theater
Antietam
Emancipation Proclamation
Gettysburg
Ulysses S. Grant
Chickamauga
William T. Sherman
Kennesaw Mountain
Atlanta Campaign
march to the sea
Andersonville
Andrew Johnson
Reconstruction
Radical Republicans
Freedmen's Bureau
Thirteenth Amendment
Fourteenth Amendment
Fifteenth Amendment
sharecropping
tenant farming
Henry McNeal Turner
Ku Klux Klan
Compromise of 1877

Multiple Choice

1. Why was the plan to blockade southern ports called the "Anaconda Plan?"
   A. It was designed to strike fast, like a snake.
   B. It involved the union army sneaking up on the Confederacy unnoticed.
   C. It was designed to squeeze the life out of the Confederacy by cutting off supplies and trade.
   D. "Anaconda" was the last name of the admiral who thought of the plan.

2. Who was William T. Sherman?
   A. He was the Confederate general who tried to invade the North twice but failed.
   B. He was the Union general who finally defeated Robert E. Lee and forced him to surrender.
   C. He was the appointed governor of Georgia during Reconstruction.
   D. He was the Union general who conquered Atlanta and marched all the way to Savannah.

3. With which of the following statements would Henry McNeal Turner have **most likely** agreed?
   A. Blacks should not be allowed to hold public office.
   B. Blacks cannot hope to get justice in the South and should leave for Africa.
   C. The Radical Republicans should mind their own business.
   D. It would have been better if the Confederacy had won the war.

4. Which of the following statements **best** describes the effects of the Civil War on Georgia?
   - A. Thousands of Georgians died fighting in the war while many others suffered at home.
   - B. Other than soldiers dying in far away battles, people in Georgia never really felt the effects of the war.
   - C. The war led to whites finally accepting blacks as their equals.
   - D. Small farmers suffered a great deal at the hands of the Union army, but people in Atlanta were spared any hardship.

5. Which of the following ended slavery throughout the United States?
   - A. the Emancipation Proclamation
   - B. Radical Reconstruction
   - C. the Thirteenth Amendment
   - D. the Fourteenth Amendment

6. Which of the following would have **least** supported the Radical Republicans?
   - A. a freed slave
   - B. a scalawag
   - C. a member of the Ku Klux Klan
   - D. a supporter of the Fifteenth Amendment

7. Which of the following battles occurred in the state of Georgia?
   - A. the battle of Gettysburg
   - B. the bloodiest one-day battle of the war
   - C. Chickamauga
   - D. Antietam

8. Which of the following helped African-Americans in the South after the Civil War?
   - A. the Ku Klux Klan
   - B. conservative Democrats
   - C. most white landowners
   - D. the Freedmen's Bureau

Chapter 6
From Reconstruction to WWI

This chapter covers the following standard(s).

SS8H7	The student will evaluate key political, social, and economic changes that occurred in Georgia between 1877 and 1918.

6.1 Politics and the Economy in Post War Georgia

The Bourbon Triumvirate and the "New South"

After Reconstruction, Democrats known as the *Bourbons* rose to power in the South. The Bourbons thought that the South needed to have more industry and rely less on agriculture for its economic welfare. In Georgia, three of these leaders in particular dominated state politics. Together, they were known as Georgia's **Bourbon Triumvirate**.

The Bourbon Triumvirate

The first was **Joseph E. Brown**. Brown was a fiery secessionist before the war and served four terms as the state's governor. During Georgia's time in the Confederacy, Brown often resisted Jefferson Davis' war policies because he believed they went too far and violated states' rights. After the war, Brown remained as governor until Republican Rufus Bullock took over and named him chief justice of the Georgia Supreme Court. He eventually served Georgia as a US Senator from 1880 –1891.

Joseph Brown

The second member of the Triumvirate was **John B. Gordon**. Gordon fought in the Confederate army and later became the leader of the Ku Klux Klan in Georgia. In 1872, he defeated Alexander Stephens to become a US Senator and played a key role in securing the Compromise of 1877. He resigned from the Senate in 1880 (Joseph Brown was appointed to take his place) and, in 1886, won the first of two terms as Georgia's governor. He later returned to the US Senate for one more term before ending his political career.

John Gordon

Finally, **Alfred H. Colquitt** was a man educated at Princeton University. He owned slaves before the South lost the war and served in the Confederate army. He believed blacks needed whites to take care of them and, as a lay preacher (untrained preacher), often taught Sunday school in black churches during and after Reconstruction. After losing his first bid for governor in 1857, Colquitt was elected in 1876 and served as the state's first Democratic governor after Reconstruction from 1877–1882.

Alfred Colquitt

The Triumvirate promoted policies that gradually replaced Georgia's former large landowning class with a new and growing middle and business class. They also expanded the railroads and increased industrialization. They promoted "white supremacy" (the idea of whites being superior to African-Americans) in order to keep the political support of white racists, and they often used their power to make money as they ran the government. One way they did this was through the *convict lease system*, in which they profited from convicted prisoners being used as slave labor.

Henry W. Grady and the "New South"

Henry Grady

Henry W. Grady was another influential figure of the time. As editor of the *Atlanta Constitution*, Grady used his newspaper to promote what he labeled the **New South**. Grady believed the South needed to be more like the North economically and stop relying so much on cotton and farming. He tried to get northern businesses to invest in the South and called for cooperation between the two regions. In 1866, he gave a speech in New England that convinced many northerners to invest in Atlanta. He also helped start a new university that focused on technology. Established in 1887, this institution ultimately became Georgia Tech. Although Grady helped bring new business and industrialization to the region, he did not get the chance to see the "New South" fully develop because he died unexpectedly of pneumonia 1889.

The International Cotton Exposition and New Industry

International Cotton Exposition

One of the ways cities make money is by attracting visitors. During the 1800s, cities often attracted visitors with fairs and expositions (expositions are public shows, often put on by businesses). In 1881, as part of his New South program, Henry Grady promoted Georgia's first **International Cotton Exposition**. The exposition attracted 200,000 paid visitors during its two and a half month run and showed the country that Georgia was ready for more industry. Georgia went on to host more expositions as well. One of them attracted business representatives from several northern states as well as Alabama and Georgia in 1895. It also featured a visit from President Grover Cleveland and a historic speech by Booker T. Washington (we will discuss Washington later in this chapter).

Textile Mill

Thanks to the Bourbons and men like Grady, Georgia's industry grew drastically following Reconstruction. **Atlanta** once again became the transportation hub of the South and its new industrial center as well. It also became the state capital in 1868. Due to the state's long tradition of growing cotton, **textile mills** became the state's number one industry and attracted lots of northern investors. Other industries also took off. By the 1890s, Georgia was number one in the world in the shipment of **naval stores** (products traditionally used to build and maintain wooden sailing ships, such as turpentine, rosin, etc.). Fertilizer production, sawmills, and even coal, marble, and iron-ore mining became growing industries in the late 1800s. Although Georgia's industry was nowhere near that of the North's, it still represented a big change. Despite the Bourbon's efforts, however, agriculture remained the state's biggest business. In fact, many small farmers grew to resent the Bourbons because they viewed industrialization as nothing more than northern businessmen coming south to drain money away from "hard working Georgians."

TOM WATSON AND THE POPULISTS

Not everyone agreed with Henry Grady's vision of the New South. Political leader, **Tom Watson**, criticized the New South program because he claimed it hurt small farmers in Georgia. In the late 1880s, the farmers certainly had reason to believe Watson was right. Most of them were suffering economically and slipping more and more into debt due to the *crop lien system*. Under the crop lien system, farmers borrowed against their upcoming harvest in order to get the supplies they needed. The only problem was that farmers usually did not harvest enough to cover everything they'd borrowed. As a result, they owed more money each year. Many of them ended up losing their land altogether. Angry and frustrated that they couldn't get out of debt, a large number of southern farmers joined the **Populist movement**. Populism was a political movement that fought to help farmers. Eventually, it became a political party known as the *People's Party*. The Populists wanted the government to do more to regulate the economy so that farmers could earn more money for their crops. They also encouraged farmers to work together for their cause through *cooperatives* or *alliances*. Most of these farmers were white, but there were some African-American Populists as well.

Tom Watson

Tom Watson became the most powerful voice for Populism in Georgia and one of the most powerful in the nation. Originally elected to Congress in 1890 as a Democrat, Watson became frustrated that the Democrats weren't doing enough to help the farmers and eventually left the party to become a Populist. He turned down a request to be the People's Party candidate for governor in 1892, choosing instead to run for re-election to Congress (this time as a Populist candidate). He lost. Then, in 1894, he ran again and, once more, was defeated. Although he was popular, Watson couldn't overcome the Democratic Party's domination of Georgia politics. He and his fellow Populists also found it hard to defend themselves against white racism. Since Populists often courted black voters and preached that poor white and black farmers should come together to help themselves economically, many white supremacists (even among poor farmers) refused to support Populist candidates in the South. The Populists did, however, win some seats in the state legislature.

THE ELECTION OF 1896 AND THE DECLINE OF POPULISM

In 1896, the Populists realized that they did not have enough support to win the US presidential election. On the other hand, their movement was popular enough that its support could decide which major party's candidate did win. The party decided to back the Democratic candidate, William Jennings Bryan. Even though Bryan did not fully support the Populists' ideas, his views were at least closer to what the Populists wanted than Republican William McKinley's. However, the Populists chose not to support Bryan's vice presidential running mate, Arthur Sewall. Instead, they nominated none other than Tom Watson for vice president. The Democrats refused to remove Sewall as their nominee, but they did allow Watson's name to appear on the ballot as well. Despite an energetic campaign by Bryan, McKinley won the election. The Republican took office in 1897, and the Populist movement was all but over. Watson actually ran as the Populist candidate for president in 1904 and 1908, but the party never again had the

William J. Bryan

same momentum as it did in the 1890s. Once criticized for trying to appeal to blacks and advocating cooperation between white and black farmers, Watson spent his last few years trumpeting white supremacy to sell his publications and win white, rural votes. He won a seat in the US Senate in 1920, but died less than two years later in September 1922.

THE COUNTY UNIT SYSTEM

As businessmen in Atlanta gained more power, rural Georgians began to fear that they were being pushed out of the political process by northern influences. In response, the state established the **county-unit system** for its political primaries in 1917 (a primary is a vote to see who will represent a political party in an upcoming election). Under the unit system, whichever candidate won the most unit votes won the election. The eight most populous counties got six votes, with each of the remaining counties receiving less. Whoever won the most votes in a given county got *all* of that county's unit votes. The effect was that small, rural counties ended up having more say over who won the primary than heavily populated counties. Even though two-thirds of the population lived in fewer than 40 counties, the remaining counties had enough unit votes to determine the winner all by themselves. Since only Democrats really stood a chance of winning a general election (election in which the Republicans and Democrats run against one another), whoever won the Democratic primary was bound to win the election as well. Many people saw the county-unit system as unfair because it meant that candidates could win even if the majority of the state voted for someone else. African-Americans especially did not like it because it kept power in the hands of rural Georgians and politicians who normally supported racist policies to win votes.

Practice 6.1 Politics and the Economy in Post War Georgia

1. Political leaders who dominated Georgia after Reconstruction, supported new industry, and often appealed to white supremacy were called what?

   A. Radical Republicans
   B. Populists
   C. The Bourbon Triumvirate
   D. Alliance Democrats

2. A small farmer in Georgia who was suffering economically during the 1890s would have most likely been drawn to which of the following?

   A. the Bourbons
   B. the Populists
   C. the New South
   D. Henry Grady

3. Who was Tom Watson, what impact did he have on the Populist movement, and how did some of his views change towards the end of his life?

6.2 Race Relations and Reform

Rebecca Latimer Felton

Rebecca L. Felton

The late nineteenth and early twentieth century is remembered as the *Progressive Era* in US history because it was a time when many "progressive" reformers called for change. Georgia was no different. One of the state's most noted reformers was **Rebecca Latimer Felton**. Felton was the wife of a progressive congressman and an activist. At times, she wrote articles for newspapers that challenged the Bourbon Triumvirate. She and her husband, William, also publicly criticized the convict lease system and helped bring it to an end around the turn of the century. In addition, Felton fought fiercely for *women's suffrage* (the right for women to vote). Although Georgia disappointed her by becoming the first state to reject the Nineteenth Amendment (amendment to the US Constitution giving women the right to vote), enough states eventually ratified it and women won their right to vote in 1920. Two years later, 87-year-old Rebecca Latimer Felton served as one of Georgia's US Senators when the governor appointed her to fill the seat of deceased Senator Tom Watson. Although she served just two days before a special election chose a permanent replacement, Felton made history as the first woman ever to sit in the United States Senate.

Segregation in the South

Separate Entrances for Movie House

Like many states, Georgia practiced **segregation** in the years following Reconstruction. Segregation meant that blacks and whites were not allowed to be together in public places. Whites liked segregation because it meant that they did not have to associate with blacks. Also, since they were the ones in power, whites normally got to enjoy the best seats and facilities, while African-Americans had to make due with inferior ones. Often, poor whites also wanted segregation because they resented black advancements in education and economics. By the early 1900s, more whites were poor sharecroppers than blacks. Segregation allowed these whites to still feel some sense of control and superiority even though they were falling behind some blacks economically. Ironically, "progressives" tended to view segregation as a positive reform. They believed it was the best way to limit racial violence and allow African-Americans to develop culturally.

Homer Plessy

To ensure segregation, many southern states, including Georgia, passed **Jim Crow laws**. These laws required blacks and whites to remain separated. Georgia's first Jim Crow Law required whites and blacks to ride in separate railroad cars. Eventually, some even made it illegal for blacks and whites to be buried in the same cemeteries. The Supreme Court said that such laws were okay in a famous 1896 court case known as ***Plessy v. Ferguson***. Louisiana had a law saying that blacks and whites could not share the same railway cars. Homer Plessy, a man who was part African-American, violated this law by sitting in a "whites only" car and was arrested. He sued all the way to the Supreme Court. The Court, however, ruled against Plessy. With the exception of just one dissenting judge ("dissenting" means that he disagreed with the Court's decision), the Court ruled that segregation was constitutional so long as African-Americans' facilities are equal to white facilities. The case upheld Jim Crow laws and established a legal doctrine known as "separate but equal."

KEY AFRICAN-AMERICAN FIGURES

Booker T. Washington

W.E.B. DuBois

Two important men during this time period were Booker T. Washington and W.E.B. DuBois. **Booker T. Washington** was a former slave who believed that blacks should focus on learning a trade, like farming, teaching, or some other form of manual labor, such as carpentry and construction. He felt that by proving themselves in such fields, African-Americans would eventually be treated as equal citizens. He founded a school called the *Tuskegee Institute* in Alabama that focused on just such training.

Another key figure was **W.E.B. DuBois**. DuBois taught at Atlanta University and strongly disagreed with Washington. He believed that African- Americans should strive to be intellectuals (well-educated and scholarly) and promoted liberal arts education within the black community. He felt that blacks needed to achieve positions of leadership and influence if they were going to change their standing in society.

John and Lugenia Burns Hope

John and Lugenia Burns Hope provided intellectual leadership and social activism in Atlanta's African-American community. John Hope was born to a white father and black mother. He was so light-skinned that, had he wanted to, he could have taken the easy road and passed for a white man. He was proud of his African-American heritage, however, and presented himself to people as a black man. Hope served as the first African-American professor at Morehouse College and became the first black president of Atlanta University in 1929 (Atlanta University was the first black institution in the South to offer graduate degrees). During World War I, the YMCA appointed him as special secretary to improve the welfare of US African-American soldiers serving in France. Meanwhile, his wife, Lugenia, was a social activist and welfare worker. She organized the Atlanta Neighborhood Union in 1908, which included a health clinic, clubs for boys and girls, and vocational classes for children. She also appealed to the city to improve schools, streets, and sanitary facilities. In addition, Lugenia Hope helped change policies in the YWCA that discriminated against blacks and served in the Association of Southern Women for the Prevention of Lynching.

Alonzo Herndon

Economically speaking, **Alonzo Herndon** was arguably the most influential African-American of the early twentieth century. Born a slave, he grew up to become a barber. By 1907, he owned three barber shops in Atlanta. Eventually, Herndon had enough wealth to start the *Atlanta Life Insurance Company* on Auburn Avenue in 1922. As one of the few companies that would insure African- Americans, the Atlanta Life Insurance Company made Herndon an incredibly rich man and helped Auburn Avenue win the nickname, "black Wall Street" (Wall Street in New York City is the country's center of business and finance). He gave large sums of money to various charities and causes and became the largest black donor to Atlanta University, where he served on the Board of Trustees. At the time of his death in 1927, Alonzo Herndon was the wealthiest African-American in Atlanta.

THE "ATLANTA COMPROMISE"

Auburn Avenue, Atlanta

In 1895, Booker T. Washington gave a controversial speech to a mostly white audience in Atlanta. In the speech, Washington supported segregation. He said that blacks and whites could be, "as separate as fingers, yet... one as the hand." Whites loved the speech. They enjoyed hearing a leader in the African-American community say segregation was okay. Many blacks, however, were upset with Washington. W.E.B. DuBois was especially mad. He thought Washington's ideas were outrageous and labeled the speech the **Atlanta Compromise** because he believed Washington had sold out his own people to win favor with whites.

NIAGARA AND THE NAACP

Niagara Movement

In response to views like those held by Washington, a number of African-American intellectuals gathered on the Canadian side of Niagara Falls in 1905 to discuss how they might better help the black cause (they weren't allowed any hotel rooms on the US side). W.E.B. DuBois, John Hope, Alonzo Herndon, and Norris Herndon (Alonzo's son) were among the group. Their meeting gave birth to the Niagara Movement and eventually led to the establishment of the NAACP (National Association for the Advancement of Colored People). DuBois moved to New York and became editor of the organization's key publication, *The Crisis.* Even today, the NAACP remains a key political voice for the African-American community.

ETHNIC VIOLENCE AND DISFRANCHISEMENT IN GEORGIA

VOTING RESTRICTIONS ON BLACKS

Although the Fourteenth Amendment made African-Americans citizens and the Fifteenth Amendment protected black men's right to vote, many southern whites came up with creative ways to keep blacks **disfranchised** (unable to vote). Like many southern states, Georgia enacted a *grandfather clause* in 1908. States often passed grandfather clauses to keep blacks from voting in elections. Georgia's law stated that voters in Georgia had to be a veteran of the Confederate army or a descendant of a veteran. Since African-Americans generally did not fight for the Confederacy (except for a few slaves forced to towards the end of the war) the law effectively meant that blacks could not vote.

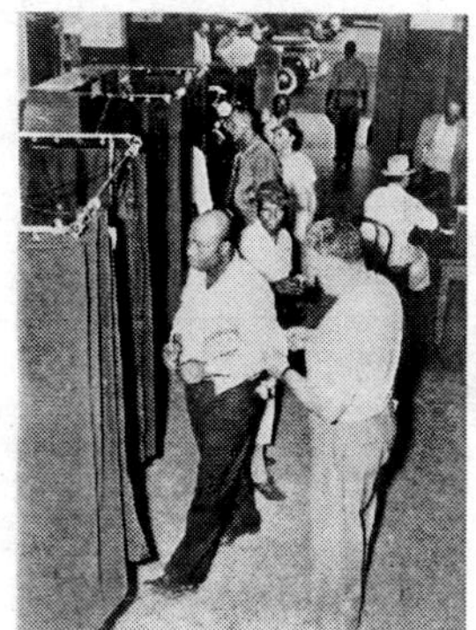
Paying a Tax to Vote

In addition, the legislature and various local governments passed laws requiring voters to pay a *poll tax* and/or pass *literacy tests*. In other words, before someone could vote, they had to pay a special tax and/or prove they could read and write. Since many African-Americans in the South were poor and illiterate (unable to read and write) the laws were effective at keeping them from voting. Even African-Americans who could read often failed the literacy tests because the questions were intended to keep them from passing. Combined with grandfather clauses that said whites did not have to pay a tax nor take these tests, such laws denied blacks the right to vote while still allowing poor and illiterate whites to participate. When these laws failed to disfranchise African-Americans, groups like the Ku Klux Klan often used violence, intimidation, and lynchings to keep blacks from exercising their Fifteenth Amendment rights. The period from 1890 to 1930 was the bloodiest period of **racial violence** in Georgia's history.

The 1906 Atlanta Race Riot

In September 1906, growing racial tensions in Atlanta resulted in the three-day **Atlanta Race Riot**. A white, drunken mob started the riot on September 22, in part due to unproven reports that black men had assaulted several white women. Hoke Smith, a candidate for governor that year, also contributed to the racial tension with his appeals to white racism in an attempt to win votes. The mob attacked black-owned businesses and killed several business owners. Over 20 African-Americans and at least two whites died during the violence.

Atlanta Race Riot

The Leo Frank Case

Leo Frank

Mary Phagan

African-Americans were not the only targets of ethnic violence in the early 1900s. In Atlanta on April 1913, someone murdered a thirteen-year-old girl from Marietta named Mary Phagan. Authorities arrested, tried, and convicted Leo Frank, the Jewish factory superintendent whom Phagan worked for. The court sentenced Frank to hang for the crime, but Georgia Governor John M. Slaton commuted (reduced) Frank's sentence to life in prison after personally investigating the evidence. The governor believed Frank did not commit the murder and that his innocence would eventually be proven. Many Georgians were outraged because they believed Frank had escaped justice for the murder. Meanwhile, Frank's Jewish heritage only served to fuel their anger. Finally, on a dark night in 1915, a group of citizens from Phagan's hometown traveled to the prison in Milledgeville where Frank was housed, kidnapped him, drove through the night back to Marietta, and hanged him from an oak tree. Frank remains the only known case of a Jewish person being lynched in the United States. Decades later, new evidence revealed that the murder was most likely committed by someone else who worked at the factory. The state pardoned Frank 71 years after his lynching, but the **Leo Frank case** remains a sad injustice in Georgia's history.

Practice 6.2 Race Relations and Reform

1. Which notable African-American leader believed that blacks should strive to be intellectuals and helped found the NAACP?

   A. W.E.B. DuBois　　C. Jim Crow
   B. Booker T. Washington　　D. Leo Frank

2. What were grandfather clauses, poll taxes, and literacy tests intended to do?

   A. end segregation
   B. protect African-American voting rights
   C. discriminate against Jewish Georgians
   D. disfranchise blacks

3. What was the "Atlanta Compromise" and why did it upset certain African-Americans?

6.3 Georgia and World War I

World War I began in Europe in 1914 after the heir to the throne of a country called Austria-Hungary was assassinated in Bosnia. Austria-Hungary blamed the nation of Serbia for the murder and threatened war. Since both nations were allies with other countries in Europe, the whole continent got involved in the war. Germany and Austria-Hungary fought on one side and were called the *Central Powers*. Meanwhile, Russia, Great Britain, and France lined up against them as the *Triple Entente*.

Archduke Ferdinand of Austria-Hungary

The US Enters the War

It became known as a a "world war" because most of the world's more powerful nations took part. At first, President Woodrow Wilson and most of the US public did not want to go to war. They believed the war was a European matter and should not involve the United States. People changed their minds for two key reasons. First, **German U-boats** (fighting ships that travel under water and are also called submarines) kept sinking US ships in the Atlantic because they believed the ships were carrying military supplies to England (some of them were). The most famous ship sunk was the **Lusitania**. It was a commercial cruise ship attacked by German U-boats in 1915. The attack outraged people in the United States because 128 US passengers died when the ship went down. Little did those passengers know that the ship also had military supplies on board intended to help Great Britain defeat Germany.

RMS Lusitania

Second, the United States learned that Germany sent a telegram promising Mexico territory in the western United States in exchange for its help in a war with the US. Mexico never agreed to the deal, but the **Zimmerman Telegram** (Zimmerman was the name of the official who sent it) still made people in the US furious with Germany. The telegram, combined with more U-boat attacks, led the United States to declare war in April 1917.

Breaking the code of the Zimmerman Telegram

GEORGIA'S CONTRIBUTIONS TO THE WAR

FIGHTING GEORGIANS AND THE SELECTIVE SERVICE ACT

President Wilson

When the war began, thousands of Georgians joined the armed forces. By war's end, over 100,000 Georgians had served and roughly 3,000 had died contributing to the war effort. President Wilson knew, however, that volunteers would not be enough. The nation needed more soldiers if it hoped to help Great Britain and France win the war (Russia pulled out of the war after going through its own revolution and was no longer fighting). In May 1917, he approved the *Selective Service Act*, which instituted a draft. A **draft** is when the government selects people (in this case, men ages 21– 30) to serve in the military rather than waiting for them to volunteer. The act was very controversial. Many people did not want to serve in the military. It caused division in Georgia as well. Tom Watson and Rebecca Latimer Felton both criticized the policy publicly. Before winning his Senate seat in 1920, Watson returned to his law practice and defended two African-Americans who were jailed for failing to register for the draft. So many people came to the trial that it had to be held outdoors.

World War I trenches

One reason the Selective Service Act was so unpopular in Georgia was because it took able-bodied men off the farms and put them in the military. The value of Georgia's cotton crop tripled between 1900 and 1916. Georgia farmers were more prosperous when the war began than they had been in over 60 years. They wanted to keep growing more and more cotton so they could make as much money as possible. The draft, however, threatened to take away the workers these farmers needed. Some planters refused to deliver draft notices to their employees. Sometimes, when laborers were illiterate, farmers refused to read them the notice or pretended it said something different. As a result, some sharecroppers didn't even know they'd been drafted. In a few cases, some planters did not tell their workers that they had been drafted on purpose, then turned them in for failing to report for duty so they could collect the reward. The state was so concerned about possible labor shortages that it passed a *"work or fight"* policy. Georgia required each man between 16 and 55 to prove that he was either serving in the war effort or gainfully employed. Those that couldn't often got arrested.

Military Bases

General Pershing

A number of **military bases** in Georgia played key roles in preparing US troops for war. Fort McPherson, located just outside Atlanta, was the oldest and dated back to 1889. Other key bases included Fort Gordon in Augusta, and the newly opened Fort Benning near Columbus. *General John Pershing*, the general Wilson appointed to command the army in Europe, ordered the opening of Benning in 1917 to train thousands of troops. The state also had additional camps that provided specialized services. Georgia bases ultimately trained many of the men who fought in Europe during World War I.

Barracks at Fort McPherson

War Time Production

Georgia also **contributed to the US war effort** in other ways. The state's textile mills produced fabric that was used for uniforms and blankets. Farmers produced needed food, livestock, cotton, and tobacco (farmers actually did well during the war despite fears about reduced manpower). Georgia's railroads proved valuable for transporting men, weapons, and supplies. Meanwhile, citizens volunteered to help in organizations like the Red Cross and sacrificed by growing much of their own food or trying to get by on less so that the troops could have what they needed.

Red Cross Poster

The War Ends

In November 1918, Germany and the Allies (the US, Great Britain, France, and Italy) signed an **armistice** (agreement to stop fighting) that effectively ended the war. The Allies ultimately forced Germany to sign a humiliating treaty and take full blame for the war despite President Wilson's belief that the Germans should not be punished. Back home, people in Georgia and across the nation celebrated the allied victory and the return of the soldiers. At the same time, however, they also mourned those who had died and hoped that they would never witness such a terrible war again. Unfortunately, many of them did just two decades later.

Armistice Signed on train

Practice 6.3 Georgia and World War I

1. Which of the following is a reason why the US decided to enter World War I?

   A. Mexico was planning to attack the US.

   B. The heir to the throne of Austria-Hungary was assassinated.

   C. The Triple Entente kept attacking US ships.

   D. German U-boat attacks made many Americans angry.

2. How did Georgians feel about the Selective Service Act?
   A. Georgia was one of the few states where the act did not cause controversy because people were so eager to serve.
   B. Many Georgians opposed the act because they feared it would hurt farmers.
   C. Georgians did not worry about the act because it only applied to northern states.
   D. Georgians refused to obey the act because most people in the state believed the war was wrong and very few agreed to serve in the armed forces.

3. In what ways did Georgia contribute to the war effort in World War I?

Chapter 6 Review

Key Terms, People, and Concepts

Bourbon Triumvirate
Joseph E. Brown
John B. Gordon
Alfred H. Colquitt
Henry W. Grady
New South
International Cotton Exposition
Atlanta
textile mills
naval stores
Tom Watson
Populist movement
Rebecca Latimer Felton
county unit system
segregation
Jim Crow laws
Plessy v. Ferguson
Booker T. Washington
W.E.B. DuBois
John Hope
Lugenia Burns Hope
Alonzo Herndon
Atlanta Compromise
disfranchise
Atlanta Race Riot
Leo Frank case
World War I
German U-boats
Lusitania
Zimmerman Telegram
draft
military bases
Georgia's wartime contributions
armistice

Multiple Choice Questions

1. Which of the following statements **best** describes the Bourbon Triumvirate?
   A. They were Radical Republicans who led Georgia during Reconstruction.
   B. It was an organization founded by African-American intellectuals.
   C. They were Bourbon Democrats who dominated post-Reconstruction Georgia politics.
   D. It was the name of a US ship sunk by German U-boats before the United States entered WWI.

2. Which statement would Henry Grady have **most likely** agreed with?
   A. Agriculture is the backbone of the South and Georgians must do more to promote small farming.
   B. The South must become industrialized, like the North.
   C. Southern culture must be protected; therefore, northerners should leave and go back where they came from.
   D. Georgians should support the Populist movement.

3. What effect did the International Cotton Exposition have?

A. It demonstrated that Georgia had come out of Reconstruction ready for industry.
B. It led to the US entering World War I.
C. It encouraged the Atlanta Race Riot of 1906.
D. It demonstrated the injustice of Jim Crow laws.

4. Who would have been **most likely** to say the following quote?

> *"Farmers must unite if they are going to overcome and survive. Black farmers and white farmers must understand that they have a common enemy: big business. The Democrats will not save us! We must start a new party and save ourselves!"*

A. Booker T. Washington
B. William Jennings Bryan
C. Tom Watson
D. Henry Grady

5. A law which forbids a white man and a black man from sitting together on a train would be considered what?
A. a grandfather clause
B. a draft
C. a Jim Crow law
D. disfranchisement

6. Which of the following **best** describes the relationship between Booker T. Washington and W.E.B. DuBois?
A. They were close friends who worked together to win racial justice for African Americans.
B. They were both leaders in the Populist movement
C. They did not like each other because DuBois supported poll taxes but Washington did not.
D. They disagreed over what role blacks should strive to play in society and the issue of segregation.

7. Alonzo Herndon was an example of which of the following?
A. the role Georgia farmers played in World War I
B. the financial success some African-Americans achieved despite racism in the early 1900s
C. the success the Populist movement in Georgia
D. the important role played by the Bourbons in the "New South"

8. Which of the following is **true** regarding Georgia's contributions to WWI?
A. Georgia provided needed textiles, food, and military bases for the war effort.
B. Georgia could only supply soldiers because times were hard for farmers.
C. Georgia only allowed African-Americans to be drafted because whites were needed to work on farms.
D. Thousands of Georgians were drafted, but only a few hundred served in the armed forces because the state refused to officially support the war.

Chapter 7
Georgia Between the Wars

This chapter covers the following Georgia standard(s).

SS8H8	The student will analyze the important events that occurred after World War I and their impact on Georgia.

7.1 The Boll Weevil and Depression

The Wrath of the Boll Weevil

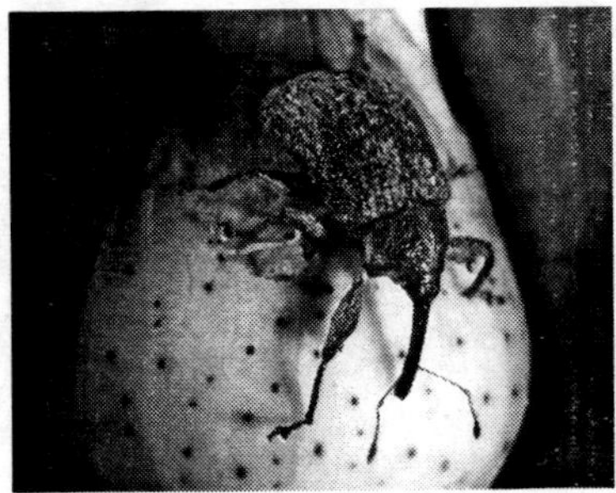
Boll Weevil

After World War I, much of the nation enjoyed good economic times. Farmers, however, faced some challenges. Despite increased industrialization, the majority of Georgians still lived and worked on farms. One of their biggest challenges came in the form of a tiny insect known as the **boll weevil**. The boll weevil made its way north from Mexico in the early 1900s and, by 1915, reached Georgia. These bugs were especially devastating to the South because they destroyed cotton crops. In addition to calling for more industry, promoters of the "New South" had preached for years that southern farmers needed to **diversify** (grow more than just cotton). Cotton was so profitable, however, that most farmers didn't listen. They kept raising cotton because it made them the most money. When the boll weevil struck in the 1920s, it hit Georgia farmers hard. Many of them lost their crops, their money, and their land! Not only did the farmers suffer, but so did the state's economy. As farmers went under, the loans they failed to repay meant hard times for banks, creditors, and businesses who depended on the farmers.

Drought

In addition to the boll weevil, **droughts** also produced hard times for farmers. A drought is when there is no rain, or at least not nearly enough. Without rain, farmers could not grow as much as they normally did. Because the state still relied heavily on agriculture, hard times for farmers meant hard times for the region. In the 1920s, Georgia was beginning to feel some of the economic hardship that would soon hit the whole country.

More and more Georgians left farms to work in cities and factories during the 1920s and '30s. In fact, by the 1930s, at least half of all workers in the state worked in non-farming jobs. Those who remained on the farms tended to be extremely poor. Many were sharecroppers or tenants, and most were drowning in debt.

The Great Depression

Consumerism and Prosperity

Flapper and New Car

While farmers in the South and Midwest struggled, most of the rest of the nation enjoyed prosperity during the 1920s. People were happy. The war had led to increased production and more money. Businesses enjoyed lots of freedom as the government did little to regulate them. Meanwhile, people's personal spending habits changed a lot as **consumerism** became normal. Consumerism means that people started focusing more on buying things than on saving money. Advertisers used new inventions like the radio and new national magazines and catalogues to convince people they "needed" to buy the latest products. At the same time, *installment plans* (plans that allowed people to pay for things a little at a time) and *easy credit* (people buying things with borrowed money) allowed people to buy goods and appliances right away, rather than having to save to afford them.

New York Stock Exchange

Finally, more people began buying **stocks** as well. When people buy stock, they purchase part ownership in companies they believe will make money. As the companies do well, the stockholders earn more wealth. During the '20s, people often bought stock *on the margin*, which means they only paid for part of a stock and then borrowed to buy the rest. Other times, they bought on *speculation,* meaning that they made high-risk investments they hoped would pay off.

Farmers and Overproduction

Meanwhile, businesses and farmers were trapped by **overproduction**. In other words, they were producing more than people could buy. Farmers were especially suffering as a result. The war years had been so good that many farmers produced way too much. With the war over, prices for their products fell drastically, making it hard for farmers to earn a profit. As a result, many of them borrowed money to buy new equipment and raise more crops. They hoped that by raising more crops they could sell more and make up for the lower prices. Unfortunately, this only meant more overproduction and prices continued to fall.

Black Tuesday

Resident of a Hooverville
Library of Congress

Finally, on October 29, 1929, the **stock market crashed**! Stock prices dropped so much that it set off a financial panic. The day became known as **Black Tuesday**, and is generally considered to be the beginning of the **Great Depression** (the worse financial crisis in US history that lasted throughout the 1930s). Many banks and businesses failed. Back then, bank deposits were not insured. Therefore, when the banks closed, people who had money in them lost their savings. Some of the nation's wealthiest families suddenly found themselves dirt poor. Those who owed money or who bought stocks on speculation went broke. At one point during the Great Depression, roughly a fourth of all US citizens were out of work. Many people had to rely on soup kitchens (places that served food to the poor) in order to eat. Others lived in *Hoovervilles* (villages of homemade shacks where the homeless lived; they were named after President Herbert Hoover whom most blamed for the Depression).

Depression in Georgia

Farm Foreclosure

The Depression hit Georgia especially hard. After Black Tuesday, cotton prices fell fast and hard! Within a year, many farmers lost their land and moved to the cities in search of work. Some moved to places like Atlanta. Between 1900 and 1940, Atlanta's population grew by more than 200,000! Other Georgia cities grew as well. Many residents, however, left Georgia altogether. A large number of the state's African-American population moved to northern cities as part of the **Great Migration**. Although many African-Americans migrated (moved) north during WWI, the numbers increased during the Great Depression. Blacks left both to seek new employment opportunities and to escape the radical racism of groups like the Ku Klux Klan. Although Klan membership shrank in the early years of the twentieth century, the order rekindled after WWI and resumed its violent ways. It grew into a nationwide organization by targeting not only blacks, but Jews, Catholics, and foreign immigrants as well.

Sharecropper Family

Many of those who remained on the farms (both whites and blacks) were illiterate and trapped in poverty. When the '30s began, fewer than 5% of Georgia farms had electric lights or indoor plumbing. Most rural farm families lived in shacks. Already struggling to survive, many of these families went hungry and were unable to buy food and other basic necessities once the Depression hit. Despite advances in state education during the early years of the century, many schools closed during the Depression. Even those that didn't saw a drop in students as children had to find work to help support their families.

Practice 7.1 The Boll Weevil and Depression

1. What is a boll weevil?
   A. a farmer who refused to move to the city despite hard times economically
   B. someone who buys more than they save
   C. an insect that destroyed cotton crops in the South
   D. an African-American who moved north during the 1920s and '30s

2. What impact did overproduction have on Georgia farmers?
   A. It raised farm prices and made them prosperous right before the Depression.
   B. caused farm prices to drop and made it difficult for farmers to get out of debt.
   C. It had little effect on farmers because most of them did not buy stocks.
   D. It almost wiped out farmers because most of them had diversified their crops.

3. What was the Great Depression and what are three factors that helped cause it?

7.2 Eugene Talmadge, FDR, and the New Deal

Franklin Delano Roosevelt and the New Deal

FDR

In 1932, voters in the United States elected **Franklin Delano Roosevelt** (commonly referred to as "FDR") to be their president. Roosevelt had a positive attitude the nation desperately needed at a difficult time. He was also ready to use government regulation to try and fix the economy. Roosevelt launched a series of government programs he called the **New Deal**. Although the New Deal did not end the Depression, it did provide some relief until World War II actually brought the crisis to an end in the 1940s.

The Agricultural Adjustment Act

Planting peanuts

Roosevelt understood that overproduction of farm products was the main reason farmers could not get out of debt. He also knew it contributed greatly to the Great Depression. In 1933, he successfully encouraged Congress to pass the **Agricultural Adjustment Act**. The law actually paid farmers *not* to produce certain crops in an effort to raise farm prices (such payments are called **subsidies**). It also encouraged farmers to plant products like peanuts, corn, and tobacco rather than relying so much on cotton. The act led to farmers raising more livestock as well. By 1940, Georgia was the nation's leader in peanut production and, just ten years later, its leader in poultry (chicken farms). The state's peach harvesting industry also made a comeback after years of decline (Georgia is known as the "Peach State"). Some Georgia farmers took the subsidies and raised fewer crops. Others diversified and bought new farming equipment. Still others used the money to leave the farms altogether and go to the cities.

The Civilian Conservation Corps

Young member of the CCC
Library of Congress

Another New Deal program was the **Civilian Conservation Corps (CCC)**. This government agency hired unmarried men ages 17 to 23, as well as war veterans of all ages, to plant trees in national forests, build trails, and work on environmental conservation projects. The agency was active in Georgia because it had so much rural land and so many men in need of work. Although the CCC did not officially exclude blacks, the number of African-Americans remained very low. Since whites ran the CCC, they tended to make sure that members of their own race got jobs before blacks did. Also, since the men who worked for the CCC usually lived together in camps located near their work site, whites often refused to be housed together with African-Americans.

Social Security

President Roosevelt also introduced *Social Security* as part of the New Deal. Prompted by the president, Congress passed the **Social Security Act** in 1935. The law established the Social Security Administration and provided retirement pay and other government benefits for workers. One important benefit was unemployment insurance, which provided money to people who were out of work. Although Social Security and other New Deal programs were originally opposed by Georgia's governor, **Eugene Talmadge**, the state's legislature finally passed legislation that allowed Georgia to participate in Social Security once Governor Eurith D. Rivers took office in the late 1930s. Social Security is the only New Deal program still around today.

Roosevelt signs Social Security Act

Rural Electrification Administration

Roosevelt also created the **Rural Electrification Administration (REA)** in 1935. The REA provided electricity to people who previously didn't have any. A year later, Congress passed the Norris-Rayburn Act, which provided funds to supply the nation's small farms with electricity. Within 15 years, most of Georgia's farms had electricity. Together, the REA, Social Security, the CCC, and farm subsidies provided much needed help for Georgians during the Great Depression.

Dairy Farmer uses Electricity to Chill Milk

GOVERNOR EUGENE TALMADGE

Eugene Talmadge

At the same time FDR emerged as a national symbol of hope, another colorful political figure arose in Georgia. Governor **Eugene Talmadge** won the first of four terms in 1932. Since the state constitution did not allow him to serve more than two consecutive terms, his time in office was actually divided. He first served consecutive two-year terms from 1933 –1937. Then, after four years out of office in which he lost two senatorial campaigns, he returned to the governor's office from 1941–1943. Talmadge was a tireless politician whose fiery speeches and personality earned him the nickname, "the wild man from Sugar Creek." Talmadge appealed mainly to rural farmers and took advantage of the county-unit system to win his bids for governor despite not always winning the popular vote. Ironically, despite his reputation for fighting for the interests of farmers, he often backed ideas that hurt them rather than helped. For instance, Talmadge opposed much of the New Deal. He thought that the federal government should keep its hands out of state matters and refused to back many of Roosevelt's policies. As a result, much of the aid offered by New Deal programs did not affect Georgia until after Talmadge left office for the first time in 1937. Still, because he preached white supremacy and related well to "country folk," Talmadge became the most popular rural candidate since the days of Tom Watson.

Talmadge Campaigns

In 1942, Talmadge ran for a fourth term and lost. He returned in 1946, however, promoting white supremacy and declaring, "Poor dirt farmers in Georgia ain't got but three friends on this earth: God Almighty, Sears Roebuck, and Gene Talmadge!" Sugar Creek's wild man won his fourth term, but he died before he could take office. Before his death, however, Talmadge helped strengthen racism in Georgia and reinforced the idea that the federal government was something for white southerners to fear.

Practice 7.2 Eugene Talmadge, FDR, and the New Deal

1. What was the name of President Roosevelt's programs designed to help people during the Great Depression?

   A. the New Deal
   B. the Great Migration
   C. Consumerism
   D. the CCC

2. Which of the following provided money for people who were out of work as well as retirement pay during and after the Great Depression?

   A. the CCC
   B. the Agricultural Adjustment Act
   C. the REA
   D. Social Security

3. How did Eugene Talmadge feel about FDR's federal programs? How did he manage to win the support of poor, white farmers despite his views on the New Deal and backing policies that sometimes hurt farmers rather than helped them?

Chapter 7 Review

Key Terms, People, and Concepts

boll weevil
diversify
droughts
consumerism
stocks
overproduction
stock market crash
Black Tuesday
Great Depression
Franklin Delano Roosevelt
New Deal
Agricultural Adjustment Act
subsidies
Civilian Conservation Corps (CCC)
Social Security Act
Rural Electrification Administration (REA)
Eugene Talmadge

Multiple Choice Questions

1. Which of the following would FDR and Eugene Talmadge have **most agreed** on?
   A. farmers needing relief during the Great Depression
   B. Georgia needing the New Deal to help it economically
   C. Social Security
   D. the federal government's proper role during an economic crisis

2. Which of the following would a cotton farmer in Georgia **most** have feared in the 1920s?
   A. The Great Migration
   B. prosperity
   C. the boll weevil
   D. subsidies

3. A farmer who grows more than one crop has done what?
   A. subsidized
   B. consumed rather than saved
   C. overproduced
   D. diversified

4. Overproduction, falling stock prices, and consumerism all contributed to what?
   A. the boll weevil
   B. the Great Migration
   C. the Great Depression
   D. droughts

5. Which of the following **best** describes President Roosevelt's approach to dealing with the Great Depression?
   A. He wanted the government to do as little as possible because he believed the economy would eventually fix itself.
   B. He believed in using government programs to end the crisis.
   C. He believed the states, rather than the federal government, should be responsible for dealing with economic problems.
   D. He wanted farmers to produce more cotton so that they could get out of debt.

6. How did the Agricultural Adjustment Act help Georgia's farmers?
   A. It paid them not to produce certain crops in an effort to raise farm prices.
   B. It paid them to produce more cotton so they could make more money.
   C. It ended subsidies.
   D. It paid farmers to move to Georgia as part of the Great Migration.

7. Which of the following is still around today?
   A. the Great Depression
   B. Social Security
   C. the CCC
   D. the REA

8. Which statement is **true** regarding Eugene Talmadge?
   A. He was governor of Georgia when the boll weevil arrived.
   B. He was a huge supporter of the New Deal.
   C. He caused great controversy by claiming that blacks had the same rights as whites.
   D. He was the biggest political hero to Georgia's white, rural farmers since Tom Watson.

Chapter 8
World War II

This chapter covers the following Georgia standard(s).

SS8H9	The student will describe the impact of World War II on Georgia's development economically, socially, and politically.

8.1 The World Goes to War

Fighting Begins

Totalitarian Dictators in Europe

Adolf Hitler

Benito Mussolini

The Great Depression did not just happen in the United States. It was a worldwide disaster that affected most countries. Germany felt the depression especially hard because it was still trying to recover from having to pay for WWI. As a result, Germans were very bitter. A talented but ruthless leader named **Adolf Hitler** took advantage of this discontent to lead his Nazi Party to power. He blamed Germany's troubles on its enemies in WWI, the betrayal of its former government, and Jews whom he blamed for the country's economic woes. By 1933, Hitler firmly controlled Germany as a **totalitarian dictator** (leader who holds all the power and does not allow any political opposition). Meanwhile, even before Hitler's rise, another totalitarian leader seized power in Italy as well. His name was **Benito Mussolini**. Hitler and Mussolini eventually became allies and led Europe into a second, bloody world war.

Japan's Aggression

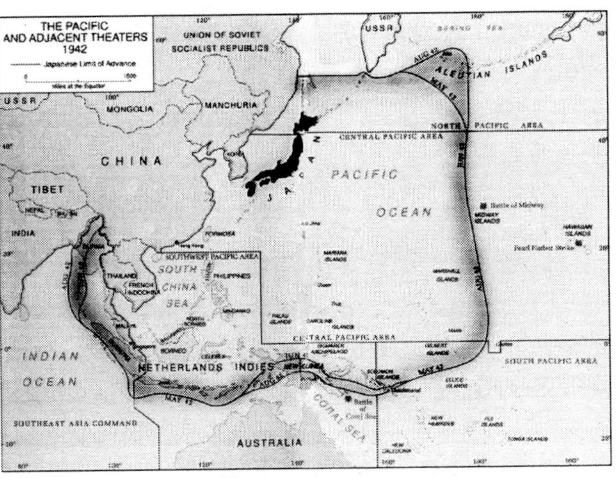

Japanese Line of Advance, Pacific Theater

While Hitler and Mussolini gained power in Europe, Japan grew increasingly aggressive in the Pacific. As a tiny series of islands, Japan did not have access to many natural resources despite being a fairly modernized country. To get the resources it needed, Japan's leaders decided to conquer territory in the South Pacific. Japan's aggression made the US very nervous and created great tension between the two countries.

Europe Goes to War

British soldiers fight in Europe

More than anything, Hitler desired to invade the Soviet Union. The Soviet Union no longer exists today, but at the time, it was a huge country in Eastern Europe that included Russia. He wanted its land for what he called *lebensraum* (living space). However, to defeat the Soviets, he felt he first must defeat France. Otherwise, Hitler feared France would attack Germany from the west while it tried to fight the Soviets in the east. In 1939, Hitler began **World War II** in Europe when he ordered his German troops to attack Poland (the only territory standing between him and the Soviet Union). The following spring he attacked France, conquering the country in a matter of days. Finally, when Great Britain refused to make peace and accept Germany's advances, Hitler went after it as well. Thanks to the heroics of the British Royal Air Force, however, Germany was never able to launch its planned invasion. With his western advance halted, Hitler now turned his attention east. In June 1941, he attacked the Soviet Union. All of Europe was at war and crumbling before the Nazis. Meanwhile, the United States sat an ocean away with one eye on Europe and the other on Japan.

Roosevelt Confronts Isolationism

Hideki Tojo

Many US citizens did not want to go to war. They supported **isolationism**. In other words, they wanted the US to stay as "isolated" as possible. Citizens who lived through World War I remembered the death and destruction and did not want to experience it again. They felt like Europe and the South Pacific should handle their own problems while the US kept to itself. Besides, the Great Depression was raging, and citizens wanted their government focused on economic matters at home, not fighting overseas. President Roosevelt, however, thought differently. While he understood the nation's isolationist feelings, he also saw that Hitler, Mussolini, and **Hideki Tojo** (Japan's military leader) were dangerous men. Prime Minister Winston Churchill of Great Britain begged the US to join the fighting before his country and the Soviets fell to Hitler. Roosevelt wanted to help, but until December 1941, he did not have enough support to commit US troops to action.

Lend-Lease

Roosevelt

Churchill

In the meantime, Roosevelt did what he could. He supported an oil embargo against Japan, refusing to ship oil to the Japanese in protest against their military aggression. He also won support for **Lend-Lease**. Under Lend-Lease, the US agreed to send supplies and aid to any nation whose defense was important to the national security of the United States. If the country couldn't pay for the supplies, then the US would give it to them anyway and not expect payment until after the war. Roosevelt felt Lend-Lease was necessary in order to save Great Britain. If Britain fell, Roosevelt believed the United States would find itself "living at the point of a gun."

Not everyone supported Lend-Lease because they wanted to remain neutral (not taking either side). They feared it would drag the country into the fighting. Still, Roosevelt won support for the policy using the example of a house on fire. "If your neighbor's house is on fire," explained Roosevelt, "you don't sell him a hose, you give it to him. Then, you take the hose back once the fire is out. This helps your neighbor and makes sure the fire doesn't spread to your own house."

Pearl Harbor

Eventually, however, it was Japan, not Hitler, who changed public opinion regarding the war. Japan wanted to continue expanding its empire, but it feared the US naval fleet at **Pearl Harbor**, Hawaii. The Japanese decided to launch a surprise attack in hopes of destroying most of the fleet. In the early morning hours of Sunday, December 7, 1941, hundreds of Japanese planes bombed US ships as they sat anchored in the harbor, killing or wounding thousands of US citizens. The next day, President Roosevelt went before Congress and asked for a declaration of war against Japan. Congress agreed. A short time later, Germany and Italy honored a pact they had with Japan and declared war on the United States. After years of avoiding war, the US now found itself thrust into the middle of the greatest military conflict in history.

US ships attacked at Pearl Harbor

Practice 8.1 The World Goes to War

1. Who was the totalitarian dictator who rose to power in Germany and started WWII in Europe?
   A. Benito Mussolini
   B. Adolf Hitler
   C. Tojo Hideki
   D. Franklin Roosevelt

2. Why did Japan bomb Pearl Harbor?
   A. They feared the US would join forces with Hitler.
   B. They were responding to the fact that Congress had declared war on them.
   C. They feared the US naval fleet anchored there and wanted to destroy it.
   D. They wanted to invade the Soviet Union.

3. What was "Lend-Lease" and why did Roosevelt support it?

8.2 Georgia and the War

On Land, Air, and Sea

Citizen Sacrifice and Military Bases

A woman machines aircraft parts during World War II

Georgia contributed to the war effort in many ways. Both men and women flocked to join the military after Japan bombed Pearl Harbor. Before the war ended in 1945, roughly 320,000 Georgians served in the armed forces. Meanwhile, those who remained in Georgia helped as well. Like many US citizens, they sacrificed, recycled, grew more of their own food, and did anything else they could to make sure the soldiers got all they needed. Many women left home and worked jobs traditionally held by men so that production could continue while the men went off to fight. Some US women even joined the armed forces, serving in almost every role except combat (fighting in battle).

As in World War I, Georgia's **military bases** played a crucial role in preparing the nation's soldiers for war. Of the millions of citizens who served as soldiers, sailors, and aviators, many were trained in Georgia before shipping out to fight overseas. Fort Gordon (Augusta), Fort Benning (Columbus), and Fort Stewart (Savannah) all served as some of the nation's largest training bases. Several of these bases also served as prisoner of war camps and housed captured Germans and Italians. Some of these prisoners chose to remain in Georgia and make the state their home after the war.

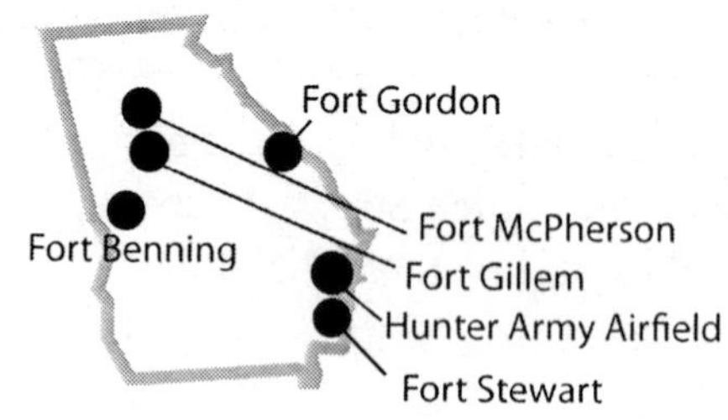

Map of Georgia's military bases

Bell Aircraft

The wartime surge was also good for Georgia's economy. Robins Air Service Command not only served as a training facility for the army air corps (the army air corps later became the US Air Force), but it also employed 15,000 civilians and gave birth to a new town: Warner Robins. Meanwhile, in Marietta, the federal government established **Bell Aircraft**. By the time WWII began, airplanes had become an important part of warfare. In fact, Hitler conquered much of Europe largely due to his effective air force. The US knew it needed planes to win the war. Bell produced many of the planes the nation needed, including over 600 B-29 bombers (planes designed to drop bombs on cities or military targets). Not only did the Bell plant help win the war, but it also helped pull Georgia out of the Great Depression. The plant created hundreds of jobs in the Marietta area and, like other wartime industries, produced economic growth.

B-29 Bombers

SHIPYARDS

Many historians (people who study history for a living) believe that Georgia's greatest military contribution to the war was its **shipyards**. As you might have guessed, shipyards are places where ships are built. Roosevelt recognized that naval power would be an important part of winning World War II. Georgia had two major shipyards. The Southeastern Shipbuilding Corporation was in **Savannah** and constructed over eighty ships. Meanwhile, the J.A. Jones shipyard in **Brunswick** turned out almost 100 ships. Many of these ships came to be called *"Liberty Ships"* because Roosevelt said they would, "bring liberty to Europe!"

Constructing a Ship

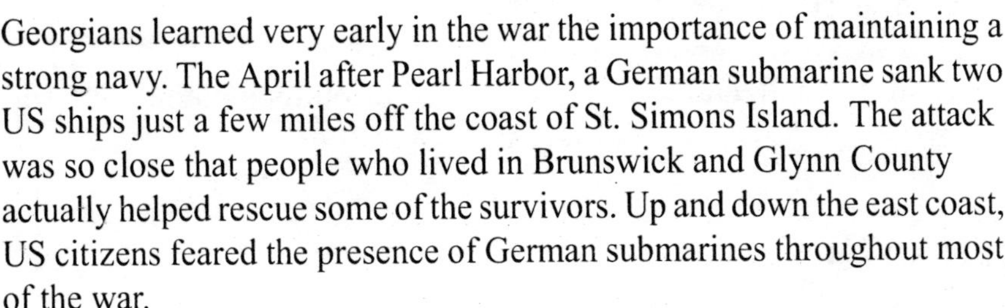

Georgians learned very early in the war the importance of maintaining a strong navy. The April after Pearl Harbor, a German submarine sank two US ships just a few miles off the coast of St. Simons Island. The attack was so close that people who lived in Brunswick and Glynn County actually helped rescue some of the survivors. Up and down the east coast, US citizens feared the presence of German submarines throughout most of the war.

German Submarine

FARMING AND INDUSTRY

Shipyards and aircraft plants were not the only industries that did well during the war. Georgia's textile industry also got a boost as it produced goods to support the war effort. Meanwhile, farmers finally did well because the nation needed as much food as possible to feed the troops and citizens at home.

CARL VINSON AND RICHARD RUSSELL

Georgia was fortunate to have two powerful leaders in Congress during the war years. One was **Richard Russell**. Russell served as the youngest member of the state legislature, the youngest governor in Georgia's history, and the youngest member of the United States Senate when he was finally elected to that office in 1933. Once in the Senate, he worked hard to push Roosevelt's New Deal programs through Congress. He also served on the Senate Naval Affairs Committee and eventually became chairman of the Senate Armed Services Committee. During WWII, he often traveled with other senators to visit US troops. Influenced by these visits, Russell was one of the first officials to argue that the US needed military bases in foreign territories in order to help secure international stability. Such bases played a vital role in the years following WWII, and many still exist today.

Richard Russell

Carl Vinson was Russell's counterpart in the House of Representatives. First elected to the House in 1914, he served 50 years, longer than any other congressman in US history. Vinson served on the House Naval Affairs Committee where he won the nickname, "the father of the two-ocean navy." For nearly two decades before Pearl Harbor, Vinson argued that the US must strengthen its navy if it hoped to remain secure. Admiral Chester Nimitz, who led much of the US war effort against Japan, actually credited the United States' ability to win in the Pacific to Vinson's efforts in Congress.

Carl Vinson

Together, Russell and Vinson not only provided strong leadership in Washington, they also used their positions to help Georgia. Each used his influence to direct as much war-time industry to Georgia as possible. Their efforts not only strengthened the nation's military, they helped heal their state's economy and lift it out of the Great Depression as well.

Practice 8.2 Georgia and the War

1. What were "Liberty Ships"?
   - A. ships sunk at Pearl Harbor
   - B. German submarines lurking off the Georgia coast during WWII
   - C. ships constructed at Georgia shipyards
   - D. ships built at the Bell plant in Marietta

2. Who were Carl Vinson and Richard Russell, and what were their contributions both to the war effort and Georgia?

8.3 Victory and Aftermath

Victory in Europe and Japan

Churchill Waves to Crowd on V-E Day

In June 1944, Allied troops (the US and the nations it supported) successfully invaded France and made their way towards Germany. Meanwhile, the Soviet Union kept attacking Germany from the east. Hitler shot himself the following spring once it became evident that Soviet troops would soon invade the German capital of Berlin. Finally, on May 8, 1945, US citizens celebrated *V-E Day* (Victory in Europe Day). Just over three months later, Japan surrendered after the US dropped the world's first atomic bombs on Hiroshima and Nagasaki. At last, World War II was over.

The Holocaust

Railroad to Auschwitz Concentration Camp

Sadly, as the world was celebrating the end of the war, it was also learning about the **Holocaust**. The word *holocaust* means, "complete or great destruction," and refers to the mass murder of more than six million Jewish people by Hitler's Nazi government. Although millions of other people the Nazi's considered "unfit to live" died at the hands of Hitler's regime as well (gypsies, Slavs, homosexuals, the mentally ill, and physically disabled), no one group suffered as badly as the Jews. The Nazis arrested many Jews and shipped them off to *concentration camps*. There, they either killed them immediately or used them as slave labor before eventually executing them. As allied soldiers liberated these camps, they often found mass graves, gas chambers for carrying out the murders, and dying prisoners. Eventually, the Allies tried more than 20 Nazi leaders for war crimes due to their role in the Holocaust. Some were convicted and received long prison terms; others were hanged.

THE EFFECTS OF THE HOLOCAUST IN GEORGIA

Prominent Jewish Atlantan William Breman, founder Jewish Heritage Museum

Like most people, when Georgians learned about the Holocaust, they were angry and amazed that such cruelty could exist. Nowhere in the state was the horror of this event felt more than Atlanta. In the decades leading up to WWII, Atlanta grew to have a large **Jewish community**. Many Jewish families immigrated to Georgia in the late 1800s and early part of the twentieth century. Most of them moved to Atlanta and started their own businesses. By the 1940s, the Jewish community in Atlanta had grown tremendously. As a result, the Holocaust caused more sadness and horror in Atlanta than anywhere else in the state. It also sparked increased fears of *anti-Semitism* (prejudice against Jews) and support for a Jewish homeland. Many Jewish Georgians thrilled when the United Nations formally recognized the nation of Israel as a Jewish state in 1948.

FAREWELL TO FDR

FDR

Little White House

Franklin Delano Roosevelt is the only president in US history to serve more than two terms in office. He was elected four times and served from March 1933 until his death in 1945. He guided the nation through some of its darkest days — first at home during the Great Depression, then abroad during the war. Yet, he always seemed confident and positive. To many, he seemed almost like the nation's "dad." Few even knew that Roosevelt actually spent most of his time in a wheelchair. As a young man, he contracted polio, a disease which left him partially paralyzed. Back in the 1930s and '40s, politicians did not appear on television like they do today. As a result, Roosevelt was able to hide his disability from the public and maintain his image as a symbol of strength. Today, society recognizes that someone can have a disability and still do a good job or be an effective leader, but back then, things were different. Interestingly, it was because of his disability that FDR developed a special relationship with the state of Georgia. Before he became president, Roosevelt learned about **Warm Springs** in Meriwether County. The area features natural spring waters and pools of warm water. Roosevelt liked Warm Springs because he found that the waters helped sooth some of the discomfort he felt from his polio. In 1932, he built a vacation home there and frequently visited. FDR spent so much time at his Warm Springs home that it eventually became known as the **Little White House**.

Sadly, after doing so much to lead the nation through depression and war, Franklin Roosevelt did not live to see the country experience peace and prosperity at the same time. He died on April 12, 1945, while vacationing at Warm Springs. Perhaps it is fitting that he spent his final moments in one of his favorite places and a state that his New Deal policies did so much to help. As the president's funeral procession made its way through the streets of Washington a few days later, citizens across the nation wept. Georgians wept as well. Not only did the state mourn the loss of a president, it mourned the loss of a friend.

Practice 8.3 Victory and Aftermath

1. What does the term "Little White House" refer to?
   A. Roosevelt's home in New York
   B. the portion of the White House where Roosevelt spent most of his time
   C. Roosevelt's vacation home in Warm Springs, Georgia
   D. the governor's mansion in Atlanta

2. Describe Roosevelt's relationship to Georgia. Why did many in the state feel they had lost a friend when Roosevelt died?

3. What was the Holocaust and how did it affect Atlanta's Jewish community?

Chapter 8 Review

Key Terms, People, and Concepts

Adolf Hitler
totalitarian dictator
Benito Mussolini
Japan's aggression
World War II
isolationism
Tojo Hideki
Lend-Lease
Pearl Harbor
military bases in Georgia
Bell Aircraft
shipyards at Savannah and Brunswick
Richard Russell
Carl Vinson
Holocaust
Atlanta's Jewish community
Warm Springs
Little White House

Multiple Choice

1. Which of the following led to World War II in Europe?
   A. the bombing of Pearl Harbor
   B. the sinking of US ships off the coast of Georgia
   C. Japan's aggression
   D. the rise of totalitarian leaders

2. Which one of the following people would have been **most** supportive of Lend-Lease?
   A. a British general B. an isolationist C. an Italian soldier D. Tojo Hideki

3. What was President Franklin Roosevelt talking about when he referred to December 7, 1941 as, "…a day which will live in infamy"?
   A. Hitler's invasion of France
   B. the bombing of Pearl Harbor
   C. Germany's surrender
   D. the beginning of the war in Europe

4. What role did Bell Aircraft play during WWII?
   A. It made many of the ships that fought in the Atlantic.
   B. It produced most of the ships that fought in the Pacific.
   C. It employed many civilians and gave birth to the town of Warner Robbins.
   D. It produced more than 600 bombers and created new jobs in Marietta.

5. Many historians consider which of the following to be Georgia's **greatest** military contribution to the war effort?
   A. Liberty Ships produced at the Brunswick and Savannah shipyards
   B. prisoner of war camps
   C. small businesses started by Atlanta's Jewish community
   D. Warm Springs

6. Who is the following quote talking about?

> *"Good thing Georgians elected him to Congress. If it weren't for him, our navy never would have been able to defeat the Japanese. No wonder they call him, 'the father of the two ocean navy.'"*

   A. Franklin Roosevelt
   B. Carl Vinson
   C. Richard Russell
   D. Benito Mussolini

7. The Holocaust **most** impacted which of he following groups?
   A. residents in Brunswick and Glynn County
   B. prisoners of war who chose to remain in Georgia after the war
   C. the state's Jewish community
   D. women serving in the military

8. Which of the following is **true** regarding FDR's relationship with Georgia?
   A. He was extremely unpopular in Georgia and never won a majority of votes in the state.
   B. He was loved by many in Georgia thanks to his New Deal programs and attachment to Warm Springs.
   C. Roosevelt never visited Georgia but was glad the New Deal helped its farmers and was grateful for its war-time contributions.
   D. Roosevelt had to end his visits to Georgia after he contracted polio and was confined to a wheelchair.

Chapter 9
Postwar Economic, Political, and Social Change

This chapter covers the following Georgia standard(s).

SS8H10	The student will evaluate key post-World War II developments of Georgia from 1945 to 1970.
SS8H11	The student will evaluate the role of Georgia in the modern civil rights movement.

9.1 Postwar Economics and Growth

Industry, Agriculture, and the Growth of Atlanta

Economic Changes

Georgia-made Hercules C-130 Lockheed Aircraft Co., Marietta

New industries continued to grow in Georgia following the end of World War II. Atlanta benefited most from this surge, as people continued to move to the city looking for jobs in its many new businesses. In 1947, Ford Motors opened a new plant in Hapeville. A year later, General Motors also opened a plant in Doraville. Of all the new businesses, **Lockheed** arguably had the most impact. After the war, Bell Aircraft closed. It reopened a few years later, however, as Lockheed. Lockheed continued to produce needed aircraft and, by the end of the 1950s, was Georgia's largest employer. Atlanta also pioneered the idea of *office parks*. Office parks are places built in the outlying areas of a city specifically to house offices. With so many businesses moving into and starting in Atlanta, new office parks allowed the city to accommodate them even if they could not find places to locate downtown. By the end of the 1940s, more Georgians actually worked in industry and manufacturing jobs, such as textiles and lumber production, than worked on the farms.

Not only did Atlanta grow due to migration (people moving to the city from other places), it also grew due to *annexation.* Annexation is when a city expands, and land that used to be on the outskirts of the city becomes part of that city. In 1952, Atlanta grew by over 100,000 new residents when it annexed over 80 square miles formerly outside the city. As more and more people left rural areas and other parts of the country to move to Atlanta, the city had to get new land in order to keep growing.

Early Atlanta suburb, Ansley Park

The **GI Bill** also contributed to Georgia's growth. Congress passed this bill to help war veterans readjust to society once they returned from the war. It allowed them to get loans for homes and provided money for education. As a result, Atlanta and other cities' suburbs grew tremendously as returning soldiers bought new homes and started families. The University of Georgia and other colleges in the state also saw their enrollments increase as the GI Bill allowed more people to attend college than ever before.

Changes in Agriculture

While manufacturing and other businesses grew, **agriculture** still remained an important postwar industry for Georgia. New technology, such as tractors and processors, helped those who remained on the farms by making planting and harvesting faster and more efficient. In addition, FDR's New Deal and the wartime demand for crops finally gave farmers the financial motive and opportunity they needed to diversify their crops. As a result, the state no longer depended on cotton to be the main source of its agricultural income. Other crops, like peanuts and pecans, became increasingly important to Georgia beginning in the '30s and '40s. In fact, today, nearly half of the US peanut crop comes from Georgia. The state's livestock industry (raising animals like cows, chickens, hogs, etc.) also became increasingly important after the war.

The National Highway Act

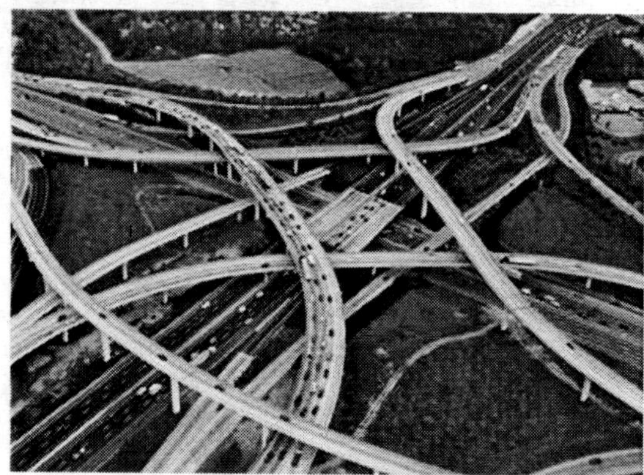

Interstates 85 and 285

When World War II ended, the US entered what came to be called the *Cold War.* It was a period that lasted from 1945 until the end of the 1980s. It was called a "cold war" because, while the US and Soviet Union never went to war (they came close at times), each country distrusted the other and each had nuclear weapons. Therefore, people on both sides lived each day with the possibility of a nuclear war that could destroy the whole world. The Cold War led President Dwight Eisenhower to support the *National Highway Act* in 1956. The act impacted Georgia and states across the nation because it authorized the construction of new **interstate highways,** many of which we still drive on today, such as I-75 that runs from Florida, through

Georgia, all the way to Michigan. Eisenhower believed such roads were necessary to move military personnel efficiently and evacuate cities quickly in the event of a nuclear attack. These highways also allowed for the growth of cities and suburbs by making it easier for people in places like Atlanta to travel back and forth between home, work, and other activities.

INFLUENTIAL ATLANTA MAYORS

WILLIAM HARTSFIELD

Atlanta also thrived during the postwar years, thanks largely to progressive mayors who had the wisdom and vision to lead the city into a new age. The first and longest serving of these was **William Hartsfield**. Hartsfield served six terms as mayor beginning in 1937 and lost only one mayoral election before retiring from office in 1961. As a city alderman in the 1920s, he saw the potential for Atlanta as an aviation hub. He played a major role in the city transforming an old speedway into Candler Field, the city's first regional airport. Eventually, Candler grew to become the busiest airport in the country and one of the busiest in the world. It made Atlanta a major hub for US and international air travel and provided yet another major economic boost to the state. Because of his efforts and the role he played in the airport, Hartsfield earned the nickname, "the Father of Atlanta Aviation." So connected is Hartsfield's legacy to the airport, that Atlanta named it after him in 1980.

William B. Hartsfield

Even more progressive, however, was Hartsfield's leadership when it came to race relations. Although he did not personally desire integration (ending segregation of the races), he cared greatly about Atlanta's reputation and his own political career. As racial tensions and the influence of black voters grew following the war, Hartsfield built a coalition of white businessmen and key African-American leaders who worked behind the scenes to bring about integration and deal with racial issues as orderly and peacefully as possible. Hartsfield believed that Atlanta needed to avoid the bad publicity and ugly racial conflicts that appeared in other southern states if it hoped to do well economically. Although he angered many middle- and lower-class whites who felt the mayor abandoned them to serve business interests and win African-American votes, Hartsfield did a masterful job of keeping racial conflict under control in Atlanta during the late '40s and 1950s. As a result, he achieved his goal of presenting Atlanta as a model southern city and won national praise for his progressive efforts. When asked on one occasion how Atlanta managed to avoid much of the racial strife that plagued the rest of the South, Hartsfield responded with his famous quote: "Atlanta is the city too busy to hate."

IVAN ALLEN, JR.

Ivan Allen, Jr.

In 1961, William Hartsfield decided to retire rather than run for another term as mayor. One of his most trusted supporters, **Ivan Allen, Jr.** succeeded him and continued leading Atlanta down a progressive path. His first day in office, Allen ordered city offices desegregated and the "colored" and "white" signs removed from city hall (these signs designated what facilities could only be used by whites and which ones were for African-Americans). He also gave African-American policeman the authority to arrest whites. Before he took office, black policemen could only arrest other blacks. Allen also led Atlanta through another economic boom. Under his *Forward Atlanta* program, the city experienced even more development.

PROFESSIONAL SPORTS

Like Hartsfield, Allen was a visionary, meaning he had great plans for the city. One of his visions involved making Atlanta the South's center for professional sports. He led the way in securing a new stadium that ultimately became Fulton County Stadium. Mayor Allen broke ground on the facility in 1964 and proclaimed, "The World Series will be played here!" Before the stadium closed in 1996, it was — in 1991, 1992, 1995, and 1996.

Atlanta Braves' Hank Aaron

Atlanta's first professional sports team was the **Braves**, a major league baseball team that moved from Milwaukee in 1966. The team brought with it a spectacular hitter named **Henry (Hank) Aaron**. On April 8, 1974, Hank Aaron made history in Fulton County Stadium when he knocked his 715th home run. The hit broke Babe Ruth's previous record and made Aaron an Atlanta hero. It was also significant because Aaron is African-American. He achieved his historic feat despite death threats from racists who did not want him to break the record. Although Fulton County Stadium has since been torn down, the section of its wall that Aaron's hit sailed over still stands as a tribute to his great accomplishment. The only event in Braves history that compares to Aaron's homer also occurred in Fulton County Stadium when Atlanta beat the Cleveland Indians to win the 1995 World Series!

Atlanta Falcons' Tommy Nobis, 1966

Nineteen sixty-six also featured the birth of professional football in Atlanta. That fall, the Atlanta **Falcons** played their first season. They also played in Fulton County Stadium until a new, indoor facility known as the *Georgia Dome* opened in the 1990s. In 1968, the **Hawks** moved from St. Louis to become the city's basketball team. After a brief period of playing their home games at Georgia Tech, the Hawks moved into a new facility called the Omni in the early '70s. In 1972, Atlanta's first hockey team, the **Flames**, skated onto the ice and played in the Omni as well. They were called the Flames to commemorate Sherman's burning of Atlanta. They later moved to Calgary, Canada and the city eventually started a new hockey team called the **Thrashers**. Atlanta's athletic facilities not only made it a southern sports capital, they also fueled its economic rise as the city gained prestige and attracted major events.

Practice 9.1 Postwar Economics and Growth

1. Which of the following best describes Georgia's economy after World War II?
   - A. It featured new industries and more diversified farming.
   - B. Thanks to wartime demands and the New Deal, cotton became Georgia's key crop.
   - C. Agriculture no longer played an important role thanks to the growth of cities and industry.
   - D. Rural farmers did well thanks to more diversified crops, but the cities suffered from a decline in population and business.

2. Which of the following statements best describes William Hartsfield and Ivan Allen, Jr.?
   - A. As governors of Georgia, they led the state through a time of economic growth.
   - B. They both brought professional sports teams to Georgia that helped the city grow.
   - C. Both were progressive mayors of Atlanta who guided the city through times of change.
   - D. Both accomplished historic feats in Fulton County Stadium as members of the Atlanta Braves.

3. What sports teams came to or started in Atlanta during the 1960s and early '70s? How did they impact the city's reputation and economy?

9.2 Postwar State Politics

Ellis Arnall

In 1942, Georgians elected **Ellis Arnall** to be their new governor. Thanks to a change in the state constitution, Arnall was the first Georgia governor to serve a four-year term (up until then, the governor only served two-year terms). Arnall was much more progressive than Eugene Talmadge, and he supported a number of measures designed to help African-Americans, such as ending the poll tax. He also improved Georgia's prison system and led Georgia to become the first state to grant 18 year-olds the right to vote. Arnall built a reputation as an efficient and honest politician, and many throughout the country admired him for the job he did in Georgia.

Ellis Arnall

The Gubernatorial Election of 1946

One of the most controversial episodes in Georgia politics was the **gubernatorial election of 1946**. Under the state constitution, Ellis Arnall could not run for re-election. After a tough campaign, Eugene Talmadge finally won the Democratic nomination for governor and, eventually, the general election as well. However, Talmadge died before he could take office, setting off a political firestorm. Talmadge's supporters wanted the state legislature to name his replacement based on who had the highest number of write-in votes during the election. Thanks to a suspicious recount in his home county, Eugene Talmadge's son, **Herman Talmadge**, had more write-in votes than any other candidate. If elected, he would no doubt continue his father's policies. Governor Arnall, however, detested Eugene Talmadge and did not want his son sitting in the Governor's Mansion.

Herman Talmadge

He vowed to only give his seat up to Lieutenant Governor Melvin Thompson. After the legislature elected Talmadge governor anyway, Arnall refused to leave office. Finally, Talmadge's supporters took the governor's office by force and seized control of the Governor's Mansion. Undeterred, Arnall formally named the lieutenant governor his successor and Thompson set up an alternate governor's office in downtown Atlanta. The state supreme court finally stepped in to end the feud and clean up the political mess. It ruled that Thompson was to serve as acting governor, but only until a special election could be held to settle the matter. Much like his father, Herman Talmadge ran a race based on white supremacy and states' rights that won the Democratic nomination. He served as governor from 1948 – 1955 and was incredibly popular in the state of Georgia. He also managed to make significant advances in state education during his time in office. Talmadge eventually won a seat in the United States Senate in 1956, where he served until his surprising defeat in 1980.

THE 1956 GEORGIA STATE FLAG

Georgia's flag, 1956-2001

Ten years after the state's most controversial governor's race, the Georgia Assembly approved the state's most controversial flag. The **1956 flag** greatly offended African-Americans and frustrated progressive whites who hoped to see progress in race relations. The flag caused problems because two-thirds of it looked like a Confederate battle flag (flag used by southern, pro-slavery states during the Civil War). Most understood the legislature's decision to be a protest against rulings by the supreme court aimed at striking down segregation. The flag represented Georgia for 45 years before it was finally replaced in 2001. Even then, many whites were outraged, arguing that the flag simply honored their southern heritage. Critics pointed out, however, that because groups like the Ku Klux Klan had long used the battle flag as a symbol of racial hatred, the state had a responsibility to its minority citizens to remove it from the state flag.

DEATH OF THE WHITE PRIMARY AND THE COUNTY-UNIT SYSTEM

Two major institutions helped rural, white supremacists keep their grip on Georgia state politics despite the growing African-American and progressive urban white populations: the white primary and the county-unit system. The **white primary** system only allowed whites to vote in statewide primaries. A primary is an election in which a political party chooses its candidate for the general election. Since the primary was sponsored by a private organization (the Democratic Party of Georgia), Democrats argued that they could run their elections any way they wanted. In reality, however, the white primary completely cut blacks out of the political process because, in the South, whoever won a Democratic primary was almost assured of winning the general election. Due to the **county-unit system**, statewide primaries were usually won by candidates who backed racist policies in order to secure the rural votes they needed to win. (Review chapter 6, section 6.1 concerning the county-unit system.) As a result, elections were basically decided before African-Americans ever got to vote. In 1944, however, the Supreme Court struck down a similar primary system in Texas, ultimately leading to the end of Georgia's white primary a couple of years later. Meanwhile, the county-unit system survived until the Supreme Court finally struck it down as well in 1962. With the end of these institutions, the political importance of black and urban white voters greatly increased.

Practice 9.2 Postwar State Politics

1. Who was a progressive governor who ended the poll tax and helped 18-year-olds win the right to vote in Georgia?
   A. Ellis Arnall
   B. Herman Talmadge
   C. Melvin Thompson
   D. Eugene Talmadge

2. What made the 1946 gubernatorial election so unusual?
   A. It was the first time a governor was elected to a four-year term.
   B. It was the first time a Republican ever became governor of Georgia.
   C. It resulted in a power struggle over the office of governor that had to be settled by the state supreme court.
   D. It was the first election after the Supreme Court struck down the county-unit system.

3. What was the "white primary" and how did it affect both political campaigns and African-American voters?

9.3 Georgia and the Civil Rights Movement

The Movement Takes Off

Benjamin Mays

Born the son of former slaves, **Benjamin Mays** grew up to be a very educated man. After serving as a dean at Howard University, he became the president of Atlanta's Morehouse College in 1940. Mays taught his students to challenge rather than accept the segregation that surrounded them. He also preached to them the sad difference between the freedom US citizens said they believed in and the racial injustices many of them allowed. He was a very intelligent and influential man, and he became known for expressing his views at a series of morning lectures attended by students.

Benjamin Mays

Dr. Martin Luther King, Jr.

Perhaps Mays' greatest achievement was the impact he had on one student in particular: **Martin Luther King, Jr.** King went on after Morehouse to earn a Ph.D. and become an ordained minister. He also became a national hero and the recognized leader of the **Civil Rights Movement**. The Civil Rights Movement was a political and social movement that many believe began just after World War II. Many African-Americans returned from serving their country no longer content to be treated as second-class citizens or humiliated by segregation. For the first time, a number of African-Americans began demanding better treatment and more respect for their civil rights. National attention shifted to the movement in 1955 after an African-American woman named *Rosa Parks* refused to give up her seat on a Montgomery, Alabama bus to a white passenger. The bus driver had Parks arrested, setting off a massive bus boycott by the African-American community. Blacks in Montgomery refused to ride city buses, costing the city lots of money. The

Martin Luther King, Jr.

boycott eventually ended after the Supreme Court ordered Montgomery to desegregate their public transportation. It also made Martin Luther King, Jr. a well-known figure because he led the boycott. Soon he was leading protests throughout the South as the head of one of the most effective movements in US history.

Raised in Atlanta, Martin Luther King, Jr. eventually returned to his home city and made it the center of the Civil Rights Movement. He was an extremely gifted man who believed in non-violent protest. Even if black protestors were beaten, arrested, or killed, King believed that African-Americans would win their rights the quickest by refusing to engage in violence. He was right. As people around the country saw peaceful black marchers and protestors being beaten by white mobs and policeman, the movement gained support.

King speaking at the Lincoln Memorial

King and others also benefited from international pressure caused by the Cold War. Due to fears that communism might spread to African and South Asian countries, the federal government knew it could not afford to have foreign nations view the US as unjust or a land of racial hatred. Taking advantage of such pressure, King shined in what many feel was his greatest public moment: his "I Have a Dream Speech," delivered before the Lincoln Memorial during the 1963 **March on Washington**. The "march" consisted of 200,000 civil rights activists demanding equality for all citizens.

Over the next two years, King's efforts proved worthwhile. In addition to winning the Nobel Peace Prize, Dr. King saw Congress pass the **Civil Rights Act of 1964**, which made it illegal for public accommodations like hotels, theaters, and restaurants to segregate. That same year, the states ratified the **Twenty-fourth Amendment** to the Constitution, ending the poll tax and making it easier for African-Americans to participate in elections. The following year, Congress passed the **Voting Rights Act of 1965**. The law authorized the president to end literacy tests and to use federal officials to make sure that all citizens had an equal opportunity to register and vote. Sadly, Dr. King's enemies did not share his belief in non-violence. In April 1968, Martin Luther King, Jr. was shot and killed as he stood on the balcony of a Memphis motel. His legacy, however, continues to inspire millions who believe in social justice.

THE ALBANY MOVEMENT

Registering to Vote after the Albany Movement

Students were a very important part of the civil rights movement. In February 1960, four black college students held the very first *sit-in* at an all-white lunch counter in Greensboro, North Carolina. Sit-ins were protests in which African-Americans would sit in segregated places and peacefully refuse to leave until they were either served or arrested. They quickly became popular with students throughout the South and inspired many young leaders to organize mass movements. One of the first major movements was the **Albany Movement**. In 1961, students arrived in Albany, Georgia to help register black voters. Dr. King even visited Albany and offered the assistance of his Southern Christian Leadership Conference. Although many were frustrated that the movement did not achieve more of its goals regarding desegregation, the Albany Movement played an important role in paving the way for future protests and showed leaders like Dr. King the potential of mass demonstration as an effective means of resistance.

INTEGRATION AND BACKLASH

BROWN V. BOARD OF EDUCATION (1954)

In 1954, the United States Supreme Court handed down a unanimous decision that greatly impacted Georgia and the entire US South. (*Unanimous* means that all nine justices on the court agreed with the decision.) The Court ruled in ***Brown v. Board of Education*** that segregation in public schools is unconstitutional. The case involved a young African-American girl who was not allowed to attend an all-white school in Kansas. In response, the NAACP sued for her right to attend the school and won. The Court said that school segregation was wrong because white and black facilities did not offer the same opportunities. Since the Court said that segregated schools could not be equal, its decision reversed the 1896 decision in *Plessy v. Ferguson*.

Celebrate Integration Ruling

INTEGRATION AT UGA

Integration means to "join together, or unify." In the South, the term referred to the process of ending segregation because it brought blacks and whites together in social settings and public spaces rather than separating them. The Court's ruling in *Brown v. Board of Education* required segregated public schools to integrate. The University of Georgia was one of the institutions impacted by this decision. African-Americans attempted to enroll at UGA as early as 1952, but the university always found reasons to deny their applications. Finally, in 1961, UGA integrated when two African-American students, **Hamilton Holmes** and **Charlayne Hunter**, enrolled in the university. Despite a great deal of protest from those who opposed integration, Holmes and Hunter both eventually graduated from the University of Georgia and went on to very successful careers (Holmes also became the first African-American admitted to Emory's school of medicine). Interestingly, however, while Holmes and Hunter were the first blacks admitted to the university, they were not the first to earn degrees. Mary Frances Early became the first African-American to receive a degree from the University of Georgia when she received her master's in music education in 1962.

Hunter and Holmes enroll inUGA

INTEGRATION IN ELEMENTARY AND SECONDARY SCHOOLS

After World War II, many veterans returned home to a prosperous economy. As a result, African-Americans bought homes in record numbers as the black population in cities like Atlanta continued to grow. This growth in population, along with court decisions that protected black voting rights, meant that politicians in urban areas had to care more about what African-Americans wanted. In Atlanta, racial tensions increased because more and more blacks were buying homes in previously all-white neighborhoods. When the city failed to intervene to "protect" white communities, many whites began selling their homes and leaving for the surrounding suburbs. The trend became

Integrated student body

known as **white flight** and resulted in a large urban black population, while the suburbs remained mostly white. Because children tended to go to public schools based on where they lived, changes in Atlanta's housing patterns also affected school integration. Atlanta was more progressive, and its political leaders preferred to find a way to obey the Court's rulings in as peaceful a way as possible. Rural areas, however, were more traditional and strongly resented the Court telling them how the state should run its schools. They favored resistance to integration.

THE SIBLEY COMMISSION

Gov. Ernest Vandiver

By 1960, the debate over integration in Georgia divided the state into two camps. On one side were people like Mayor Hartsfield who believed segregation could not last. They favored a "local option plan," which would allow individual school districts to decide whether or not to keep their schools open. If they did, then they would have to provide a limited amount of integration in order to say that they had complied with the Supreme Court's rulings. On the other side were segregationists who wanted to keep blacks and whites separated. They favored a "private school plan." This plan called for closing all state schools and running only private schools (some of which would get some state funding). By making all schools private, Georgians would not have to obey rulings from the Supreme Court striking down segregation in public schools. Governor Vandiver was very concerned about the division. He felt trapped because he won re-election promising to maintain segregation in public schools. At the same time, however, he knew that Georgia's laws would not stand up in court. He also wanted to avoid the ugly scenes that occurred in other southern states when they tried to integrate their public schools. In Arkansas, for instance, protests were so out of control that the president had to send in federal troops to protect the first African-American students at Little Rock's Central High School. Vandiver decided that citizens might better accept the state's decision if they felt they had a say in the matter. He authorized a special commission set up by the General Assembly to travel around the state and hold hearings on the issue.

The **Sibley Commission** (named for John Sibley, the lawyer and businessman who led it) traveled to every congressional district and held meetings where citizens could come and voice their opinions. The most heated meeting occurred in the gymnasium of Atlanta's Grady High School. Most at the gathering favored the "local option." However, the most memorable speech was delivered by segregationist, Thomas Wesley, on behalf of the "private school" plan. What made Wesley's speech notable was that he did not base his arguments on racial differences, but on constitutional rights. He claimed that the federal government was violating every citizen's basic right to freely choose whom to associate with. Therefore, according to Wesley, the Court itself had behaved in an "unconstitutional" fashion. Ultimately, the state voted to keep the schools open and the "local option" plan won. Wesley's argument, however, was quickly adopted by many conservative southerners and eventually helped end the Democratic Party's tight hold on southern politics.

The Axe Handle Governor

Maddox and son threaten African-American man at Pickrick Restaurant

Without a doubt, **Lester Maddox** was one of the most interesting characters in all of Georgia's history. Maddox grew up poor but worked hard and became the owner of a popular Atlanta restaurant called the *Pickrick*. He believed strongly in segregation and refused to serve African-Americans. He believed even stronger in *property rights*. Maddox felt that no one, not even the government, had the right to tell him how to run his own restaurant. When Congress passed the Civil Rights Act of 1964 requiring businesses like his to integrate, Maddox stood his ground. He met the first African-Americans who tried to enter his restaurant and threatened them with a gun. He then beat the top of their car with an axe handle as they drove away. After that, axe handles became the symbol of Maddox's feisty resistance. Many even started referring to them as "Pickrick drumsticks." The government eventually filed a lawsuit against Maddox, forcing him to either integrate or close. With the strength of the federal government mounting against him, the fiery segregationist ultimately chose to shut his doors rather than serve blacks. He eventually opened a new restaurant only to be forced to close again. Finally, he leased his business to a former employee who integrated the establishment in 1965.

Carl Sanders

"Bo" Callaway

Lester Maddox

Maddox also took his fight into politics. He ran for mayor twice, losing to Mayor Hartsfield in 1957 and Ivan Allen, Jr. in 1961. After a failed attempt to win lieutenant governor in 1962, Lester Maddox went after the ultimate prize in Georgia politics four years later: he ran for governor, hoping to succeed the moderate Carl Sanders. At first, many leaders dismissed him as just "some crazy guy with an axe handle." Many thought his ideas were backward and would only embarrass Georgia if he won the state's highest office. Maddox shocked everyone, however, by defeating former governor, Ellis Arnall, to win the Democratic primary in 1966. For the first time since Reconstruction, the Republican Party thought it now had a chance to win the governor's race. Their candidate, Howard "Bo" Callaway, had already won a seat in Congress and was a popular conservative. They hoped he could win the votes of progressive Democrats unable to stomach the thought of Maddox in the Governor's Mansion. Callaway actually won the popular vote, but due to a write-in campaign by Arnall, he did not win a majority (more than half). As a result, the election was decided by the General Assembly which voted for Maddox. To the delight of segregationist whites and the horror of progressives, axe-handle-toting Lester Maddox was the new governor of Georgia.

Despite his segregationist views, Maddox actually appointed more African-Americans to state offices than any governor before him. Since the constitution did not allow the governor to serve back-to-back terms at that time, Maddox could not run for re-election in 1970. Instead, he ran for lieutenant governor and won. He ran for governor again in 1974 and 1990, losing both times. Maddox died in 2003 of cancer, leaving behind one of the most unusual legacies in political history.

Practice 9.3 Georgia and the Civil Rights Movement

1. Which of the following describes Dr. Martin Luther King, Jr.?
   A. He was a segregationist who based his arguments against integration on constitution rights rather than racial differences.
   B. He was a world-famous figure who led the civil rights movement of the 1950s and '60s.
   C. He made history when he refused to integrate his restaurant despite rulings by the Supreme Court.
   D. He was the first black president of Morehouse College and used his position to lead the first sit-ins.

2. Which of the following statements would Lester Maddox have most likely agreed with?
   A. People should be treated the same, regardless of the color of their skin.
   B. Hamilton Holmes is a great example; the University of Georgia needs more students just like him.
   C. Dr. King is perhaps the greatest Georgian in history.
   D. A man has the right to do with his own property as he sees fit, without the government telling him what to do.

3. What was the Albany Movement and what was its impact?

4. What was the Sibley Commission and what was its purpose?

Chapter 9 Review

Key Terms, People, and Concepts

new postwar industries
Lockheed
GI Bill
postwar agriculture
interstate highways
William Hartsfield
Ivan Allen, Jr.
Braves
Henry "Hank" Aaron
Falcons
Hawks
Flames
Thrashers
Ellis Arnall
gubernatorial election of 1946
Herman Talmadge
1956 flag
white primary
county-unit system
Benjamin Mays
Dr. Martin Luther King, Jr.
civil rights movement
March on Washington
Civil Rights Act of 1964
Twenty-Fourth Amendment
Voting Rights Act of 1965
Albany Movement
Brown v. Board of Education
integration
Hamilton Holmes and Charlayne Hunter
white flight
Sibley Commission
Lester Maddox

Multiple Choice

1. The economic changes that occurred in Georgia after the war are **best** represented by which of the following events?
   A. the opening of the Pickrick restaurant
   B. continued cotton farming
   C. the opening of Lockheed
   D. the 1946 gubernatorial election

2. Why did the General Assembly form the Sibley Commission?
   A. to settle the controversy over the 1946 gubernatorial election
   B. to decide on a new state flag
   C. to build a new sports stadium
   D. to address school integration

3. Who of the following would have **most likely** agreed with the views of Lester Maddox?
   A. William Hartsfield
   B. Herman Talmadge
   C. leaders of the Albany Movement
   D. Benjamin Mays

4. Which of the following is credited to Ivan Allen, Jr.?
   A. the birth of Atlanta as an aviation hub
   B. the promotion of professional sports in the South
   C. shifting the case for segregation from racial language to arguments over constitutional rights
   D. breaking Babe Ruth's record

5. Who of the following would **most likely** agree with the quote below:

> *"US citizens have a basic right to freely decide who they will, and will not, associate with. It is not only unconstitutional, it is indecent, for any government official to force any citizen to mix with those he, or she, prefers not to."*

   A. Lester Maddox
   B. Benjamin Mays
   C. William Hartsfield
   D. Hank Aaron

6. Which of the following would an African-American citizen **most likely** be supportive of?
   A. the policies of Herman Talmadge
   B. integration
   C. segregation
   D. the 1956 state flag

7. What challenge did Hamilton Holmes and Charlayne Hunter face in 1961?
   A. They were the first African-Americans admitted to Atlanta's public schools.
   B. They were the first African-Americans to attempt to enter Lester Maddox's restaurant after the Civil Rights Act of 1964.
   C. They were the first African-Americans admitted to the University of Georgia.
   D. They were the first African-Americans to play professional sports in the South.

Chapter 10
Georgia's Modern Age

This chapter covers the following Georgia standard(s).

SS8H11	The student will evaluate the role of Georgia in the modern Civil Rights Movement.
SS8H12	The student will explain the importance of significant social, economic, and political developments in Georgia since 1970.
SS8G2	The student will explain how the Interstate Highway System, Hartsfield-Jackson International Airport, and Georgia's deepwater ports help drive the state's economy.
SS8E1	The student will give examples of the kinds of goods and services produced in Georgia in different historical periods.
SS8E2	The student will explain the benefits of free trade.
SS8E3	The student will evaluate the influence of Georgia's economic growth and development.

10.1 Shifts in Political Power

Reapportionment

African-Americans Waiting to Vote in Atlanta

The end of the county-unit system meant that Georgia elections were finally decided by popular vote rather than unit points. In 1964, the Supreme Court went even further and ruled that states had to make sure their voting districts were equal in population and representation. As a result, Georgia had to undergo **reapportionment**. Reapportionment is when representation in government is re-determined to make sure that citizens are represented fairly. Often, it involves redistricting (redrawing voting districts). Together, the end of the county-unit system and reapportionment greatly transformed how candidates campaign and which voters most influence elections. Since most Georgians live in cities and suburbs, political candidates now focus on **urban voters** in places like Atlanta. They realize that winning urban votes gives them a good chance of winning office as well. The influence of **African-American voters** also increased. Thanks to the end of the white primary and the county-unit system, African-Americans (many of whom live in urban areas) now have more say over who wins elections. In fact, in the city of Atlanta, it is nearly impossible for anyone to win an election without solid support from the African-American community.

Atlanta's First African-American Mayors

Maynard Jackson

Maynard Jackson

African-Americans began to rise to key political positions as a result of such changes. In 1969, **Maynard Jackson** won his bid to become vice-mayor of Atlanta. Four years later, he made history when he won election as the city's first African-American mayor. During his time in office, Jackson sought to make sure minority businesses received their fair share of city contracts, sometimes upsetting established white business leaders. Under his leadership, MARTA (Atlanta's mass transit train system) began service and Hartsfield Airport added a new international terminal that further helped the economy and continued to improve the city's image. Since the law did not allow Jackson to run for a third consecutive term, he left office for the first time in 1982. In 1990, however, Jackson returned for a third and final term. Following Jackson's death in 2003, the city of Atlanta honored him by adding his name to the airport he'd done so much to improve.

Andrew Young

Andrew Young

Andrew Young first became well known as a civil rights activist and aide to Dr. Martin Luther King, Jr. He was well respected within the civil rights movement and was present when Dr. King was assassinated in Memphis. In 1972, he won a seat in Congress and became Georgia's first black representative to the House since Reconstruction. In 1977, President Carter appointed Young to be US ambassador to the United Nations, where he served for two years before resigning. Finally, in 1981, he ran for mayor of Atlanta in hopes of succeeding his close friend, Maynard Jackson. With Jackson's support, he won, making Atlanta the first major US city in which one African-American mayor succeeded another. Young served two terms in which he successfully increased international investment in the city and brought the 1988 Democratic Convention to Georgia. Following his second term as mayor, he ran for governor in 1990 but lost to Democratic rival, Zell Miller. Since leaving office, Young has continued to have impact. He played a key role in bringing the 1996 Olympic Games to Atlanta and currently co-chairs a consulting firm focused on encouraging US investments in developing African and Caribbean nations.

Rise of the Two-party System in Georgia

Barry Goldwater

While many understood that new voting laws and civil rights legislation would lead to an increase in urban and African-American voting power, the social changes of the 1960s also had an unforeseen impact on southern politics: the **rise of the two-party system**. For nearly a century, only Democrats stood any real chance of winning major elections in Georgia. However, Supreme Court rulings striking down segregation and civil rights laws supported by Democratic presidents like Harry Truman, John Kennedy, and Lyndon Johnson, began causing deep resentment among southern Democrats after WWII. The first cracks in Georgia's Democratic Party appeared in 1962 when Republican **Howard "Bo" Calloway** won a seat in Congress. Then, when Lyndon Johnson ran for election as the Democratic presidential nominee in 1964, Georgia broke a hundred years of tradition and voted for the Republican, Barry Goldwater. Goldwater was a senator from Arizona, and his views sounded very much like those of conservative, southern Democrats. Although Goldwater himself contributed to organizations like the NAACP and personally did not support segregation, he believed firmly in states' rights and property rights. He believed it was wrong for the federal government to tell private owners how to run their own businesses. Meanwhile, many southern Democrats viewed their own party as favoring more government intervention and supporting minorities over whites. Despite Johnson's easy victory in the November election, the fact that Goldwater won parts of the South over a Democratic president showed that the days of the "solid South" were over. Since 1964, Georgia has only voted Democratic in three presidential elections: 1976, 1980, and 1992.

Important Georgia Republicans in the Modern Age

Gingrich (upper right) presides over the House during Clinton's State of the Union speech

Although he did not win in Georgia, Republican Ronald Reagan's lopsided victory over Jimmy Carter in the 1980 presidential election marked a new day in US politics. Not only did Reagan win the White House, the Republicans won the Senate as well. Despite an increase in conservatism during the '60s, it wasn't until southerners decided to forsake their traditional party loyalties that the Republican Party was able to get a dominant grip on US politics (conservatism is a political philosophy that values property rights, personal liberties, freedom from government regulations, and limited government funding by as few taxes as possible). Georgia experienced the effects as well. After 24 years in the United States Senate, Democrat Herman Talmadge lost to Republican Mack Mattingly in 1980. Two decades later, in 2002, Georgians elected **Sonny Perdue** as their first Republican governor since Reconstruction. By 2004, Republicans were in control of the General Assembly as well. In 2006, Perdue easily won re-election and currently the lieutenant governor and both US Senators from the state of Georgia are Republicans. In national politics, no Georgian represents the huge shift in political influence more than **Newt Gingrich**. Gingrich is a conservative Republican who first won a

Sonny Perdue

congressional seat from Georgia in 1978. Seventeen years later, in 1995, he became the speaker of the House. No longer in politics, Gingrich remains a major conservative spokesman and many believe he would make an excellent candidate for president one day.

Some claim that the Republican Party managed to gain influence in the South by taking advantage of the racial fears of middle-class whites. Many Republicans respond, however, that Southerners support their party for the same reasons as people in other parts of the country: because it promotes limited government and personal rights. Regardless of the reasons, the balance of power in Georgia politics has clearly shifted over the last 40 years.

Practice 10.1 Shifts in Political Power

1. Redetermining representation in state legislatures to make sure that citizens are represented fairly is called
   A. conservatism.
   B. urbanization.
   C. reapportionment.
   D. power shifting.

2. Who was Maynard Jackson?
   A. Georgia's first African-American governor
   B. Atlanta's first African-American mayor
   C. Mayor of Atlanta during the 1996 Olympics
   D. the first Republican elected to Congress in Georgia since Reconstruction

3. How did the end of the county-unit system and the white primary change political campaigns in Georgia? What impact did the end of these institutions have on African-Americans in politics?

10.2 Jimmy Carter

From Governor to President

In 1976, **Jimmy Carter** became the first and only Georgian to win the presidency. Before he moved into the White House, however, Carter got his political start at home. After a career as a naval officer, he returned to Plains, Georgia and successfully managed his family's peanut business. He then served two terms in the state legislature before winning the 1970 governor's race. Limited to one term by law, Carter used his four years to reform state government and make it more efficient. He favored integration and often feuded with his predecessor and lieutenant governor at the time, Lester Maddox. He also favored the continued growth of business and industrial development. In 1971, *Time* magazine featured Governor Carter on its cover as a symbol of the "New South."

Victory and Crisis

When Carter announced his candidacy for president, very few people outside of Georgia knew who he was. Thanks to an effective campaign, however, he won the Democratic nomination and faced Republican Gerald Ford in the November election. Ford was the only man in history to serve as both vice president and president without winning election to either office. President Nixon appointed him vice president in 1973 after his former vice president resigned. Then, in August 1974, a stunned nation watched as President Nixon also resigned rather than face impeachment for Watergate (a huge scandal that involved supporters of the president breaking into Democratic headquarters). In less than two years, Ford went from being a respected congressman from Michigan to being president of the United States.

President and Mrs. Carter Walk Down Pennsylvania Avenue

Carter defeated Ford in a relatively close election. On inauguration day (the day the president is sworn into office) US citizens cheered their new president as he walked down Pennsylvania Avenue hand-in-hand with his wife, Rosalynn, rather than riding in the traditional limo. Unfortunately, the celebration did not last long. Many citizens blamed Carter for the nation's double-digit inflation and hurting economy. Even worse, many perceived him as weak. Not long after the president signed a new arms treaty with the Soviet Union, the Soviets invaded the neighboring country of Afghanistan in 1979. Although Carter responded by ordering a grain embargo against the Soviets and a boycott of the 1980 Olympic games in Moscow, many US citizens questioned whether or not the president was capable of being tough enough with the Soviets.

Even more damaging for Carter was the **Iran Hostage Crisis**. In 1979, Iranian students stormed the US embassy in Tehran (Iran's capital) and took those inside hostage. The students were part of a revolution that overthrew the former ruler, the Shah of Iran, and replaced him with a Muslim government. They were angry at Carter for letting the Shah enter the US for medical treatment and demanded the president return the Shah to Iran to stand trial in exchange for the hostages. When Carter refused, a long stand-off followed.

Eventually, five months into the crisis, Carter authorized a rescue attempt that failed when a military helicopter collided with a transport plane, killing several US soldiers. Not until after Carter lost the 1980 election did the Iranians agree to let the hostages go. In the meantime, people in the US felt angry and humiliated. Many of them blamed the president for "letting it happen." Finally, within hours of Carter leaving office, the Iranians released the hostages and the long nightmare was over.

American hostage held by Iranians

THE CAMP DAVID ACCORDS

Sadat, Carter, Begin sign Camp David Accords

Carter did, however, have at least one monumental success while in office: The **Camp David Accords**. For centuries, Arabs and Jews have fought bitterly of the region of Palestine in the Middle East. A new chapter in this conflict opened in 1948 after the United Nations formally recognized the Jewish state of Israel in the disputed territory. Jewish people welcomed the decision and felt that such a homeland was needed after the horrors of the Holocaust. Arab nations, however, were furious! They believed the land given to the Jews rightfully belonged to an Arab people called the Palestinians. As a result, many of these Arab nations and Israel soon fought a series of wars against one another. One of the countries that fought Israel was Egypt. Egypt was largely viewed as the most powerful and influential Arab nation at the time. In 1977, Egypt's president, Anwar Sadat, shocked everyone by traveling to Israel to meet with its prime minister, Menachem Begin. President Carter was encouraged by the gesture and invited the two leaders to Camp David (the president's personal retreat) to try and come up with a lasting peace agreement between the two nations. At first, the meetings were unproductive because Begin and Sadat could not agree on a number of key issues. Eventually, however, thanks largely to Carter's tireless efforts, Egypt and Israel came to a historic peace agreement. The three leaders signed the Camp David Accords on September 17, 1978. Many saw the event as a diplomatic miracle and credited Carter for his ability to help negotiate a treaty between two nations that had been bitter enemies for so long.

FAREWELL TO WASHINGTON

Carter receives the Nobel Peace Prize

Despite his accomplishments at Camp David, President Carter could not overcome the nation's economic troubles or the crisis in Iran. On election night, 1980, the nation overwhelmingly voted for his opponent, Ronald Reagan. However, since leaving office, President Carter has become one of the most admired ex-presidents in history. Rather than retreating to a quiet life of retirement, Carter has remained active in charitable projects like Habitat for Humanity (a non-profit organization that builds houses for lower-income families) and has often been called on by some of his successors in the White House to represent the United States in diplomatic efforts. In addition, he has authored several books and continues to be active in social causes. Due to his hard work and accomplishments, he was awarded the Nobel Peace Prize in 2002.

Practice 10.2 Jimmy Carter

1. Which of the following statements describes Jimmy Carter?

   A. He is the only Georgian to serve as president.

   B. As lieutenant governor, he often feuded with Governor Lester Maddox over integration.

   C. He is the only man to serve as vice president and president without winning election to either office.

   D. After he left the White House, he returned to Georgia to become governor rather than retire.

2. Which of the following hurt Carter's chances for re-election in 1980?
   A. Watergate
   B. a healthy economy
   C. the Iranian Hostage Crisis
   D. the Camp David Accords

3. What were the Camp David Accords and why were they seen as so important?

10.3 IMAGE, GROWTH, AND INDUSTRY

GEORGIA'S TRANSPORTATION SYSTEMS

Over the past forty years, Georgia's economy has continued to grow and expand. It has produced millions of new jobs while, at the same time, helping the state develop an impressive international reputation.

THE BUSIEST AIRPORT IN THE WORLD

Hartsfield-Jackson International Airport

One of the reasons for Georgia's growth is its accessible **transportation systems**. Transportation systems include airports, railway lines, sea ports, and highways. Such systems prove valuable to states and cities because they allow goods to be hauled, imported, and exported much more efficiently. They also increase tourism and business, both of which help the local economy. **Hartsfield-Jackson International Airport**, located just outside Atlanta, contributes greatly to the state's economy. In 2006, it was named the "busiest airport in the world," servicing millions of passengers each year and shipping tons of cargo. Having one of the world's most sophisticated and active airports helps the city attract major events and additional business. Furthermore, the airport employs, either directly or indirectly, over 50,000 people a year. It literally produces billions of dollars a year for Georgia.

INTERSTATE HIGHWAYS

Interstate 85

Georgia also benefits from its **interstate highways** (review chapter 9, section 9.1 regarding the National Highway Act). These highways make it easy for Georgia businesses to transport goods throughout the country or to airports or seaports for trade overseas. They also make it easy for suppliers outside the state to ship products to Georgia as well. Georgia has four interstate highways. Interstate 95 runs along Georgia's east coast and stretches from Miami to Maine. Interstate 75 runs from Florida, through western Georgia, and ends in Michigan. Finally, I-85 runs from Virginia to Alabama, and I-20 runs west from South Carolina into Texas. Of the four, only I-95 does not cut through the heart of Atlanta.

Deepwater Ports

Port of Savannah

As a coastal city, Georgia also depends heavily on its **deepwater ports**. These ports allow ships to import and export many of the products Georgia depends on. Savannah and Brunswick are the two major ports, with each providing billions of dollars in revenue and thousands of jobs for the state. Both are located close to rail lines which make it easy for ships to be unloaded and their cargo transported to cities further inland. Savannah is the fifth largest port in the United States and the fourth busiest US port overall. Meanwhile, Brunswick's port specializes in shipping automobiles and heavy equipment, such as tractors and other machinery.

Railroads

Georgia Railroad

You may remember from earlier chapters that **railroads** became very important to Georgia in the 1800s. Although other forms of transportation have replaced railroads to some degree, they still play an important role in Georgia. The state still has roughly 5,000 miles of track, used to haul cargo to and from shipyards, farms, warehouses, etc. Georgia's railroads help businesses effectively transport their products while at the same time serving to preserve an important part of Georgia's past.

Georgia's Modern Economy

Economics refers to how nations and states use their limited resources (money, raw materials, labor, etc.). **Georgia's economy** has to do with how much the state produces, how much debt it has, how many of its citizens are employed, etc. The better a state's economy is doing, the happier and more secure its citizens tend to be. As a result, political leaders always try to encourage economic growth.

Trade: Past and Present

Historic trade

From the time King George II first granted Oglethorpe and the trustees their charter, **trade** has always been an important part of Georgia's economy. Trade is the importing and exporting of products between different nations or regions. *Imports* are the products a state or nation buys from another region or country, while *exports* are the products it sells to foreign territories. Like most of the southern colonies, England founded Georgia to produce goods for trade. Although the colony never produced the amount of silk Great Britain hoped, other agricultural products eventually turned out to be very profitable. The port of Savannah became very important as Georgia shipped rice, indigo, lumber, tobacco, and eventually tons and tons of cotton to England and places like the West Indies. As the colony shipped agricultural products across the Atlantic, it also relied on manufactured goods from England and products like rum, sugar, and molasses from the Caribbean. In the 1770s, Georgia proved more hesitant than most other colonies to break away from England largely because it depended so heavily on trade with its "mother country." Over time, cotton and textiles became major exports as the South came to rely on cotton and cotton-related industries as the foundation of its economy. Naval stores (products like turpentine that come from trees and are used to make ships), also became increasingly important. Meanwhile, since industries in the South were limited in the 1800s, the state relied on imports from England and other parts of the US for many of its manufactured goods. So important was international trade to Georgia's survival in the 1800s that the Union attempted to cripple the state during the Civil War by blockading its coast to interfere with shipping.

Carpet industry in Dalton

Today, Georgia continues to rely heavily on trade. Agricultural products and agriculture-related industries (businesses that depend on agriculture, such as textiles, meat packing, or retail foods) continue to be a major portion of Georgia's exports, bringing in billions of dollars each year. In particular, peanuts, tobacco, cotton, soybeans, corn, and poultry all produce a great deal of income for the state. However, other industries have become important as well. Georgia's exports include paper and forest products, various manufactured goods, and machinery, to name a few. Meanwhile, its imports include clothing, furniture, and foreign manufactured goods. Trade allows Georgia to earn money by selling to the rest of the world those goods it most efficiently produces, while at the same time purchasing products from other places that Georgians want or need.

Key Industries and International Business

Despite occasional challenges, Georgia's economy has continued to grow since 1970. Although agriculture still makes up over 10% of the state's income every year, other industries have become major parts of Georgia's economy as well. Non-food wholesale and retail industries, banking and finance, music and entertainment, professional athletics and major sporting events in places like Atlanta, textiles, paper products, tourism, media and television, and numerous other industries all play important parts in the state's bustling modern economy.

George Busbee

Joe Frank Harris

One key change since the early '70s has been the growth of **international business** (business involving foreign nations). Thanks largely to *Governor George Busbee* (in office from 1975 – 1983) and *Governor Joe Frank Harris* (in office from 1983 –1991), Georgia has become an international business center. There are currently between 1500 and 2000 internationally owned facilities in Georgia in addition to a number of foreign businesses and international banks. At the same time, Georgia has also established offices in a number of other countries to recruit foreign businesses and encourage them to invest in Georgia. As a result, Georgia has attracted more overseas business. For instance, Korean auto manufacturer, KIA, chose Georgia as the site for its new US plant in 2006. The decision thrilled many Georgians who were still disappointed over decisions by Ford and General Motors to close their plants in Hapeville and Doraville just months before. International investments in the state help Georgians in several ways. First, they pump more money into the state's economy. Second, they create jobs. When foreign businesses build facilities or open offices in Georgia, they usually hire local residents as employees. As a result, the state benefits from more employment.

Special Events and Facilities

Georgia World Congress Center

Part of the reason Georgia has grown economically has been its willingness to invest in adequate facilities. The **World Congress Center** opened in Atlanta in 1976 as a convention and exhibition center. It provides meeting space for regional, national, and international gatherings. In 1992, the **Georgia Dome** opened. The dome is an indoor sports arena that seats over 70,000 fans. It is currently home to the Atlanta Falcons and has hosted such events as the Superbowl, NCAA Final Fours, numerous SEC championship games, and even portions of the 1996 Olympics. Such major sporting events attract thousands of spectators who visit the state and spend millions of dollars in the local economy.

Atlanta Falcons play at the Georgia Dome

Opening ceremony of the Atlanta Olympics

Of all the spectacular events that Georgia has hosted, none has impacted the state as much as the **1996 Centennial Olympic Games**. Thanks to the efforts of Mayors Andrew Young and Maynard Jackson, as well as numerous supporters and volunteers, Georgia won the honor of hosting the summer Olympics in 1996. Although the city of Atlanta served as the official host city, the entire state contributed and benefited from this worldwide event. More than 10,000 athletes and countless media representatives came to Georgia as part of the games. The event put Georgia on a national stage and made Atlanta a world-known city. It had lasting economic benefits as well. In preparation for the Olympics, Atlanta constructed Olympic Stadium, which was later re-named Turner Field and currently serves as home to the Atlanta Braves. In addition, the state also benefited from a new horse park, state-of-the-art shooting range, a new rowing center, and an elaborate tennis facility. Even today, Georgia Tech and Georgia State University continue to use buildings and dormitories built to serve as the Olympic Village (complex the athletes live in while they compete in the Olympics). In addition, the thousands of people who came to the state for the games spent lots of money at restaurants, hotels, stores, etc., pumping millions of dollars into the local economy. Meanwhile, world leaders and businesses gained exposure to the area and witnessed Georgia's ability to successfully host one of the largest international gatherings in the world. As a result, the state's ability to attract major events and investments increased. Sadly, the games were marred by one tragic event. One evening, while visitors to the games enjoyed a concert in newly-constructed Centennial Olympic Park, a bomb exploded, killing one person and injuring others. Eventually, a man named Eric Rudolph was captured and convicted for the bombing. Despite this sad incident, however, the 1996 Olympics proved to be a success for Georgia and one of the most important events in state history.

Major Businesses and Entrepreneurs

Georgia is home to a number of major businesses, thanks to the vision and efforts of some of the most gifted **entrepreneurs** in history. An *entrepreneur* is someone who starts a business or a company, often taking great financial risks in the process. They take such risks in hopes of earning a **profit**. Profit is the amount of money a person or business earns and has left over after all costs of production are paid. In other words, say you want to mow yards during the summer for $20 per yard. If you paid $5 for gas and oil for the lawnmower, then after one yard your profit would be $15. Some of the world's riches and most successful entrepreneurs have started or located their businesses in Georgia.

Coca-Cola

Santa-themed Coke Advertisement

John Pemberton

In 1886, an Atlanta druggist named John Pemberton invented a new drink to cure headaches. The drink effectively eased people's pain in large part because it contained cocaine (a strong drug that is very addictive and illegal today). In 1892, **Asa Candler** bought the rights to the drink for $2300 and began marketing **Coca-Cola** (also known as Coke) as a regular drink rather than a medicine. He was one of the first entrepreneurs to understand the potential of nationwide advertising and used it to turn Coke into a household name. In 1919, he sold the company for $25 million to Ernest Woodruff (a profit of $24,997,700). Four years later, Woodruff's son, **Robert Woodruff**, took over and built Coke into a worldwide sensation. Woodruff became so influential that he was considered by many to be the key member of Atlanta's progressive coalition that ran much of the city's government from behind the scenes during Mayor Hartsfield's time in office (see Chapter 9). He also gave millions of dollars as a philanthropist (someone who gives money to support charitable causes and/or public projects). Today, millions of people around the world drink Coke every day.

Robert Woodruff

The Home Depot

Bernie Marcus and Arthur Blank founded **The Home Depot** in Atlanta in 1978. The store sells home improvement supplies at reduced prices. By 2004, The Home Depot's profits exceeded $5 billion! Today, The Home Depot is in all 50 states and several foreign nations as well. Arthur Blank ultimately became so wealthy that he bought the Atlanta Falcons in 2002 and is currently one of the most recognized owners in the NFL.

Bernie Marcus and Arthur Blank

Georgia Pacific

Owen Cheatham created what became **Georgia-Pacific** in Augusta, Georgia in 1927. Originally a lumber company, Georgia-Pacific is currently the largest wholesale supplier of building products in North America and the second largest producer of paper products. The company operates over 600 plants in the US and elsewhere, reporting profits of more than $250 million each year. After several years headquartered out west, Georgia-Pacific moved its home offices back to Georgia in 1982.

Delta Airlines

Delta jet at Atlanta Airport

Begun as a crop-dusting business in 1924, **Delta Airlines** grew to be one of the nation's major airlines under the leadership of **C.E. Woolman**. (Crop-dusters fly their planes low over fields of crops, dropping pesticides to kill insects.) The company began in Macon, Georgia, then moved for a brief time to Louisiana. It was eventually named "Delta" after the Mississippi River delta. In 1941, Woolman moved his headquarters to Atlanta to take advantage of its up-and-coming airport. Delta continued to grow even after Woolman's death in 1966, making its first transatlantic flight (flights to the other side of the Atlantic Ocean) in 1978. Hard economic times, the terrorist attacks of September 11, 2001, and poor customer relations have caused Delta serious problems in the last few years. In 2003, the company filed for bankruptcy, but successfully fought off takeover attempts by other airlines to re-emerge from bankruptcy in 2007.

Chick-fil-A

Founded by **S. Truett Cathy**, the first **Chick-fil-A** restaurant opened in Atlanta in 1967. It grew out of Cathy's original restaurant, the Dwarf Grill, and his innovative way of preparing chicken to be served as a sandwich. Currently, Chick-fil-A operates more than 1200 restaurants in 38 states. By 2004, it reported over $1.7 billion in profits, making it one of the nation's most prosperous restaurant chains. This feat is remarkable considering that Cathy, a devout Christian, insists that his restaurants remain closed on Sundays.

S. Truett Cathy

AFLAC

AFLAC duck

Three brothers, **John, Paul, and Bill Amos**, founded the American Family Life Insurance Company in Columbus, Georgia in 1955. Eventually they changed the name to the American Family Life *Assurance* Company, better known as **AFLAC**. Originally funded through the selling of stock, the company grew and eventually pioneered cancer insurance in 1958. Today, AFLAC is the nation's leader in supplemental health insurance and also sells policies in Japan. In recent years, AFLAC has consistently been rated as one of the best companies in the nation to work for. It has also been recognized as one of the country's best employers for minorities and working moms. Still based in Columbus, the company features one of the most popular corporate mascots in all of advertising: the AFLAC duck.

Impact of Immigration

A Multicultural State

A Multicultural Classroom

Thanks largely to **immigration**, Georgia has become a much more diverse state over the last few decades. Immigration is the process of people moving to a nation or state from somewhere else. Georgia is one of the most populous states in the nation, with thousands of new people arriving every year. In 2007, Atlanta ranked as the number one fastest growing city in the country, and several Georgia counties ranked among the nation's top ten in growth! Many of these people move to Georgia from other parts of the country, while others are foreign immigrants. There are a number of factors that draw newcomers to the state. The rising influence of international business means that foreigners often come to occupy key positions within companies headquartered in their home country. Others come as students to one of Georgia's many colleges or universities and decide to remain after they graduate. Poorer immigrants often come to find work in Georgia's factories, urban blue-collar jobs, building construction, or on farms. Quality of life often attracts people as well. Since the South traditionally has warmer weather and a lower cost of living than many other parts of the country, many immigrate to states like Georgia because it costs less money and the climate is more pleasant. Such growth creates the need for new homes, new businesses, increased construction and services, etc. This produces job opportunities which attract even more people. Such factors not only attract those from other countries but many people from other states as well.

The fastest growing immigrant community in Georgia is the **Hispanic community**. Many Hispanic immigrants come from Mexico in search of jobs and greater economic opportunities. Some trace the beginning of this rapid increase in Hispanic immigration to the years leading up to the '96 Olympics when new construction projects and renovations created lots of job opportunities and a high demand for labor. Georgia's current Hispanic population is roughly four times what it was just two decades ago. Its growth has had great impact. Schools, businesses, and public agencies now rely more on Spanish as they serve a growing population that does not speak English as a first language, if at all. Also, the number of businesses, newspapers, magazines, radio and television stations, etc. that cater specifically to Spanish-speaking people has grown tremendously in recent years.

Illegal Immigration

While greater cultural diversity is viewed by many to be a positive thing, **illegal immigration** presents serious problems for Georgia and other states. Illegal immigration is when people from another country enter the US illegally. Most illegal immigrants come from Hispanic countries and enter the US over its southern border with Mexico. Georgia's illegal immigrant population is believed to have doubled since 2000, and the state is estimated to have the fastest growing illegal immigrant population in the US. This is amazing considering Georgia, unlike several other states, does not border Mexico.

Illegal Immigrants Protest

Today, few political and social issues cause as much controversy as illegal immigration. Most citizens are especially concerned about illegal immigration after the terrorist attacks of 9/11. Most citizens believe that, until the US is aware of who is crossing its borders, it will always be vulnerable to another deadly attack. Some citizens want to build a wall along the Mexican border and close it off except for closely monitored crossing points. Some want current immigration laws made stronger and more strictly enforced. They also want to deny illegal immigrants many tax paid services, claiming that they do not pay for them and should not receive them since they are not citizens. Others disagree. They point out that most immigrants are good people just looking for a better way of life and claim that they help the economy by working manual labor, low-income jobs that many US citizens might not accept. Many Hispanics, both legal and illegal, are upset by the idea of stricter immigration laws because they see them as racist. Supporters of such laws, however, quickly respond that they favor strict immigration laws as a matter of national security and necessity, not because they are prejudiced against Hispanics.

In 2006, Georgia's General Assembly passed the *Security and Immigration Compliance Act* in an effort to clamp down on illegal immigration in Georgia. It is one of the strongest anti-illegal immigration laws in the nation and is praised by many who support a stronger stance against illegal immigration. In most cases, it requires people seeking state benefits to prove that they are a legal resident. It also requires police to confirm the legal status of anyone they arrest and penalizes employers who continue to hire illegal immigrants.

Georgia's General Assembly

Practice 10.3 Image, Growth, and Industry

1. Which of the following is true regarding Hartsfield-Jackson International Airport?

   A. It is one of the busiest airports in the world and important to Georgia's economy.
   B. It is no longer important to Georgia's economy because other forms of transportation have become more popular.
   C. It allows millions of tourist to visit the state each year but does little to help business or provide jobs.
   D. It is located in Savannah and is the fifth busiest airport in the nation.

2. S. Truitt Cathy, Asa Candler, Arthur Blank, and C.E. Woolman are all examples of what?

   A. businessmen who helped to build one of the busiest airports in the world
   B. men who made "Coke" a household name
   C. entrepreneurs who founded companies in other states and moved them to Georgia
   D. entrepreneurs who have created widely recognized businesses

3. How did the 1996 Centennial Olympics impact Georgia?

4. How has immigration affected Georgia and what are some of the arguments for and against stiffer laws to deal with illegal immigration?

Chapter 10 Review

Key Terms, People, and Concepts

reapportionment
urban voters
African-American voters
Maynard Jackson
Andrew Young
rise of the two-party system
Howard "Bo" Callaway
Sonny Perdue
Newt Gingrich
Jimmy Carter
Iran Hostage Crisis
Camp David Accords
transportation systems
Hartsfield-Jackson International Airport
interstate highways
deepwater ports
railroads
Georgia's economy
trade
international business
World Congress Center
Georgia Dome
1996 Centennial Olympic Games
entrepreneurs
profit
Asa Candler
Coca Cola
Robert Woodruff
Bernie Marcus and Arthur Blank
The Home Depot
Owen Cheatham
Georgia-Pacific
Delta Airlines
C.E. Woolman
S. Truitt Cathy
Chic-fil-A
the Amoses
AFLAC
immigration
Hispanic community
illegal immigration

Multiple Choice

1. Which of the following benefitted the **most** from reapportionment?
   A. a white farmer in rural Georgia
   B. an African-American farmer in rural Georgia
   C. registered voters living in downtown Atlanta
   D. legal immigrants

2. Andrew Young made history when he was elected mayor of Atlanta for which of the following reasons?
   A. He was the first black mayor in the city's history.
   B. It was the first time an African-American mayor had ever succeeded another African-American mayor in a major city.
   C. He was the first mayor elected after the end of the county-unit system.
   D. He was the first mayor in history to serve two consecutive terms.

3. Which of the following **most accurately** describes Georgia's modern Republican Party?
   A. It still struggles to get any Republicans elected to major offices because of the traditionally "solid South."
   B. It is the party that helped Jimmy Carter win the presidency in 1976.
   C. It has grown in power greatly over the last few decades, seizing many of the state's most powerful positions.
   D. Its candidates have won nearly every key office in Georgia except governor.

4. Someone helping President Jimmy Carter campaign for re-election in 1980 would have **most likely** tried to get voters to focus on which of the following?
   A. the Camp David Accords
   B. the Iran Hostage Crisis
   C. the economy
   D. US relations with Soviet Union

5. Georgia has traditionally relied on Brunswick and Savannah to serve as what?
   A. major railroad hubs
   B. intersections of major highways
   C. sites of key airports
   D. important deepwater ports

6. What impact has international business had on Georgia?
   A. None, because only the federal government may engage in international business.
   B. It has boosted the state's economy and increased its international reputation.
   C. It has helped lessen the state's reliance on Hartsfield-Jackson airport.
   D. It has hurt the state's ability to engage in trade.

7. Asa Candler and Robert Woodruff are associated with which of the following?
   A. Coca-Cola
   B. AFLAC
   C. The Home Depot
   D. rise of the two-party system in Georgia

8. Which of the following is a major challenge facing Georgia?
   A. the arrival of international businesses
   B. major events
   C. being stuck with facilities constructed especially for the Olympics
   D. illegal immigration

Chapter 11
Georgia's Geography

This chapter covers the following Georgia standard(s).

SS8G1	The student will describe Georgia with regard to physical features and location.

11.1 Georgia's Place in the World

Georgia as a World and National Region

Geography is the study of the earth's climate, surface, countries, peoples, industries, natural resources, etc. An area's geography greatly affects how its people live, what kinds of plants and trees grow there, what species of animal inhabit it, and what is produced. Geography also helps define what **region** an area is a part of. A *region* is a geographic area defined by some kind of trait, such as climate, culture, the people who live there, location, etc. Regions may be defined locally, such as part of a city or county, or broadly, covering large portions of the earth. The state of Georgia is part of several world and national regions.

Georgia's Location on the Globe

Globe

Georgia has its own, specific location on earth. To pinpoint it, we must first understand what world region Georgia is a part of. Georgia lies in both the **Western and Northern Hemispheres**. When you study a globe (three dimensional model of the earth) you are looking at a sphere. A *hemisphere* is simply half of a sphere. The globe consists of four hemispheres: northern, southern, western, and eastern. To help us find where places on earth are located in each hemisphere, the globe also has imaginary lines known as *parallels* and *meridians.* **Parallels** run around the globe from east to west, while **meridians** run from pole to pole. Each parallel and meridian is assigned a certain number of *degrees*. Meanwhile, the space in between each meridian and parallel consists of 60 *minutes*. Parallels start at the **equator** which is zero degrees and zero minutes (0°, 0'). The equator runs all the way around the globe at its halfway point between the north and south poles and divides the globe into its northern and southern hemispheres. As you get closer to each pole, the number of degrees assigned to each parallel increases in either a northern or southern direction. You know which direction you are headed by adding either an "N" if it is the Northern Hemisphere or an "S" if it is the Southern. For example, the North Pole is located at 90 degrees north (90°, 0' N), while the South Pole is located at 90 degrees south (90°, 0' S). Any time you are discussing the location of a place on the globe and see a number followed by degrees and minutes with the letter N or S after it, you know that you are pinpointing that place's location in either the Northern or Southern Hemisphere. Such a location is called ***latitude***.

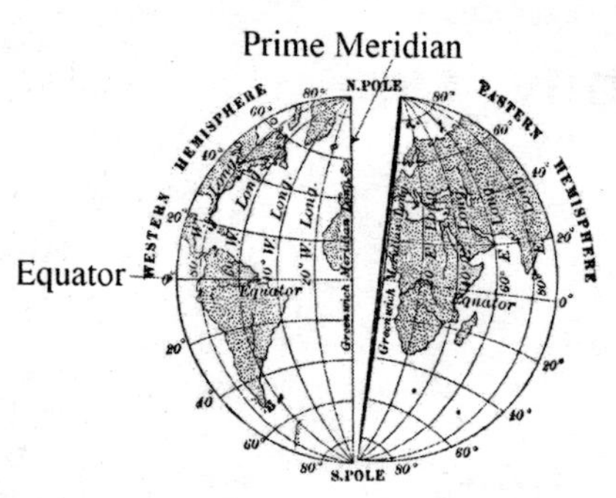

By comparison, meridians start at the **prime meridian** which runs from pole to pole through England, parts of Africa and Europe, and Antarctica. While parallels measure latitude, meridians measure ***longitude***. The prime meridian is located at zero degrees and zero minutes longitude (0°, 0' longitude). As you move east or west of the prime meridian, the meridians increase in degrees, all the way to the **International Date Line** which is located at 180°, 0' longitude. The prime meridian and the International Date Line are located directly opposite of one another on the globe and, together, form the line that divides the globe into the Western and Eastern Hemispheres. Just as degrees of latitude move in either a southern or northern direction, degrees of longitude move either eastern or western. Therefore, instead of using a N or S, you designate which direction you are moving in terms of longitude by adding either an "E" or a "W." When you know both the latitude and longitude of a place, you can find its exact location in the world. Georgia's latitude is between **32°, 02' and 35° N,** while its longitude is between **80°, 50' and 85°, 36' W**.

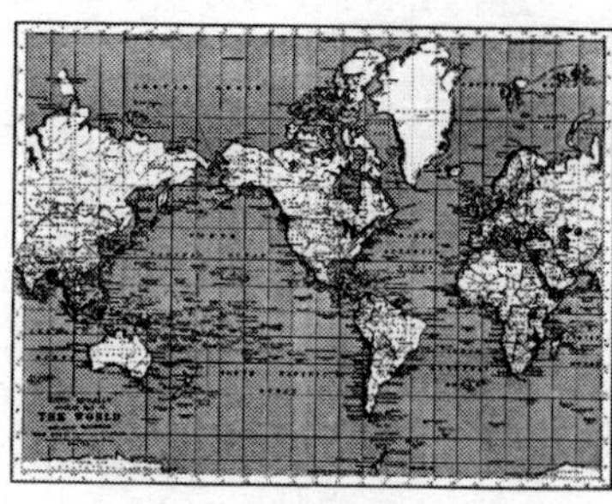

Map of world

GEORGIA AS PART OF A NATIONAL REGION

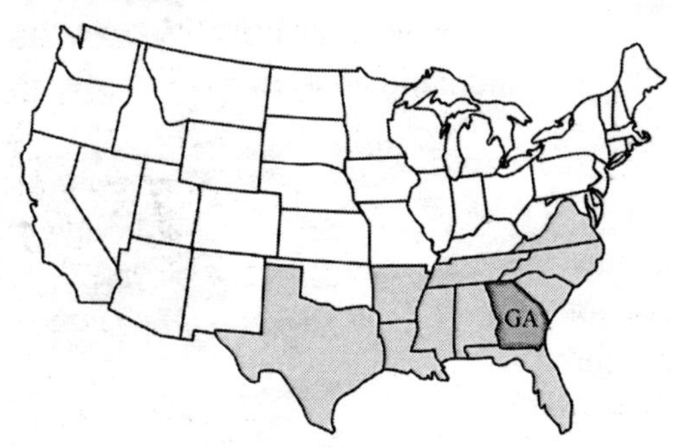

Georgia is part of the continent known as **North America**. It is also one of fifty states that make up the country known as the **United States of America**. Within the United States, Georgia is part of the **South** region. This region stretches from Virginia down through Florida and westward through Texas. The states which make up this region share similar climates, cultures, history, industries, have often depended on similar cash crops, and together formed the Confederate States of America during the Civil War. Georgia is also part of a number of "sub-regions." For instance, it is part of the **Sun Belt** which is the fastest growing part of the country and stretches from the Carolinas across the nation's south to California.

Georgia's Climate

North Georgia Mountains

Climate refers to an area's consistent weather patterns over a long period of time. Georgia enjoys a relatively mild climate with summers that average 80° F and winters averaging just above 40° F (although it is not unusual for some regions to reach 100° F in the summer and the mountains to dip close to 0° F in the winter). The state also experiences four distinct seasons with notable temperature changes. Springs are warm and mild and usually feature heavy amounts of pollen from the many varieties of plants and trees that begin to bloom. As a result, it can be a difficult time for people who have allergies. Summers are hot, with the highest temperatures usually falling in July. July also has the highest amount of rainfall on average, although both spring and summer can experience severe droughts (shortages of rain) as well. Falls start out warm and gradually cool. The leaves change to a beautiful variety of colors, making places like the Blue Ridge Mountains popular tourist sites during this part of the year. The fall also includes what is on average the state's driest month: October. Finally, winters are cold, with temperatures in the mountains usually dropping lower than those in the lower elevations. Although snow is rare for Atlanta and regions further south, the Georgia mountains commonly experience snowfall during this part of the year. January is traditionally the state's coldest month.

A number of factors affect Georgia's climate. Wind and ocean currents from the Gulf of Mexico and the Atlantic Ocean often impact how much precipitation (rainfall, snow, etc.) there is and what the temperature will be. Since climate is fairly stable, such factors are usually predictable depending on the time of year. However, *El Niño* (warmer than normal Pacific Ocean current) and *La Niña* (colder than normal Pacific Ocean current) can greatly alter climate patterns worldwide and affect Georgia in unusual ways (such as unusual storms, unseasonable temperatures, floods, droughts, etc.).

Wild Horses on a Georgia Beach

Climate and Economic Development

Georgia's climate has helped its **economic development** tremendously. Its scenic mountains, sunny beaches, rivers, forests, and mild temperatures make it an enjoyable destination for tourists who spend money in the local economy. Even more importantly, Georgia's climate also attracts new businesses and industries, military bases, and people who move to the state permanently from other parts of the country. Its rivers, inland waterways, and accessibility to the ocean also make it a key location for shipping and trade (see chapter 10). Finally, Georgia's soil, forests, and temperatures make it an ideal state for growing various agricultural products and producing other natural resources, many of which have been discussed in earlier chapters. Without question, Georgia owes much of its economic and population growth to its favorable climate.

HURRICANES, TORNADOES, AND DROUGHTS

Hurricane

Lightning

Georgia's climate can be challenging, however. **Hurricanes** (violent storms that form over the Atlantic Ocean with winds of more than 75 mph) can strike Georgia's east coast or come ashore elsewhere and pass through the state as **tropical storms** (hurricane-like storms with winds less than 75 mph). Although modern technology allows meteorologists (people who study the weather for a living) to know when and where hurricanes and tropical storms will hit days ahead of time, the power and fury of these storms can still cause massive damage and loss of life. **Thunderstorms** are also common in Georgia during the spring and summer months. These are storms that often strike fast and hard, producing thunder, large amounts of rain, and lightning. Georgia consistently ranks in the nation's top ten states for lightning strikes each year. *Lightning* is electrical current that is produced during intense storms and can cause serious injury or death. When such current makes contact with objects on the ground it is referred to as a "lightning strike." Extremely severe thunderstorms can result in **tornadoes**. Tornadoes are large, potentially deadly storm clouds that rotate, often producing a spinning column that touches and moves along the ground. Large tornados can travel for miles and produce winds of more than 200 mph. Tornadoes are especially dangerous because they form quickly and often allow only a few minutes warning before people need to take cover. On average, Georgia experiences more than 20 tornadoes per year, most of them occurring in the middle and southern portions of the state.

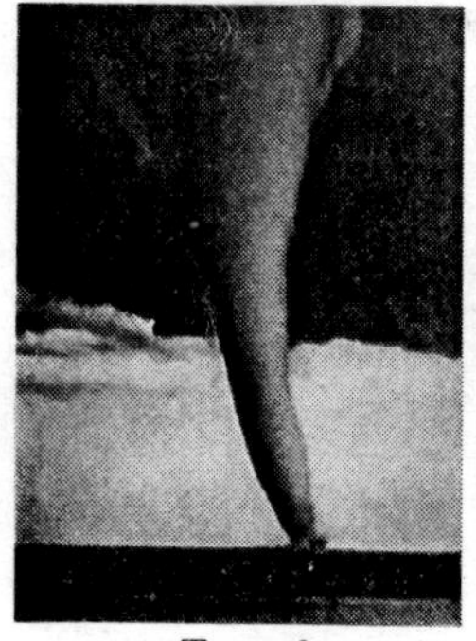
Tornado

Droughts can also cause problems. From time to time, Georgia does not get the rainfall it needs to maintain comfortable levels of water for public use or to effectively grow crops. In spring 2007, Georgia experienced one of the most severe droughts in state history. Not only did it affect how citizens use water and hurt crop production, but it also allowed massive wildfires to burn out of control for weeks on end in south Georgia, destroying millions of dollars in property and causing areas as far away as North Carolina to experience smoke-filled skies.

Dried Soil During Drought

Practice 11.1 Georgia's Place in the World

1. What two hemispheres is Georgia located in?

   A. Northern and Eastern
   B. Western and Southern
   C. Western and Eastern
   D. Northern and Western

2. Which region of the United States is Georgia located in?

   A. South
   B. Sun
   C. North
   D. Confederate

3. Describe Georgia's overall climate and tell how it has impacted the state economically.

11.2 Regions Within Georgia

The Appalachian Plateau

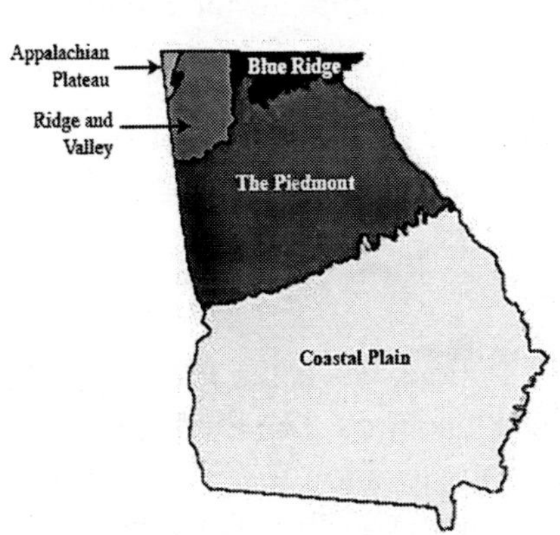

Just like the United States, Georgia also consists of several officially recognized regions. The first is the **Appalachian Plateau** (a plateau is a flat area of land that sits at a higher elevation than the surrounding land). It is the state's smallest region and is located at its very northwest corner. It is sometimes called the *"TAG corner"* because it is where Tennessee, Alabama, and Georgia meet. Also known as the Cumberland Plateau, this region features a long, narrow valley with Sand Mountain on one side and Lookout Mountain on the other. It has two beautiful waterfalls and a number of underground caves, including Ellison Cave which is the deepest cave east of the Mississippi River. Once a profitable area for mining coal and iron ore, the region is covered in forests and is home to historic Civil War battle sites like Chickamauga. Its highest elevation is roughly 2,000 feet with average summer time temperatures around 70° F and an average winter temperatures just above 40° F.

Appalachian Plateau

Ridge and Valley

The **Ridge and Valley** region is located in northwest Georgia, east of the Appalachian Plateau, and consists of a series of high, narrow ridges and low, open valleys. The region ranges in elevation from 700 to 1,600 feet and features forests of oak, hickory, and pine trees. Farming is limited with large portions of land used for pastures. Meanwhile, agricultural products include corn, soybeans, wheat, and cotton. In addition, abundant apple orchards make Ellijay, Georgia the "apple capital" of the state. However, some consider Ellijay to be part of the Blue Ridge rather than the Ridge and Valley region.

Blue Ridge

The **Blue Ridge** region, in the northeast corner of Georgia, is made up of part of the Blue Ridge Mountains that also extend into Tennessee and the Carolinas. These mountains are part of the larger **Appalachian Mountains** that run from Maine to Alabama. They are called the "Blue Ridge Mountains" because the vegetation that covers them gives them a blue hazy color when viewed from a distance. This region is home to Georgia's highest peak, Brasstown Bald, which rises to 4, 784 feet. It is also the site of Springer Mountain, the southern end of the world-famous *Appalachian Trail*. The Appalachian Trail stretches 2,175 miles from Georgia to Maine and is traveled by thousands of hikers

Blue Ridge region

each year. Waterfalls, gorges, and canyons are found in this region, including *Amicalola Falls* (the tallest waterfall east of the Mississippi River) and *Tallulah Gorge*, which is two miles long and 1,000 feet deep. The Blue Ridge receives the most rainfall in Georgia, and often gets snow in the winter due to its high elevation. Many of Georgia's rivers, including the Savannah and Chattahoochee, begin in this region, and minerals such as copper, marble, talc, and gold, have historically made the region important for mining. The average high temperature is 69 °F, while the average low temperature is 45° F. The climate and mountainous terrain prevent much agriculture from taking place, but vegetables, grapes, and apples are grown in this region. Due to its scenic beauty, hiking trails, and outdoor recreational activities, this region attracts thousands of tourists each year.

The Piedmont

South of the Appalachian Plateau, Ridge and Valley, and the Blue Ridge regions lies is the **Piedmont**. It is the second largest region in the state, taking up roughly 30% of the state's land area. The Piedmont, which means "foot of the mountains," is made up of low rolling hills and ranges in elevation from 500 feet at the Fall Line to 1700 feet at its northern border (we will discuss the Fall Line more shortly). This region is known for its famed "Georgia red clay," which is a soil rich in iron minerals. The region also has large amounts of granite and marble, enabling Georgia to be the nation's leading producer of both (Pickens County is famous for its marble production while Stone Mountain is the largest exposed mass of granite in the world).

Before the Civil War, the Piedmont region was responsible for most of Georgia's cotton production, which means it produced much of the South's cotton as well. Today, it is still an important region for agriculture, producing large amounts of wheat, soybean, corn, cattle, and poultry. The region also features the bulk of Georgia's industry and population thanks to cities like Atlanta, Athens, and Milledgeville. Roughly one half of all Georgians live in the Piedmont.

Stone Mountain

The Coastal Plain

Coastal Plain

The **Coastal Plain** covers approximately 60% of the state's total area and is the state's largest region. It stretches from the barrier islands and beaches along the coast across southern Georgia to Alabama. The Coastal Plain features good farmland, underground water, abundant sources of pulp, naval stores, and produces most of Georgia's crops. Peanuts, pecans, corn, and world-famous Vidalia onions all grow in this region. Thanks to its beaches and historic sites like Savannah, the Coastal Plain region attracts large numbers of tourists each year, while serving as an important source of industry for the economy due to its important shipyards (review chapter 10, section 10.3).

Practice 11.2 Regions Within Georgia

1. How many officially recognized regions does Georgia have?

   A. 4 B. 3 C. 5 D. 6

2. Which of the following regions gets the most snowfall?

   A. Piedmont B. Blue Ridge C. Coastal Plain D. Atlanta

3. Which of Georgia's regions covers the most territory in the state? Which one has the greatest population?

11.3 Other Geographic Features

The Fall Line

The area where the Piedmont and Coastal Plain regions meet is known as the **Fall Line**. It is about twenty miles wide and extends from the city of Columbus in the west, through Macon and Milledgeville, to Augusta in the east. It is called the "Fall Line" because it marks that part of the state where the elevation begins to drop drastically towards sea level. As a result, water runs down hill at an increased rate, picking up speed and momentum. That's why early Georgians built cities like Augusta here, because the increased rate of water flow made the Fall Line great for harnessing water power for mills in the days before electricity. The Fall Line also features some of the state's most beautiful waterfalls.

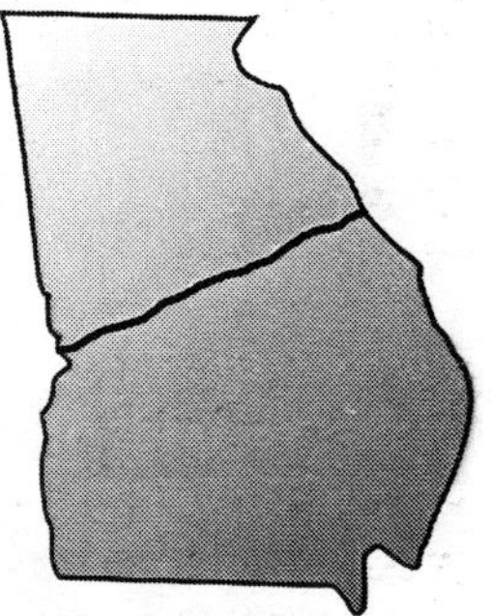

Fall Line

Barrier Islands

Along Georgia's coastline are a series of islands known as the state's **barrier islands**. They are referred to as "barrier islands" because they protect the mainland from much of the ocean wind and waves that would otherwise erode its coast. Some of these islands, like Jekyll, St. Simons, and Tybee islands, are open to the public and serve as popular tourist attractions for thousands of visitors who come to enjoy their beaches and activities. Others are protected as wildlife reserves and wilderness sanctuaries (a reserve or sanctuary is a place protected by the government so that animals' habitats, trees, bodies of water, plants, etc. are not disrupted or destroyed by man-made development).

Georgia's Barrier Islands

GEORGIA'S RIVERS

Georgia has always relied heavily on its rivers for drinking water, travel, trade, power, and recreation. Georgians built cities such as Macon, Augusta, and Columbus along rivers because they offered both a source of power and transportation. Most of Georgia's rivers flow from north to south because of the drop in elevation. Some of them flow into the Gulf of Mexico, while others flow into the Atlantic Ocean. Two of the state's main rivers are the Chattahoochee and the Savannah. The **Chattahoochee River** begins in the Blue Ridge Mountains and flows toward the southwest. It runs through the metro Atlanta area before forming part of the border between Georgia and Alabama. Historically, cities like Columbus relied on the Chattahoochee as a source of power for its mills as well as a major means of transportation and source of drinking water. Today, a number of man-made lakes help harness the river's waters for hydroelectricity, drinking water, recreation, and even flood control. The Chattahoochee is an important source of water for Alabama and Florida as well.

The Chattahoochee River at Columbus

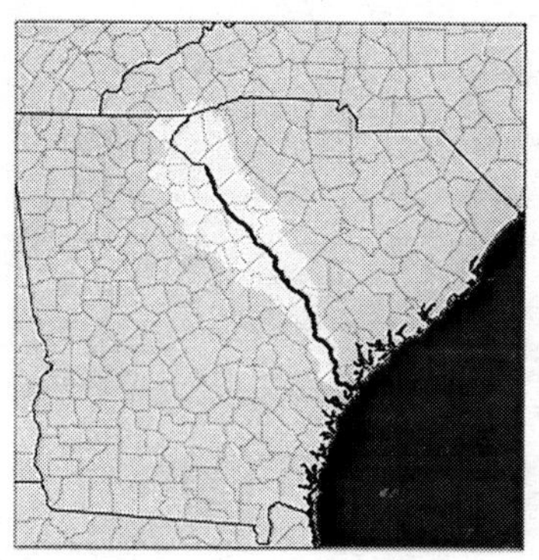

Savannah River Watershed

The **Savannah River** begins where the Tugaloo and the Seneca Rivers join in the foothills of the Appalachian Mountains. Augusta and Savannah are major cities that lie along this river. As you may remember from chapter 2, Oglethorpe chose the site for Savannah in large part because of its accessibility to the Savannah River, which allowed the colonists to engage in travel and trade more easily. The river also forms most of the border between Georgia and South Carolina and, like the Chattahoochee, features a number of man-made lakes intended to supply Georgians with water, recreation, and power. Its deep waters and width make it possible for large ships to navigate much of the lower Savannah, enabling the port of Savannah to remain one of the busiest in the US.

THE OKEFENOKEE SWAMP

Okefenokee Swamp

Covering roughly 700 square miles of Georgia's coastal plain is the **Okefenokee Swamp**. It is a freshwater wetland that lies in southeastern Georgia and part of northern Florida and is one of the largest swamps in North America. Its name comes from a Seminole word meaning "land of the trembling earth" (the Seminoles are a Native American tribe that once occupied much of the region). The name probably refers to the unstable, marshy ground beneath the swamp. Although the swamp is not deep (its average depth is only 2 to 4 feet), it is home to hundreds of different species of plants and a wide variety of animals. Much of the swamp is protected as the *Okefenokee Wildlife Refuge*, established by President Franklin Roosevelt in 1937 to protect the swamp from destruction due to development and the logging of cypress and pine trees.

Practice 11.3 Other Geographic Features

1. The area where the Piedmont and Coastal Plain meet that features a drop in elevation and beautiful waterfalls is called what?

   A. The barrier islands
   B. Tallulah Gorge
   C. Amicalola Falls
   D. the Fall Line

2. Which of the following is **true** regarding Georgia's barrier islands?

   A. They protect the mainland from erosion.
   B. They feature most of the state's waterfalls.
   C. The public is not allowed to visit any of them because they are wildlife reserves.
   D. They receive more snowfall than any other region.

3. In what ways are the Chattahoochee and Savannah rivers important to Georgians?

4. Describe the Okefenokee Swamp and tell why much of it is protected as a wildlife refuge.

CHAPTER 11 REVIEW

Key Terms, People, and Concepts

geography
region
Western and Northern Hemispheres
parallels
meridians
equator
latitude
prime meridian
longitude
International Date Line
Georgia's latitude and longitude
North America
United States of America
South
Sun Belt
climate
climate's effect on Georgia's economic development
hurricanes
tropical storms
thunderstorms
tornadoes
droughts
Appalachian Plateau
Ridge and Valley
Blue Ridge
Piedmont
Coastal Plain
Fall Line
barrier islands
Chattahoochee River
Savannah River
Okefenokee Swamp

Multiple Choice Questions

1. Which of the following represents Georgia's latitude?
   - A. The state's distance from the prime meridian
   - B. The state's distance from the equator
   - C. 32°, 02' – 35°W
   - D. 80°, 50' – 85°, 36' W

2. Georgia is located in which of the following?
   - A. the prime meridian
   - B. the US Fall Line
   - C. the Western Hemisphere
   - D. the Southern Hemisphere

3. Which of the following statements **best** describes the effect of Georgia's climate on its economic development?
   - A. Its climate has discouraged businesses from locating in Georgia because they view the state as primarily a tourist attraction.
   - B. The state's mild climate has helped to attract new industries and residents to Georgia.
   - C. The state's population and economic growth is decreasing due to the tornadoes and thunderstorms that are common in the spring and summer.
   - D. Since climate deals with long-term weather patterns, it has very little effect on the state's economy.

4. In less than 45 minutes, Jeff rode his motorcycle through parts of Alabama and Tennessee before stopping at a restaurant in Georgia. The restaurant Jeff stopped at is **most likely** located in which of the following regions?
   A. Blue Ridge
   B. Ridge and Valley
   C. Appalachian Plateau
   D. Coastal Plain

5. Emily hates living in a crowded place and can't stand snow. She prefers wide-open, flat spaces with lots of farm land and warm weather. Which of Georgia's regions would Emily **most likely** enjoy living in?
   A. Appalachian Plateau
   B. Coastal Plain
   C. Piedmont
   D. Ridge and Valley

6. Which of the following projects would Georgia and South Carolina **most likely** work together on?
   A. building a dam on the Chatahoochee River
   B. starting a project to ensure that the Savannah River stays clean
   C. trying to protect the Okefenokee Swamp
   D. developing a plan to help the Seminoles

7. A rural settler in the early 1800s would have been **least likely** to start a new town in which of the following areas?
   A. the Fall Line
   B. along the Chattahoochee River
   C. where the Piedmont and Coastal Plain meet
   D. the Okefenokee Swamp

Chapter 12
Georgia's Government

This chapter covers the following Georgia standard(s).

SS8CG1	The student will describe the role of citizens under Georgia's constitution..
SS8CG2	The student will analyze the role of the legislative branch in Georgia state government.
SS8CG3	The student will analyze the role of the executive branch in Georgia state government.
SS8CG4	The student will analyze the role of the judicial branch in Georgia state government.
SS8CG5	The student will analyze the role of local governments in the state of Georgia.
SS8E4	The student will identify the revenue sources and services provided by state and local governments.

12.1 Georgia's Constitution

In chapters 1–10, we studied Georgia's history. Now we will study how Georgia's state and local governments operate today. The structure and powers of state government are defined by the state constitution. Therefore, before we can understand Georgia's government, we must first examine its constitution.

Principles on Which Georgia's Constitution Is Founded

Georgia Capitol Building

Georgia's constitution is the highest body of laws in the state. Georgians adopted their first state constitution in 1777 (see chapter 3) and ratified their current constitution in 1983. It is the state's tenth constitution overall and is based on many of the same principles as the United States Constitution. For instance, the Georgia Constitution contains a bill of rights to ensure limited government and establishes a government based on popular sovereignty (serving the will of the people). *Limited government* means that the government must respect the rights of its citizens, while *popular sovereignty* means that Georgians get to elect which leaders they want to represent them. If they feel the government is failing, the constitution allows them to replace their existing leaders and/or change the state constitution. The Georgia Constitution also provides for **separation of powers** and a system of **checks and balances**. Like the federal government, it divides power between three branches: executive, legislative, and judicial. Each branch has specific powers that only it can exercise. For instance, only the legislative branch may pass new laws, only the governor may appoint state officials and enforce state laws, and only the judicial branch may decide whether or not state laws are constitutional. However, each branch also has ways to *check* the other branches and keep them from becoming too powerful. The governor cannot make laws, but he/she can *veto* (reject) a law passed by the legislature, keeping it from becoming law. Only the governor may appoint public officials, but the Senate must often approve them before they can take office. Meanwhile, the judicial branch may declare laws passed by the legislature and signed by the governor to be "unconstitutional," in which case they are no longer laws. These are just some of the ways checks and balances work.

STRUCTURE OF THE GEORGIA CONSTITUTION

The Georgia Constitution begins with a **preamble** (opening sentence that says why the document was written) that reads as follows:

> *"To perpetuate the principles of free government, insure justice to all, preserve peace, promote the interest and happiness of the citizen and of the family, and transmit to posterity the enjoyment of liberty, we the people of Georgia, relying upon the protection and guidance of Almighty God, do ordain and establish this Constitution."*

Following the preamble are eleven articles addressing the different branches and duties of government. They are listed below:

Article I	Bill of Rights	**Article VII**	Taxation and Finance
Article II	Voting and Elections	**Article VIII**	Education
Article III	Legislative Branch	**Article IX**	Counties and Municipal Corp
Article IV	Const. Boards and Comm.	**Article X**	Amend. to the Constitution
Article V	Executive Branch	**Article XI**	Miscellaneous Provisions
Article VI	Judicial Branch		

GEORGIA'S BILL OF RIGHTS AND THE AMENDMENT PROCESS

Two articles worth noting are Article I and Article X. Article I of the Georgia Constitution contains the state's **Bill of Rights**. Section I of this article lists the rights of citizens. Some of these rights include: right to life, liberty and property, freedom of speech, freedom of the press, and the right to defend oneself in court. Section II addresses the "Origin and Structure of Government" and establishes the principles of Georgia's government.

Meanwhile, Article X defines how Georgia's constitution may be **amended** (changed). Under Article X, the Georgia Constitution may be amended in one of two ways. The first is through *Proposals by the General Assembly.* Under this method, a state senator or representative must introduce the proposed amendment in the General Assembly. If two-thirds of both houses accept the change, then it must go before the people of Georgia for a vote at the next general election. If the majority of voters ratify the amendment, it becomes part of the constitution.

The second way the constitution may be amended is by *constitutional convention*. If two-thirds of each house of the General Assembly agrees to call such a convention, then delegates to the convention will meet to discuss and vote on possible changes to the constitution. If the convention votes in favor of a proposed amendment, then the amendment goes before the state's citizens for a vote. If the majority of voters vote in favor of the change, then it becomes part of the Georgia Constitution.

Practice 12.1 Georgia's Constitution

1. Which of the following is **true** regarding the Georgia Constitution?

   A. Georgia has had the same constitution since 1777.
   B. Georgia's constitution is based on limited government instead of popular sovereignty.
   C. The laws in the Georgia Constitution are final and cannot be amended or changed.
   D. It is the highest body of state laws in Georgia.

2. What is meant by the terms "separation of powers" and "checks and balances"? Give some examples of how we find these principles in Georgia's constitution.

12.2 Branches of State Government

The Legislative Branch

Georgia Senate

In Georgia, the **General Assembly** acts as the state's **legislative branch** of government. It consists of two houses: the **House of Representatives** and the **Senate**. Under the constitution, the House must have at least 180 members and the Senate must have at least 56. Senators and representatives each serve **two-year terms** after winning elections in their own House or Senate *district*. Thanks to reapportionment, all House and Senate districts are similar in size and/or population to ensure that citizens are represented equally. There is no limit on how many consecutive terms senators and representatives may serve.

In order to serve in the General Assembly, individuals must meet certain **qualifications**. Under Article III, Section II, members of the General Assembly must:

- be at least 21 years old to serve in the House
- be at least 25 years old to serve in the Senate
- be a US citizen and a citizen of Georgia for at least two years
- be a legal resident of the House or Senate district they wish to represent
- not be on active duty as part of the armed forces
- not hold any civil appointment or office

Duties, Powers, and the Legislative Process

Glenn Richardson
Speaker of the House

The General Assembly's main responsibility is to make the laws that govern Georgia. It meets each year beginning the second Monday in January for a 40-day session that typically ends in mid-March. During that time, it debates and passes legislation (new laws) addressing a number of issues. In order for a **bill** (proposed law) to become a law, it must go through a specific **legislative process**. It begins when either a senator or representative introduces a bill for consideration. The bill then goes to a **committee** in the house where it was introduced. The committee consists of several members and one chairperson (leader), all of whom have been appointed by either the speaker of the House (House committees) or the lieutenant governor (Senate committees). The committee then considers the bill and recommends whether or not the bill should become a law. Eventually, after considering the committee's recommendation, the entire House or Senate votes on the bill. If the majority votes "no", then the bill dies and will not be considered again without changes. However, if the majority votes "yes", then the bill goes to the other house where the process is repeated. If the bill passes both houses, it goes to the governor for his/her signature. If the governor signs it, the process is over and the bill becomes a law. However, if the governor **vetoes** (rejects and refuses to sign) the bill, then it goes back to the General Assembly where senators and representatives will reconsider it. If two-thirds of each house votes in favor of the bill, then the General Assembly **overrides** the governor's veto and the bill becomes a law anyway. If less than two-thirds of each house votes in favor of the bill, however, the bill dies and the governor's veto stands.

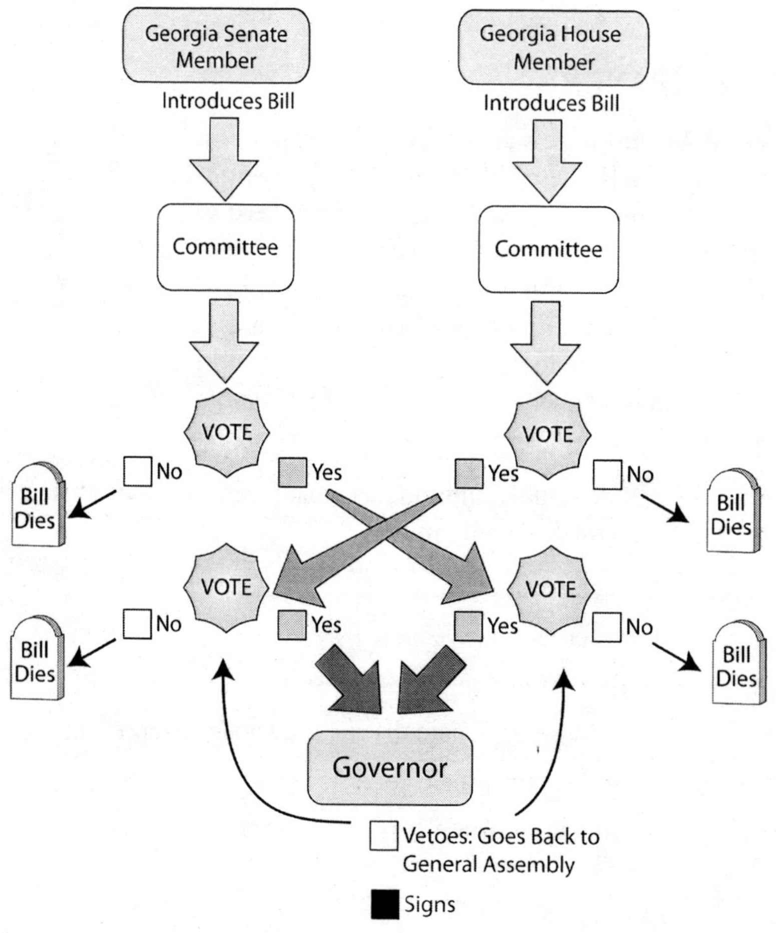

While many legislative powers are shared by the House and Senate, some powers are reserved for one house but not the other. For instance, only the House of Representatives may introduce bills designed to raise revenue (money), appropriate funds (determine state spending), or impeach (charge public officials with wrongdoing while in office). Meanwhile, only the Senate may determine the guilt or innocence of impeached officials or approve/reject appointments by the governor.

Organization of the General Assembly

Lieutenant Governor Casey Cagle

Each house of the General Assembly requires leadership and structure in order to fulfill its role. The **speaker of the House** acts as the head of the House of Representatives. Members of the House elect him/her from among their own number. Meanwhile, the **lieutenant governor** presides over the Senate. Georgians elect the lieutenant governor in a statewide election by popular vote (we will discuss the lieutenant governor more when we look at the executive branch of government). In addition, the House elects a **speaker pro tempore** and the Senate elects a **president pro tempore** to serve in place of the speaker and the lieutenant governor should they not be able to fulfill their duties. The Senate also has a *secretary of the Senate* and the House a *clerk of the House of Representatives*. Finally, as mentioned above, both the speaker of the House and the lieutenant governor appoint **committees** that focus on different issues and make recommendations about specific bills.

The Executive Branch

Governor and Lieutenant Governor

The **executive branch** is responsible for enforcing Georgia's laws and is the largest branch of state government. As chief executive officer of the state, the **governor** heads the executive branch. Under Article V, a candidate for governor must meet certain **qualifications**. He/she must:

- be at least thirty years of age by the time he/she takes office
- be a citizen of the United States for at least fifteen years
- be a resident of Georgia for at least six years.

Governor Sonny Perdue

To become governor, a candidate must win a statewide election by popular vote. Once in office, he/she serves a **four-year term** and is not allowed to serve more than two consecutive terms. In addition to presiding over the state Senate, the **lieutenant governor** serves as the state's second highest ranking executive officer and is responsible for any duties which the governor assigns to him/her. The lieutenant governor is also first in line to take the governor's place should he/she be unable to serve a complete term. Therefore, candidates for lieutenant governor must meet the **same qualifications** as those for governor. The lieutenant governor serves a **four-year term** after winning a statewide popular vote and is not limited in the number of consecutive terms he/she may serve.

Powers and Duties of the Governor

The Georgia Constitution outlines the governor's formal **powers and duties**. They include enforcing civil and criminal laws, appointing state officials and justices, signing bills into law, vetoing proposed bills, reporting to the legislature on the "state of the state," calling special sessions of the legislature, and calling for special elections to fill vacancies in the legislature. The governor also serves as commander in chief of the state's military forces (Georgia's National Guard).

Georgia's governor also enjoys a special power known as the **line-item veto**. It allows the governor to veto part of a bill without having to veto all of it. Not all governors have this power. In fact, not even the president of the United States enjoys the privilege of a line-item veto. Instead, the president and a number of other governors must either veto or accept entire bills without having any power to make changes. Thanks to the line-item veto, Georgia's governor has greater power and flexibility than many other chief executives.

Other Elected Executive Officials

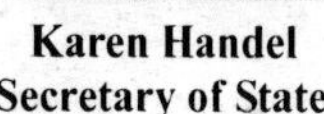

Karen Handel
Secretary of State

Thurbert Baker
Attorney General

In addition to the governor and lieutenant governor, Georgians also elect several other public officials who serve as part of the executive branch. They include: the secretary of state, state attorney general, commissioner of agriculture, commissioner of labor, commissioner of insurance, and the state school superintendent. These officers are elected at the same time and serve the same term as the governor. As you can tell by their titles, each is responsible for a specific area of state government. For instance, the state attorney general is the state's highest ranking legal officer, the commissioner of agriculture is responsible for overseeing policies affecting the state's agriculture, and the state school superintendent oversees the state's public educational system.

Appointed Officials, Boards, and Agencies

There are also a number of unelected officials in the executive branch. They are appointed by the governor, department heads, or department directing boards, and must often be approved by the Senate before they may take office. Examples of such officials include the director of the Georgia Bureau of Investigation, who is appointed by the governor, and the state's chief drug inspector, appointed by the commissioner of agriculture.

The executive branch also includes a large number of boards and agencies which focus on different policy areas. The State Board of Pardons and Paroles, the Board of Natural Resources, the State Personnel Board, the Board of Human Resources, and the Board of Public Safety are just a few examples. In most cases, the governor appoints members to serve on these boards or to lead such agencies.

The Judicial Branch

Georgia Supreme Court

The state's courts make up the **judicial branch** of Georgia's government. This branch makes sure that the state's laws are applied properly and upholds the constitution. The **Georgia Supreme Court** is the highest court in the state and is made up of seven justices elected to six-year terms. If one of the justices retires or dies, the governor will appoint a new justice to complete his/her term. The justices select one person from among their own number to serve as chief justice and lead the court. Since the Supreme Court is an appellate court, it only hears cases on appeal from lower courts; it does not conduct trials (we will discuss appeals and trials more in chapter 13). The Georgia Supreme Court may hear appeals involving the constitutionality of a law (this authority is called "judicial review"), questions of constitutional procedure during court trials, cases dealing with disputes over elections, titles to land, equity, wills, habeas corpus (whether or not a person should be in jail), divorces, and/or alimony (money a divorced person must pay to his or her ex-spouse). The Georgia Supreme Court also reviews all death penalty convictions to make sure the sentenced person's rights were not violated. Usually, decisions of the Georgia Supreme Court are binding, meaning that it has the final word regarding matters of law at the state level. However, parties can appeal cases from the Georgia Supreme Court to the US Supreme Court if the appeal involves a matter of federal law (for example, a claim that the government violated someone's constitutional rights).

Georgia Appellate Judges

The second highest state court in Georgia is the **Court of Appeals**. Twelve judges sit on this court. Like the state supreme court, the judges on the Court of Appeals serve six-year terms and select one of their members to serve as chief judge. The Court of Appeals is an appellate court and only hears cases appealed from lower courts rather than trying cases for the first time.

Trial courts sit below the Georgia Supreme Court and Court of Appeals. These are the courts that hear and try cases for the first time. Georgia's trial court system is made up of 188 superior courts, 70 state courts, 159 probate courts, 159 juvenile courts, 159 magistrate courts, and over 400 city and special courts. Each court exercises jurisdiction (authority) over certain types of cases.

Chart of Georgia's Trial Courts and Their Jurisdictions:	
Superior Courts:	Rule on trials in felony cases and hear appeals from lower courts. Judges are elected to four-year terms in circuit-wide elections. Judicial circuits are simply divisions within the state over which different superior courts preside.
State Courts:	Have jurisdiction over all misdemeanor violations and civil actions which occur in counties where the superior court and/or a city court do not have exclusive jurisdiction. Judges are elected to four-year terms in a countywide election.
City and Special Courts:	City courts try violations of city ordinances, while special courts may address only specific issues. Qualifications and length of terms for city judges are set by local legislation.
Probate Courts:	Rule on issues involving wills and estates after people die. Most judges are elected in countywide elections and serve four-year terms.
Juvenile Courts:	Hear cases involving crimes committed by those under 17 years of age, or cases involving deprived or unruly children under the age of 18. Judges are appointed by the superior court of the circuit.
Magistrate Court:	Civil claims of $15,000 or less; minor criminal offenses; county ordinance violations; bad checks; preliminary hearings, and arrest and search warrants. Most chief magistrates are elected in partisan, countywide elections to four-year terms.

Practice 12.2 Branches of State Government

1. Georgia's speaker of the House is part of which of the following?

   A. the legislative branch of government
   B. the highest court in Georgia
   C. the executive branch of government
   D. the key committee in the judicial branch of government

2. The governor receives a bill that has passed the General Assembly. After reviewing it, he determines that he wants to sign part of the bill, but not all of it. The governor will **most likely** use which of the following powers?
   A. report on the state of the state and ask the General Assembly to reconsider the bill
   B. the line-item veto
   C. veto the whole bill
   D. appoint more state officials that will make laws the governor favors

3. What are the responsibilities of the lieutenant governor?

4. Describe the legislative process by which a bill becomes law in the state of Georgia.

5. What is the role of the judicial branch? List the different levels of courts in Georgia and describe the role each plays.

12.3 Georgia's County and City Governments

County Governments

Counties are subdivisions of Georgia set up to perform certain government functions. There are currently 159 counties in Georgia, the most allowed under the state constitution (only the state of Texas has more counties than Georgia). **County governments** are headed by elected boards of commissioners that usually serve four-year staggered terms ("staggered" means that they don't all run for re-election at the same time). The board of commissioners establishes county policies, adopts county ordinances (laws), determines the county's budget and tax rates, and provides county services. It also appoints a county administrator, who serves as the chief administrative officer and manages the day-to-day operations of county government. Most counties also elect a clerk of superior court, judge of probate court, tax commissioner, and sheriff. Meanwhile, appointed county officials include county clerks, attorneys, tax assessors, emergency management services directors, fire chiefs, building inspectors, registrars, road supervisors, animal control officers, and surveyors.

MUNICIPAL AND SPECIAL PURPOSE GOVERNMENT

Glover Park, City of Marietta

Unlike counties, a *city* is established by charter from the state legislature. An area must meet three requirements in order to be chartered as a city. First, it must have at least 200 residents. Second, it must be located at least three miles from the boundaries of the nearest existing city. Third, at least sixty percent of its land must be divided into tracts (pieces of land) or be in current use as residential, business, industrial, institutional, or government areas. A city operating its own government is called a *municipality.* Therefore, such governments are called **municipal governments**.

A city's charter limits and defines the powers of its municipal government. Most city charters authorize cities to provide police protection, license businesses, maintain streets and sidewalks, manage parks, control traffic, and provide water and sewer services. Some cities, such as Atlanta and Marietta, also operate their own school systems under the guidelines of their charters.

DIFFERENT MODELS OF MUNICIPAL GOVERNMENT

Atlanta Mayor Shirley Franklin

Not all cities use the same model of government. The *mayor-council* form of government divides power between an elected city council that acts as the legislative branch and an elected mayor who serves as the city's chief executive. The council is responsible for passing city ordinances (laws) and the mayor is responsible for enforcing them. The mayor also often has veto power. Such a system is often referred to as a **strong mayor-council** system because the mayor has a great deal of power and influence over the council. Some cities, however, prefer not to allow their mayor to have such power. They use a **weak mayor-council** system. In a weak mayor-council system, both the legislative and executive powers lie with the city council. The mayor's powers are very limited and he/she rarely has veto power. Often, the mayor serves more as a figurehead (a person who is the head of an organization but has few powers) who presides over council meetings and engages in ceremonial duties.

A third form of municipal government in Georgia is the council-manager system. In the **council-manager** system, the elected council still makes laws and policies, but it also *hires a city manager* to oversee the day-to-day operations of the city and appoint heads of city departments. These department heads (for example, the chief of police) then answer to the city manager, who answers to the council. Sometimes, such governments will still have a mayor appointed by the council, but he/she generally does little more than preside over council meetings and/or represent the city at events.

Special-Purpose Governments

School Board Meeting

MARTA Train

Georgia has a number of special-purpose governments. **Special-purpose governments** serve to deal with a single issue or task. For example, Georgia generally divides its public schools into districts, each of which is governed by a school board. School boards are examples of special-purpose governments. Another example of a special-purpose government is the Metropolitan Atlanta Rapid Transit Authority (MARTA). MARTA runs Atlanta's bus and train system, sets its transportation schedule, and determines the cost of fares. Other special-purpose districts include community fire departments, parks and recreation authorities, and airport and port authorities.

Practice 12.3 Georgia's County and City Governments

1. Which of the following statements describes a county government in Georgia?

   A. Power is divided between a legislative, executive, and judicial branch.
   B. A strong mayor exercises most of the power.
   C. A weak mayor exercises very little power.
   D. A board of commissioners sets the policies and passes ordinances.

2. Which of the following is part of a municipal government?

   A. the governor of Georgia
   B. the president of the United States
   C. the mayor of Atlanta
   D. a probate judge

3. Describe the differences between a "strong mayor-council" system of government, a "weak mayor-council" system of government, and a "council-manager" system of government.

12.4 Spending and Revenue

State and Local Spending

Both the state and local governments spend millions of dollars each year to pay government employees and provide services to citizens. Most elected officials, teachers, law enforcement personnel, and various other government employees all depend on state or municipal money to pay their salaries. In addition, governments provide things like police and emergency services, education, medical services, trash collection, road construction, and prison/correctional facilities. Citizens depend on such services to help make sure society functions efficiently.

Spending Choices

Have you ever paid for a ticket to the movies, only to find you don't have enough money left over to buy both a drink and a bucket of popcorn? You only have enough for one or the other. If you buy the drink, then you have to miss out on that hot, buttery popcorn. On the other hand, if you buy the popcorn, then all that butter and salt will have you dying of thirst before the last preview is over. You just don't have enough money to pay for everything you want, so you have to make a decision about what to buy and what to do without. Governments face the same kinds of decisions every day. There may be lots of services the government wants to fund, but it can't pay for all of them. Therefore, the government has to make **spending choices**. According to the Georgia Constitution, the government must have a **state budget** every fiscal year (the fiscal year begins in July and ends the following June). The budget tells how much revenue the state expects to have, what it plans to spend, and what programs and services it will spend its money on. Several factors affect what the government spends money on. For instance, how much **debt** (money that a person, business, or government owes)does the government have? The greater the state debt, the less money is available to spend.

Debate on Spending

Which political party is in power is also important. Republicans tend to be more conservative and Democrats tend to be more liberal (although this is not always the case). Conservative politicians favor a smaller role for government and, therefore, often favor less spending. Meanwhile, more liberal politicians believe in a socially active government and are more likely to support more spending. How high taxes are also affects state spending. The more taxes people pay, the more money the government has. Another factor is population. The more people there are in Georgia, the greater the demand for certain services and the more taxpayers there are. Meanwhile, who makes up the population is important as well. For instance, Georgia's growing Hispanic population means that more state funds are likely to be spent on measures to accommodate for Spanish-speaking peoples and to deal with immigration issues. Also, **constituencies** can affect spending decisions. A *constituency* is a group of citizens an elected official represents and answers to. Since politicians rely on the support of their constituencies to remain in office, how their constituency feels about a certain issue greatly affects how much a leader supports or opposes spending in certain areas. These are just a few of the factors that affect spending decisions.

It is important to remember that, for every state agency or program that receives funding, another agency or program is not funded or receives less funding than it otherwise would have. Like people, state and local governments only have so much money. That's why there is often much debate and disagreement among leaders regarding what to fund and how much money to spend. For example, both Peach Care (the state's medical insurance for low-income children) and education are noble programs. However, the more the state funds health care, the less it can spend on education and vice versa. When the state has to sacrifice funding one program, either partially or in full, in order to fund another program, it is called an **opportunity cost**. An *opportunity cost* is what a person, business, or government gives up in order to spend their resources on something else.

Government Revenue

Fees, Fines, and Grants

Fee

Fine

Of course, the government must have money before it can spend it. The money which the government takes in to fund its spending is called **revenue**. The state raises revenue in a variety of ways. For instance, any time you have to pay a government *fee* or *fine*, you are giving the government money it can then spend to provide services. **Fees** are money that you pay directly for a service, license, to register for something, etc. For example, when people in Atlanta pay a fare to ride MARTA or a toll to drive on Georgia 400, they are paying a special fee to help fund the government. In the same way, people must pay a fee to get most licenses or to register their business annually with the state of Georgia. By comparison, **fines** are money you must pay as punishment for some offense you have committed. If your mom or dad gets pulled over by a policeman and issued a speeding ticket, he or she will have to pay a fine for driving too fast. Fines are often issued for traffic violations, littering, failure to abide by local ordinances, failure to obey state regulations, and any other number of offenses.

Another way state and local governments may get money is through **federal grants**. Grants are money the federal government gives to state or local governments in order to help address a specific issue. For instance, the federal government might give the state money to repair its roads, improve its schools, or invest in protecting the environment. Usually, such grants are given because the federal government believes that helping a particular state or local government will serve a national interest as well.

Taxes

The most common way the state and local governments raise revenue is through **taxes**. Taxes are money that citizens and businesses must pay the government. Georgians pay **sales taxes** on products that they buy. You've probably noticed that if you buy a candy bar at the local convenience store for $1.00, you actually end up paying more than a dollar at the register. That's because you also had to pay sales tax. Since the tax is based on a percentage of how much the product costs, the more expensive an item, the more you pay in sales tax.

Sales Tax on a Purchase

Georgians also pay **property taxes**. As you probably guessed, these are taxes you pay on property. The state requires citizens to pay taxes on the cars they drive, while county and/or municipal governments often require people to pay taxes on homes and structures they own within a county or city. Usually, property taxes are based on the value of the property. The more your property is worth, the more tax you'll pay.

Property Tax

Once a year, Georgians pay **personal income taxes** to both the state of Georgia and the federal government. Citizens pay these taxes based on how much money they make. In theory, the more money you make, the more taxes you pay. However, because the tax system can be complicated and some citizens are better than others at finding "loop holes" (legal technicalities in the tax codes that allow a person to pay less taxes), this is not always the case. Income taxes are usually taken out of people's paychecks every time they get paid. Individuals then file a tax return with both the state of Georgia and the federal government by April 15 of each year. If the return shows that a citizen has not paid enough taxes out of their paycheck, then he/she must pay the difference. However, if the return shows that the government took too much money out of a person's paycheck, then he/she gets a refund.

People pay other kinds of taxes, too; but sales, property, and personal income taxes are among the most common and consistent. Taxes provide the bulk of Georgia's annual revenue.

Practice 12.4 Spending and Revenue

1. A policeman spots Mary littering in the park and gives her a ticket. She will have to pay the government $50 for her offense. Mary is paying what?

   A. taxes
   B. a fee
   C. a fine
   D. a grant

2. The General Assembly debates back and forth whether to give more money to education or more to construct new highways. Eventually, it decides to give more money to education. Which of the following statements is true?

   A. The government has failed to make a spending decision.
   B. The additional roads that could have been built if more money had been given to highways is an opportunity cost.
   C. The state budget will not be ready on time because of this decision.
   D. The state must reduce revenue if it hopes to better fund highways in the future.

3. Describe the differences between property taxes, sales taxes, and personal income taxes.

4. What are some of the factors that affect government spending decisions and why do they have such an effect?

CHAPTER 12 REVIEW

Key Terms, People, and Concepts

Georgia's constitution
separation of powers
checks and balances
preamble to Georgia's Constitution
Georgia Bill of Rights
amendments/amendment process
legislative branch
General Assembly
House of Representatives
State Senate
terms served by representatives and senators
qualifications to serve in General Assembly
bill
legislative process
veto
override
speaker of the house
lieutenant governor
President pro tempore
Speaker pro tempore
committees
executive branch
qualifications for governor/lieutenant governor
term served by governor/lieutenant governor
powers and duties of governor
judicial branch
Georgia Supreme Court
Court of Appeals
trial courts
county governments
municipal governments
strong mayor-council government
weak mayor-council government
council-manager government
special-purpose governments
government spending choices
state budget
debt
constituency
opportunity costs
revenue
fees
fines
federal grants
taxes
sales tax
property tax
personal income tax

Multiple Choice

1. The governor appoints an official to serve in Georgia's state government. However, the state Senate rejects the appointment, preventing the person from ever taking office. The Senate's actions are an example of what?
   A. limited government
   B. popular sovereignty
   C. checks and balances
   D. constitutional convention

2. The General Assembly passes a new law making it illegal to insult government leaders in public. The governor gladly signs it. A citizen sues, claiming that he is entitled to say what he wants about government leaders under Georgia's bill of rights. The citizen is hoping the court will do what?
   A. disband the General Assembly
   B. declare the law unconstitutional
   C. appeal the case to trial courts
   D. veto the law

3. A bill to make it illegal for people to smoke in state parks must first be introduced where?
   A. in the executive branch
   B. in a municipal government
   C. in the General Assembly
   D. before a board of county commissioners

4. Which of the following affects state spending decisions the **least**?
   A. the state's growing Hispanic population
   B. the number of people living in Georgia
   C. citizens angry about high taxes
   D. term limits on the governor

5. Claudine is a state senator. She introduces a bill that she hopes will become a law. After she introduces it, the bill will probably go where next?
   A. to a Senate committee
   B. to the House of Representatives for approval
   C. to the governor
   D. to the Georgia Supreme Court

6. The governor of Georgia has which of the following powers?
   A. He/she can veto rulings by the state supreme court.
   B. He/she can order the National Guard to help in an emergency.
   C. He/she appoints all justices to the Georgia Supreme Court.
   D. He/she makes laws that then must be approved by the General Assembly.

7. Samantha serves in the branch of Georgia government that makes sure laws are applied appropriately and according to the constitution. Samantha is most likely which of the following?
   A. a state senator
   B. the governor
   C. a Court of Appeals judge
   D. an appointed department head

8. Most state revenue comes from which of the following?
   A. fees
   B. fines
   C. grants
   D. taxes

Chapter 13
Georgia's Judicial System

This chapter covers the following Georgia standard(s).

SS8CG4	The student will analyze the role of the judicial branch in Georgia state government.
SS8CG6	The student will explain how the Georgia court system treats juvenile offenders.

13.1 Criminal Law

In chapter 12, we briefly looked at the structure of Georgia's court system. We learned that the Georgia Supreme Court is the highest court in the state, with the Georgia Court of Appeals, state courts, superior courts, municipal courts, magistrate courts, probate courts, and juvenile courts below it. Each has its specific role and jurisdiction. In this chapter, we will examine the state's courts and how they work in greater detail.

Criminal Courts and Cases

Judicial matters are divided into two categories of law: criminal and civil. In this section, we will focus on **criminal law**. Criminal cases arise when the state accuses someone of violating a state or local law. Such crimes are classified as either felonies or misdemeanors. A **felony** is a more serious crime, such as murder or robbery, and is punishable by at least a year in prison and/or a fine of at least $1,000. A **misdemeanor** is a less serious crime, such as shoplifting or a minor assault, and is punishable by less than a year in prison and/or a smaller fine. Georgia's **superior courts** exercise jurisdiction over felony criminal cases, while **state courts, magistrate courts, municipal courts,** and **special courts** exercise jurisdiction over misdemeanor cases.

Robbery: a Felony

Criminal Court Proceedings

The Defendant and Attorneys

The criminal court process begins when someone is arrested and charged with committing either a felony or misdemeanor crime. Authorities may make an arrest and file charges as the result of an arrest warrant (document issued by the court stating that there is enough evidence to arrest a particular person), probable cause (law enforcement has witnessed or has good reason to believe someone has committed a crime), or an **indictment**. An indictment must be issued by a **grand jury** made up of a group of citizens who hear all

Arrest

the evidence against someone and decide if they should stand trial. In Georgia, the state is not required to get an indictment from a grand jury before charging someone with a crime. Therefore, in many cases, the state simply files charges directly with the court.

Under the Sixth Amendment to the US Constitution, citizens have the right to be represented by a lawyer at their criminal trial and to have that attorney present during any questioning by the police or prosecuting attorneys. The person accused of a crime is called the **defendant** and the attorney who represents him/her is the **defense attorney**. In 1963, the US Supreme Court ruled that defendants are entitled to lawyers even if they can't afford to hire their own. Therefore, if a criminal defendant in Georgia can't afford an attorney, the state must provide one. Larger cities and counties often have **public defenders** to represent clients who don't have enough money to hire their own defense attorneys in criminal cases. In many smaller counties and towns, however, there is no public defender's office. When this is the case, the court simply appoints a private attorney to represent low-income defendants.

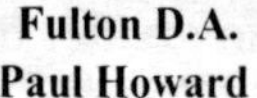

Fulton D.A. Paul Howard

Cobb Judicial Circuit D.A. Pat Head

Since the government considers criminal acts to be harmful to all of society, the state formally charges the defendant even if the crime was committed against a private citizen. The attorney for the state who presents the case against the defendant is called the **prosecutor**. In state cases, the chief prosecutor in each judicial district is known as the **district attorney (D.A.)**. Citizens elect the D.A. to be responsible for prosecuting all criminal cases in their jurisdiction. Many times, if it is a serious felony or high-profile case (case that gets a lot of publicity) the D.A. will try the case personally. However, if it is a misdemeanor or less serious felony, the D.A. often assigns the case to an **assistant district attorney**.

Pretrial Procedures

Once formally charged, the defendant will appear in court for an **arraignment** (usually within 72 hours of his/her arrest). At his/her arraignment, the defendant goes before a judge and the charges are officially read. Sometimes, the defense attorney will use this opportunity to ask the judge to dismiss (throw out) the case because of a lack of evidence or some violation of the defendant's rights. If the judge agrees, the defendant is released and set free. However, if the judge disagrees or the defense attorney does not make such a request, then the defendant enters one of four *pleas*. A **plea** is how the defendant answers the charges against him/her. The four possible pleas in Georgia are:

1. **<u>Guilty</u>** – A "guilty" plea means that the defendant admits committing the crime. Often, defendants will agree to plead guilty in order to get a less severe **sentence** (punishment issued by the court) or in exchange for a promise from the D.A. to charge him/her with a less severe crime. Such an arrangement is called a **plea bargain**. Defendants often plea bargain when they believe it is likely that they would be found guilty at trial anyway. Prosecutors like plea bargains because they save the state the time and money of having to conduct a regular trial. Plea bargains also assure the D.A.'s office of a **conviction** (a conviction is when a criminal defendant is found guilty of a crime). Once a defendant pleads guilty, the judge either sentences him/her immediately or schedules a future date for sentencing.

2. **<u>Not Guilty</u>** – A "not guilty" plea means that the defendant refuses to admit that they committed a crime. When a defendant pleads "not guilty," the state holds a criminal trial.

3. **No Contest** – "No contest" means that the defendant is not admitting guilt, but neither will he challenge the charges the state presents against him. Why would a defendant make such a plea? Usually, defendants plead "no contest" for the same reasons that they plead "guilty." However, a no contest plea is different because it prevents the defendant from having an admission of guilt on his record. By not formally admitting guilt, no one can use the plea against them in a civil case should they be sued (we will discuss civil cases in the next section). Defendant's who plead "no contest" are usually sentenced like those who plead "guilty."

4. **Mute Plea** – A "mute plea" means that a defendant does not enter an official plea. He/she "stands mute." When this happens, the court enters a "not guilty" plea on the defendant's behalf and schedules a trial.

Jury Box

Under the Sixth Amendment of the US Constitution, a criminal defendant is entitled to a **jury trial**. A jury is simply a group of the accused person's peers (fellow citizens; usually 12 in number) who hear all the evidence at trial and then decide if the defendant is guilty or not guilty. However, if the crime is a misdemeanor that carries a maximum sentence of less than six months in jail, or if the defendant chooses not to have a jury, the court will hold a **bench trial** instead. A bench trial is a trial in which the judge who sits on the bench will make any decisions about guilt or innocence, rather than a jury. If there is a jury, both the defense attorney and the prosecutor interview potential jurors (citizens who serve on the jury) at a special court session called the *voir dire.* The purpose of the voir dire is to make sure that the jury is fairly chosen and acceptable to both sides.

Criminal Trials

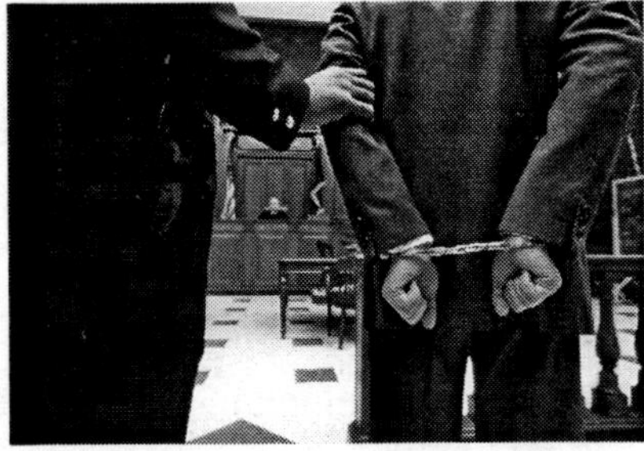
Criminal Trial

During the criminal trial, both sides present evidence and question witnesses. Once they have finished presenting their cases, both sides' attorneys make closing arguments in which they attempt to convince the jury (or judge if it is a bench trial) one last time. In the US justice system, it is up to the state to prove an accused defendant is guilty, rather than the defendant having to prove he/she is innocent.

If it is a bench trial, the judge will then render a verdict of either "guilty," or "not guilty." However, if it is a jury trial, the jury then goes into **deliberation**. In other words, they meet together in private to decide if the defendant is guilty or innocent. Sometimes deliberations are as short as an hour. At other times, they can last weeks. Once the jury reaches a decision, its members return to the courtroom and announce their verdict. If a defendant is "not guilty," then the legal proceedings are over and the defendant is free to go. On the other hand, if the defendant is "guilty," then the judge will either issue a sentence or schedule a court date to do so. The only time this is not the case is if it is a **capital offense**. A *capital offense* is a crime for which a person can be put to death. If a jury finds a defendant guilty in a capital offense case, then its members must go back into deliberation to decide whether or not the defendant should die for the crime or be sentenced to life in prison.

Sometimes, jury members cannot agree on whether, or not, a defendant is guilty. When this happens, it is called a **hung jury** and the judge declares a **mistrial**. A "mistrial" means that the state must either dismiss its charges against the defendant or start over with a new trial.

Criminal Court Appeals

Defendants who are found guilty often **appeal** following their trial. When convicted defendants appeal, they ask a higher court to review their trial/conviction and **overturn** (cancel) the lower court's decision. Misdemeanor appeals from lower trial courts are usually heard first in superior court, while felony appeals are usually heard first by the Georgia Court of Appeals. The one exception is death penalty cases. If the appeal involves a defendant who has been sentenced to death, then it goes directly to the state supreme court. Defendants may appeal claiming either that they are innocent and were wrongly convicted or that their constitutional rights were somehow violated during the trial process.

Anne Barnes, Chief Judge, GA Court of Appeals

Leah Sears, Chief Justice, GA Supreme Court

The Court of Appeals and the Georgia Supreme Court are both **appellate courts**. They do not try cases to determine guilt or innocence, nor do they have juries. Instead, they are made up of a panel of judges/justices (see chapter 12, section 12.2) who rule on whether or not the lower trial court followed proper procedures according to the state constitution. The **Court of Appeals** has twelve judges, each of whom serves on a panel of three. When it accepts an appeal from superior court, one of these panels reviews the trial court's verdict and either upholds (agrees with) or overturns its decision. If the court overturns it, then the defendant is awarded a new trial. However, if the Court of Appeals upholds it, then the conviction stands. The defendant may then appeal to the **Georgia Supreme Court**. As you likely remember from Chapter 12, this is the state's highest court and consists of seven elected justices. All seven justices discuss and rule on all appeals accepted from the Court of Appeals and superior courts. Again, if the court overturns the conviction on appeal, the defendant is awarded a new trial. However, if the court upholds the conviction, then, most of the time, the appeals process is over and the defendant's conviction stands.

State Criminal Cases in Federal Courts

Sometimes, defendants may appeal state cases to the United States Supreme Court if their conviction is upheld by the Georgia Supreme Court. In order for this to occur, the case must involve a matter relating to the United States Constitution (for example, a defendant claims that their Fifth Amendment right to due process was violated). Also, the Supreme Court must agree to hear the case (the Court is not obligated to hear every appeal). If the US Supreme Court upholds the conviction or refuses to hear the case, then the conviction stands and the appeals process is over. If, however, the Court reverses the conviction, then the state must either drop the case or hold a new trial.

Practice 13.1 Criminal Law

1. A more serious crime that carries a sentence of more than a year in prison and/or a fine of at least $1000 is called what?
   A. a felony
   B. a misdemeanor
   C. an indictment
   D. an arraignment

2. Frank is accused of armed robbery. He hires Lisa to argue before the court that he is innocent. Meanwhile, Sylvia argues on behalf of the state that he is guilty. Which of the following is true?
   A. Frank is not entitled to a jury trial.
   B. Sylvia is an arraignment judge.
   C. Lisa is a defense attorney.
   D. Lisa is a prosecutor.

3. What is a *plea bargain*? Why do both defendants and prosecutors agree to this process?

4. List and define the four possible pleas in Georgia.

5. What is an appeal and how are appellate courts different from trial courts?

13.2 Civil Law

Civil Cases

Civil law cases result from disputes between two or more persons or groups. Examples include disputes over who owns a particular piece of land or property, who is responsible for a person's injury, divorce and child custody issues, and/or whether or not a person/business lived up to its end of a contract. The state initiates criminal cases when it arrests somebody and charges them with a criminal offense. Civil cases, however, begin when one party (person or business) feels it has been wronged and files a **lawsuit** (claim that one has been wronged and is entitled to help from the courts) against another party. The party that claims they have been wronged and files the lawsuit is called the **plaintiff**. The party defending itself against the plaintiff's claim is called the **defendant**. Since no one is claiming that the defendant is guilty of a criminal offense against the state, nobody is arrested and neither the defendant nor the plaintiff is guaranteed an attorney under the Constitution. Therefore, although both parties may hire their own lawyers to represent them, the state is not obligated to provide one.

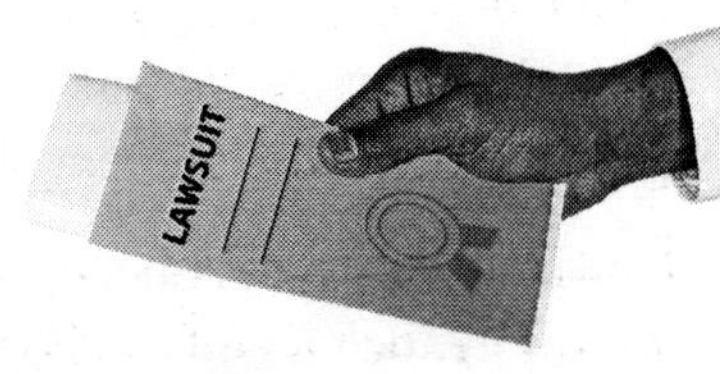

CIVIL COURTS AND TRIALS

CIVIL JURISDICTIONS

Civil cases may begin in one of several courts in Georgia. Most cases begin in **magistrate court**. These courts hear cases involving disputes over money in the amount of $15,000 or less. Examples of disputes might include unpaid rent, failure by a contractor to properly fix an electrical problem, damage to someone's house or car, dispute over who should pay a medical bill, etc. No jury trials are held in magistrate court; the judge decides the case. Also, both plaintiffs and defendants often represent themselves rather than hiring a lawyer.

Superior courts also hear civil cases. In addition to hearing appeals from magistrate courts, superior courts also have *exclusive jurisdiction* over cases dealing with land disputes, divorce settlements, and equity. They also enjoy *general jurisdiction* in all other civil matters. **Exclusive jurisdiction** means that only a certain court (in this case, superior court) may initially hear and rule on the case. **General jurisdiction** means that a court may hear the case first, but so could another court, such as a magistrate court.

Finally, **state courts** rule on civil cases as well. In fact, they may rule on any civil matter, regardless of how much money is at stake, unless it is a case in which the superior court has exclusive jurisdiction. They also may hear cases appealed from magistrate courts.

CIVIL TRIALS

As mentioned above, in magistrate courts, there are no juries, only a judge. Usually, both sides represent themselves. The judge listens and asks questions as each side presents its case, then rules in favor of either the plaintiff or the defendant. If the judge rules in favor of the plaintiff, then the defendant is usually ordered to pay **damages** (money the court orders one party in a civil case to pay the opposing party). However, if the judge rules in favor of the defendant, then the defendant pays nothing. Sometimes, a defendant *counter sues*, meaning that they ask for damages from the plaintiff as well. When this happens and the defendant wins their claim, the plaintiff has to pay damages, even though they were the ones who initially brought the case to court.

Under the Seventh Amendment to the US Constitution, US citizens are entitled to jury trials in civil cases. Therefore, defendants and/or parties that lose in magistrate courts may appeal cases to superior or state courts. Also, juries often decide cases that are initially heard in state and superior courts. Lawyers for both the plaintiff and the defendant present their case and question witnesses before the jury (or judge) deliberates and comes to a decision.

CIVIL APPEALS

The **civil appeals process** in Georgia is generally the same as the criminal appeals process. In civil cases, either party may appeal the court's decision. One of four panels that makes up the **Georgia Court of Appeals** hears appeals from lower courts. If either party is displeased with the Court of Appeals' decision, then they may appeal to the Georgia Supreme Court, which usually has the final say.

STATE CIVIL CASES IN FEDERAL COURTS

Civil cases may be heard in federal courts if a lawsuit involves a question of federal law or if the parties involved are citizens of different states and the amount in question is more than $75,000. Sometimes, such cases are filed immediately in federal courts. At other times, they may be filed in state courts, only to have the defendant request that they be transferred to federal court. The US Supreme Court may also hear appeals from the Georgia Supreme Court if the appeal involves a matter of federal law.

Chart of Judicial Appeals Process

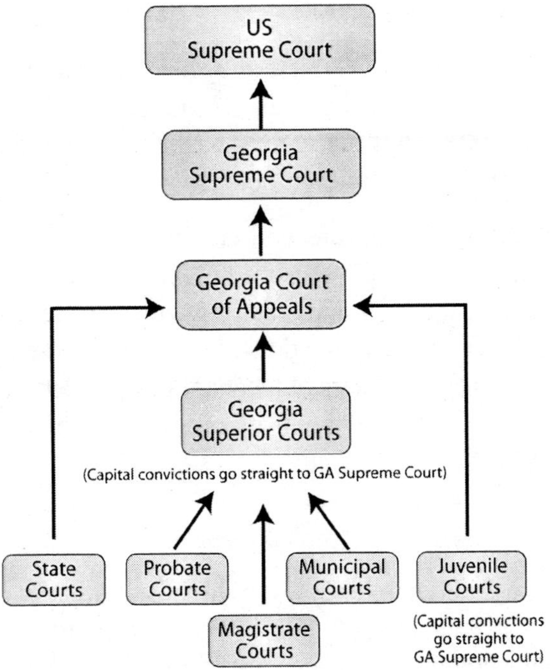

Chart of Judicial Appeals Process

Practice 13.2 Civil Law

1. The party that files a lawsuit is called
   A. the civil filer.
   B. the civil prosecutor.
   C. the defendant.
   D. the plaintiff.

2. Bill loses his case in civil court and is ordered by the judge to pay Albert $500. Which of the following is true?
   A. The court found Bill guilty of a misdemeanor.
   B. Bill has to pay Albert a fine.
   C. The judge expects Bill to pay damages.
   D. Albert was clearly the plaintiff in the case.

3. Describe the roles played by superior courts, state courts, magistrate courts, and appellate courts in Georgia's civil court system.

13.3 Georgia's Juvenile Justice System

Juvenile Courts

In 1906, the Georgia General Assembly passed a law establishing a special court for **juveniles** (those not yet considered adults). In 1911, Fulton County became the first county to set up this type of court. Georgia adopted its first **juvenile code** (set of laws especially for juveniles) in 1951, and today, every county in Georgia has a juvenile court. Currently, any citizen in Georgia under the age of 17 is considered to be a juvenile (the age differs from state to state).

The **juvenile courts** serve three main purposes. First, they help protect the well-being of children. Second, they provide the guidance and control children need while protecting the interest of the state. Third, they provide care for children who have been removed from their homes.

Juvenile Taken into Custody

Juveniles must follow the same local, state, and federal laws as all other citizens. However, due to their age, the punishments for breaking these laws are often less severe than they are for those 17 and older. Juveniles, however, must also follow certain laws that do not apply to adults. For example, they must attend school until they are at least 16 years old, cannot possess certain products, such as tobacco and alcohol, and may not hang out in public places or wander the streets between 12:00am and 5:00am.

Jurisdiction

Juvenile courts have exclusive jurisdiction over cases involving *delinquent behavior* by citizens younger than 17 and *unruly behavior* by citizens younger than 18. A **delinquent act** is anything that would be considered a crime even if it were committed by an adult (for example, burglary or car theft). An **unruly act** is usually an act that would not be a crime if committed by an adult (skipping school, running away, being continually disobedient to parents or a guardian, attempting to buy cigarettes, etc.).

The Juvenile Court Process

Technically, juveniles who commit delinquent acts or are accused of unruly behavior are not arrested in Georgia. Rather, they are "taken into custody." When this happens, the juvenile court process begins. The first step in the juvenile court process is **intake**. The juvenile is turned over to a juvenile court intake officer who investigates the case. The intake officer must look at the evidence presented against the juvenile and decide if there is enough evidence to support the charges. If there is not, the intake officer releases the juvenile. However, if there is, the intake officer must then decide whether to release the juvenile into the custody of his/her parents or legal guardian, or keep the juvenile in custody. State officials usually release juveniles into the custody of their parents/guardian. However, they will keep juveniles in custody if they believe that they are likely to run away, harm themselves or another person, have a history of breaking the law, or have no parents or legal guardian. The state is required to notify parents or a legal guardian before detaining (keeping in custody) any juvenile.

The state must hold a **probable cause hearing** within 72 hours of deciding to keep a juvenile in custody. The judge presiding over the probable cause hearing then decides whether to dismiss the case, have an informal adjustment, or hold a formal hearing. An **informal adjustment** means that the juvenile and his or her parents/guardian must admit that the juvenile committed the offense and agree to certain conditions before he/she may be released. The court then supervises the juvenile for 90 days to make sure he/she obeys the conditions (for example, attending school or going to counseling). First-time offenders or those guilty of minor offenses usually receive informal adjustments.

Formal Hearings

By comparison, the court usually orders a **formal hearing** for repeat offenders and in the case of more serious offenses. In a formal hearing, the *complaining witness* (usually the victim of the crime) files a petition detailing what happened. Once the petition is signed, the court sets a date for the hearing and issues a *summons* that requires the juvenile, his or her parents/guardian, and any witnesses to attend the hearing.

Paulding Youth Detention Center

The first part of the formal hearing is the adjudicatory hearing. An *adjudicatory hearing* is similar to a trial, but no jury is present. The judge of the juvenile court hears the case against the juvenile and arguments in the juvenile's defense. After hearing all the evidence, the judge decides whether the juvenile is guilty or not guilty. If the juvenile is found not guilty, he or she is released. If the juvenile is found guilty, the court schedules a *dispositional hearing*, where the judge will determine the juvenile's punishment. Both the prosecutor and the defense may call witnesses and present evidence to try and influence the judge's decision. After hearing any such evidence, the judge then imposes his/her sentence. Possible **consequences for unruly or delinquent behavior** include: releasing the juvenile into the custody of his or her parents/guardian; placing the juvenile on probation; placing the juvenile in a youth detention center for 90 days; or special conditions, such as paying fines, attending counseling, or performing community service. Often the court orders juveniles to fulfill certain conditions with the understanding that failure to do so could result in having to serve time in a youth detention center. **Youth detention centers** are similar to prisons, but they are specifically for juveniles who serve much shorter terms than adult inmates.

Georgia's Seven Deadly Sins

There are seven delinquent behaviors in Georgia that can transfer a juvenile's case to the adult criminal justice system. The courts will try juveniles ages 13 to 17 as adults if they are accused of: murder, rape, armed robbery (with a firearm), aggravated child molestation, aggravated sodomy, aggravated sexual battery, and/or voluntary manslaughter. The Georgia legislature named these crimes the **Seven Deadly Sins**, and each carries a mandatory ten-year prison sentence under Georgia law. If a juvenile is accused of one of these crimes, then his/her case is tried in superior court under adult guidelines rather than juvenile. If found guilty, juveniles who commit such crimes can face serious consequences. Rather than serving time in a youth detention center, all or part of their sentence is usually served in an adult prison. Since they are younger and often weaker than adult prisoners, these juveniles often find themselves the victims of violent acts once in prison.

JUVENILES' RIGHTS

Juveniles have the same basic **legal rights** as adult citizens. The state must grant them a fair and speedy trial, notify them of the charges against them, respect their right not to incriminate themselves, provide them with an attorney if they cannot afford one, allow them to question witnesses testifying against them, and so forth. In addition, they also have the right to have their parents or legal guardian present at all hearings. However, they do not have the right to a jury (unless they are tried as an adult). Finally, juveniles may appeal their convictions to higher courts, just like adult defendants.

Practice 13.3

1. Which of the following cases would always be heard in juvenile court?

   A. An 18-year-old accused of stealing a car.
   B. A 16-year-old accused of rape and murder.
   C. A 15-year-old accused of stealing sodas from a convenience store.
   D. A parent accused of abusing their 13-year-old child.

2. Any act committed by a juvenile that would also be considered a crime if it were committed by an adult is called what?

   A. A delinquent act
   B. An unruly act
   C. An informal adjustment
   D. A criminal consequence

3. List Georgia's "Seven Deadly Sins" and describe the impact they can have on a juvenile's court case.

CHAPTER 13 REVIEW

Key Terms, People, and Concepts

criminal law
felony
misdemeanor
role of Georgia's courts in criminal cases
indictment
grand jury
defendant
defense attorney
public defenders
prosecutor
district attorney
assistant district attorney
arraignment
four pleas in Georgia
sentence
plea bargain
conviction
jury trial
bench trial
deliberation
capital offense
hung jury
mistrial
appeal
overturn
appellate courts
criminal appeals process
civil law
lawsuit
plaintiff
defendant
role of Georgia's courts in civil cases
exclusive jurisdiction
general jurisdiction
damages
civil appeals process
juveniles
juvenile code
juvenile courts
delinquent act
unruly act
intake
probable cause hearing
informal adjustment
formal hearing
consequences of unruly or delinquent behavior
youth detention centers
"Seven Deadly Sins"
juveniles' legal rights

Multiple Choice Questions

1. In Georgia, the crime of murder is which of the following?
   - A. a civil offense punishable by death
   - B. a felony tried in superior court
   - C. a felony tried in magistrate court
   - D. a misdemeanor that carries a long prison sentence

2. A Georgia district attorney would be most interested in which of the following cases?
   A. someone accused of a federal crime
   B. a murder
   C. a lawsuit involving large amounts of money
   D. someone 18 years old skipping school

3. Barbara is 19 years old and accused of a misdemeanor. Which of the following rights does Barbara have?
   A. She is entitled to have her parents present at all court hearings.
   B. She is allowed to counter sue even though she is the defendant.
   C. She has the right to have her case tried in federal court.
   D. She has the right to an attorney.

4. Fernando is arrested and charged with breaking into a school and stealing computers. His attorney tells him that the state has pictures of him on video committing the crime, as well as two eyewitnesses who saw him putting the computers into his truck. Fernando will most likely do which of the following?
   A. plead "not guilty" and insist on a trial
   B. sue the state for damages
   C. plea bargain
   D. deliberate

5. Chuckie is convicted in criminal court of armed robbery. However, he asks a higher court to overturn his conviction because he believes his constitutional rights were violated. Chuckie's request is called
   A. a complaint. B. a lawsuit. C. a plea. D. an appeal.

6. The Georgia Court of Appeals and the Georgia Supreme Court are both examples of
   A. appellate courts.
   B. federal courts.
   C. superior courts.
   D. trial courts.

7. Tony is a 15-year-old accused of punching another student in the face. Meanwhile, Paul is 16 and got caught trying to use a fake ID to buy cigarettes. Where will their cases be heard?
   A. in civil court
   B. in juvenile court
   C. in an arraignment
   D. at a youth detention center

8. For which of the following reasons are murder and rape considered two of Georgia's "seven deadly sins"?
   A. People convicted of these crimes are always sentenced to death.
   B. They are crimes for which there is no appeals process.
   C. They are two of the seven crimes for which juveniles may be tried as adults.
   D. They are two of the seven crimes for which juveniles are usually sentenced to death.

Chapter 14
Responsible Citizenship and Political Process

This chapter covers the following Georgia standard(s).

SS8CG1	The student will describe the role of citizens under Georgia's constitution.
SS8E5	The student will explain personal money management choices in terms of income, spending, credit, saving, and investing.

14.1 Rights and Responsibilities of Citizens

In addition to the many rights and privileges US and Georgia citizens enjoy, there are also a number of responsibilities that people must be willing to accept in order for society to function well. Many of the rights citizens enjoy are stated in Article I of the Georgia Constitution, as well as the US Bill of Rights (Amendments 1–10 of the US Constitution). Meanwhile, **responsibilities of citizenship** include obeying laws, respecting the rights and property of fellow citizens, fulfilling civic duties, and serving local communities. Participating and voting in elections, volunteering in community projects, serving on juries in criminal and civil court cases, and remaining informed about and expressing opinions on public issues are all important aspects of responsible citizenship.

Elections and Political Involvement

One of the key ways Georgians fulfill their civic responsibilities is through **political involvement**. In other words, they educate themselves about important political and social issues of the day and attempt to influence government policies. Some make it a point to speak at forums or open legislative sessions to make their opinions known. Others participate in rallies or protests designed to influence government decisions. Some write petitions demanding the government to take some kind of action and get hundreds of other citizens to sign them. Many people actively participate in election campaigns designed to help a candidate they support win public office. A few even go so far as to run for political office themselves.

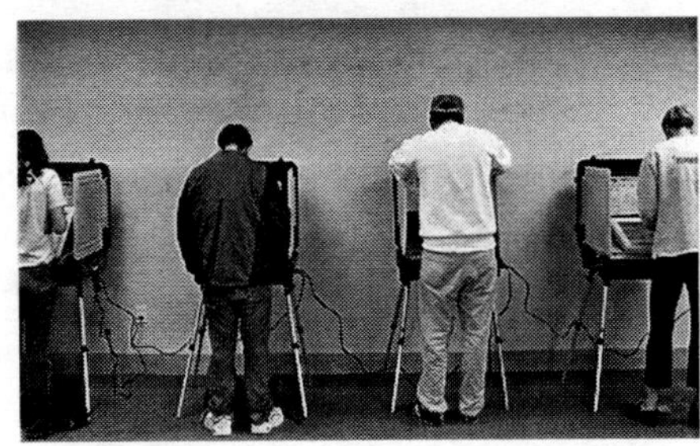

The most common way citizens become involved politically is through **voting**. When citizens vote, they officially voice their opinion about who they want to represent them in a particular office of government or about a proposed law. To vote in **elections** (an election is when voters cast their votes to elect their representatives and public officials), Georgians must first *register to vote*. The state requires people to register in order to make sure they vote for candidates in the counties and districts where they live, as well as to make sure each citizen only votes once. Under the state constitution, people must meet several requirements to vote in Georgia. They must:

- be at least eighteen years old
- be a citizen of the United States
- be a legal resident of Georgia and the county in which they live and wish to vote
- not be serving a sentence for a felony "involving moral turpitude" (an extremely wicked or shameful crime).
- not be determined by the court to be mentally incompetent

Secretary of State

Under the constitution, the **secretary of state** serves as Georgia's chief election official. He/she makes sure all candidates meet the qualifications required to run for office, schedules elections, oversees ballots, and provides Georgia's counties with all election materials. When an election is over, the secretary of state is responsible for publishing the official vote count that determines the winners.

Karen Handel
GA Secretary of State

The Role of Political Parties in Georgia's State Government

Although not mentioned in either the US or Georgia constitutions, **political parties** play an important role in state and local politics (remember the "solid South"). They are organizations that promote certain political beliefs and sponsor candidates for government offices. In Georgia and throughout the US, there are two dominant political parties: the **Republicans** and **Democrats**. Usually, the candidate who wins an election comes from one of these two parties.

Republican Elephant and Democratic Donkey

Political parties serve several functions. They nominate candidates for office and limit the list of candidates to those few that actually have a chance of winning. In addition, they help facilitate the legislative and executive branches of government working together. Instead of having to deal with each and every representative or senator separately, the governor can often deal with a large number of them by addressing the major concerns of their party. Finally, political parties also establish *party platforms*. Platforms are a party's statement of programs and policies it intends to support once its candidates are in office. In reality, however, elected officials rarely stick to every position of their party's platform. As discussed in earlier chapters, the Democratic Party dominated Georgia politics for more than a century. In recent decades, however, the Republican Party has gained a great deal of influence. Currently the state's governor, lieutenant governor, most of its legislators, and both of its US senators are all Republicans.

How Georgia Conducts Elections

US Senator Johnny Isakson Campaigns

Most Georgia elections occur in even-numbered years with primaries occurring in the spring or summer and general elections occurring on the first Tuesday in November. **Primaries** are elections between candidates of the same party to determine who will officially represent the party in the general election. For instance, if there are seven Democrats who want to be governor, then they will face each other in the Democratic primary. Whoever wins the majority of votes (more than 50%) is the primary winner and will be the official Democratic candidate for governor. In cases where there are more than two candidates and no one wins more than 50% of the vote, the state requires a **run-off election**. In a run-off, the two candidates who got the most votes—but neither got a majority—face one another again in an additional election. Whoever wins the run-off then becomes the party's nominee. If a candidate loses a primary, or if he/she does not wish to represent one of the major parties, then he/she can run in the general election as an **independent candidate**. Some candidates may represent parties other than the Republicans and Democrats. They are called **third-party candidates**. While third-party candidates rarely win major offices, they sometimes impact the state's political scene by focusing extra attention on some specific issue that inspired the party's formation or platform.

A **general election** is when the Republican candidate, Democratic candidate, and any additional third-party or independent candidates face one another in an election for public office. Like a primary, if no candidate wins a majority vote, a run-off determines the winner.

Practice 14.1 Rights and Responsibilities of Citizens

1. Obeying laws, serving the local community, and respecting the rights of other citizens are all what?

   A. guaranteed under the Georgia Bill of Rights
   B. important parts of the election process
   C. responsibilities of citizenship
   D. duties of the secretary of state

2. Which of the following is a role played by political parties?

   A. They make sure that independent candidates can't run for political office.
   B. They sponsor and support candidates for political office.
   C. They are responsible for conducting general elections.
   D. They define the responsibilities of citizens.

3. Describe the difference between primaries, general elections, and run-off elections and state the purpose of each.

14.2 Citizens and Financial Responsibility

Personal Money-Management Choices

Credit cards

Citizens need to make wise **personal money-management choices**. In other words, citizens must handle their money wisely. Failure to handle money wisely can leave citizens with too much debt. **Debt** is the amount of money that you owe. People get in debt when they spend more money than they have and are forced to borrow. Sometimes debt is not bad. High-cost items like houses and cars could rarely be afforded if it weren't for the ability to borrow money from banks or lenders on **credit**. Credit is when you borrow someone else's money with an agreement to pay it back a little over time. Usually, you have to pay an **interest rate**. The interest rate is a percentage of the amount you owe that you agree to pay *in addition* to what you borrowed. In other words, it is money you pay the lender for the privilege of using their money to make a purchase. For example, if you bought a $1000 television set using a credit card that charges 10% interest, you would actually pay $1100. Why? Because $100 is 10% of $1000, and $100 + $1000 = $1100. You paid the credit card company the extra $100 for the privilege of using their $1000 to get the television. People use credit cards for convenience or because they want to buy something they cannot afford to pay for all at once. However, it is important to remember that the longer it takes you to pay off a credit card, the more money you spend on interest.

A house in foreclosure

Unfortunately, due to undisciplined spending, many citizens today are drowning in debt. They use credit cards to buy things they cannot afford and then find that they cannot pay for all their purchases and interests. Some citizens also take out unwise loans from banks or other lenders and get into trouble. Since the year 2000, record numbers of US citizens have lost their homes because of mortgages (loans to buy homes) that allowed them to buy nice houses with little money. Over time, however, these loans became too much for them to pay back. Such loans are often known as *adjustable rate mortgages* because they start out with a monthly payment the borrower can afford, but after a set time the payment "adjusts" to a new rate the borrower cannot afford to pay. When this happens, the bank or lender **forecloses** (seizes) the person's home and sells it to get as much of its loan back as possible. When foreclosures occur, borrowers lose their house and what they've already made in house payments, while lenders lose money.

Too much debt can cause people to lose other things as well. When people can't pay back the money they've borrowed to buy cars, boats, furniture, etc. these items are often **re-possessed** (taken) by the lender. Failure to pay your debts can also damage your **credit score**. Your credit score is a number based on your history as a borrower. If you have a history of paying off loans and making monthly credit payments on time, then you will have a high credit score. If, however, you are normally late with payments or have **defaulted** (failed to pay back) loans, you will have a low credit score. Lenders use your credit score when deciding whether or not to loan you money and/or what interest rate to charge you. If you have a high credit score, then lenders are more likely to loan you money at a lower interest rate. However, if you have a low credit score, then your interest rate will be higher because you are considered to be a greater risk for the lender. Often, if your score is low enough, you won't get a loan at all. As you can see, it is very important that citizens prove trustworthy and pay back any money they owe on time. Otherwise, they run the risk of not being able to borrow in the future.

When people don't pay back their loans, it hurts the economy because lenders make less money and, therefore, have less money to lend. As a result, not as many people can get the loans they need to buy houses and other large-dollar items. If fewer people purchase homes, cars, etc. this means less income for realtors, contractors, home inspectors, car salesmen, and so on. These people then have less money to spend at restaurants, stores, or on entertainment. Sales people make less commission, waiters get fewer tips, and the guy who sells popcorn at the movies loses his job. In short, people's spending habits affect society. That's why wise money decisions are part of being a good citizen.

BANKRUPTCY

Bankruptcy is the most drastic consequence of financial irresponsibility. When a borrower or business goes "bankrupt," they acknowledge that they cannot pay their creditors (lenders) and file for legal protection. Bankruptcy allows them additional time to pay back what they can over time, while at the same time shielding them from most legal action. While this might sound like a good deal, it also has a downside. Bankruptcy stays on a person's credit record for at least seven years and makes it very difficult for them to get any kind of future loan or credit.

BUDGETS

The best way for citizens to remain responsible with their money is to have a **budget**. A budget is simply a record of how you plan to spend your money. It helps ensure that you don't lose track of your spending and get into too much debt. The first step to having an effective budget is to know your **income**. Your income is how much money you have or make. For most people, their income is the amount of money they are paid by their employer or, if they are self-employed, the money they make through their own business. A regular allowance from your parents is also considered a form of income. Since most people are paid every two weeks or once a month, most people operate on a weekly or monthly budget. It is important to know your income first so that you accurately know how much money you have to spend.

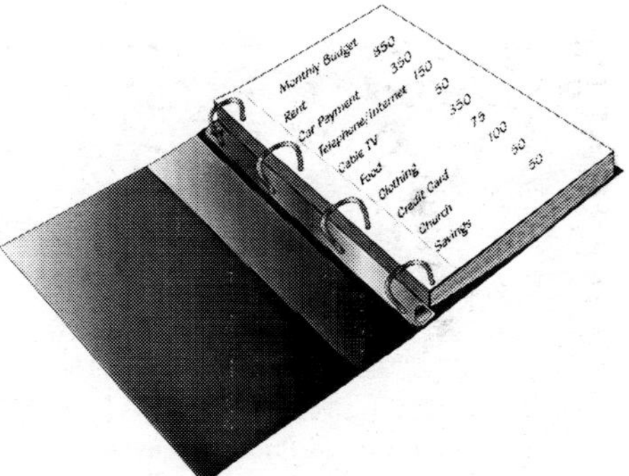

A budget in progress

Once you know your income, the second step is to write down all of your **expenses**. Expenses are the things you spend money on. Some expenses are consistent because they require money every month. Buying groceries, paying your electric bill, and making a monthly mortgage payment are all examples of consistent expenses. Other expenses might only be temporary. For instance, paying to get your television fixed or to cover a trip to the dentist might require money this month but not the next. Still others are flexible expenses. How much to spend on eating out or on clothes are examples of flexible expenses because you have some freedom to decide how much money, if any, to spend on them. When you knows your income and expenses, you can then decide how much income will go to cover each expense. The key is to make sure

Writing a check for expenses

that expenses are not more than income. Once you have a budget that works, you then need **financial discipline** to stick to it. In other words, spend only what your budget allows because you know you can afford it. When people don't stick to a budget, they run the risk of getting into financial danger.

SAVING AND SPENDING

Spending

In general, the United States tends to be a **consumer society**. In other words, most US citizens (including Georgians) spend more money than they save. People get into debt when what they spend is greater than the amount of money they can afford to pay. **Spending** is when you give money to someone or something in return for a good or service. You spend money to buy a video game, go to Six Flags, purchase new clothes, etc. **Saving** is when you take money you *could spend* and, instead, put it in the bank, a special savings account, or even your top drawer until you need it sometime in the future. There are several ways citizens save money (and many reasons why they should).

SAVINGS ACCOUNTS AND INVESTING

Georgia Railroad Bank, Augusta

Many people save by putting money in **savings accounts**. These are accounts people have with banks, credit unions, or even on-line institutions that allow them to put money into savings, while at the same time having access to their money any time they want it. They also allow a person's money to gain interest. Remember, interest is the amount a borrower pays a lender for the use of their money. When you put your money in a savings account, you are actually lending it to that bank or institution in return for interest. The bank, credit union, etc. then uses your money to finance loans, make investments, and so on. Later, you can withdraw the money and interest. However, in most cases, the interest rate you earn on savings accounts is very little. Therefore, many citizens choose to save in other ways as well.

New York Stock Exchange

Investing is one of the most popular ways people save money. Investing is when you allow businesses to use part of your money in return for interest or a share of their profits. The better the business does, the more money you make on your investment. It could be your own business that you invest in. Often, however, it is other peoples' businesses. People invest in a variety of ways. Many buy stocks, which make them part owner of a company. Others buy bonds, which does not give them ownership but rather allows them to lend money to a business or institution. Many participate in mutual funds, which are made up of many companies so that, if one company does poorly, investors still make money off of those that are doing well. Still others might invest in CDs (certificates of deposit) which keep their money in a special account for a set period of time before allowing them to withdraw it with interest. Such forms of investment are popular because they tend to pay investors much more interest than simple savings accounts. However, they also offer investors less immediate access to their money and/or require greater financial risk.

Reasons to Save

There are lots of reasons why people save. Sometimes, they save for a specific item they want to buy. Young couples often save to buy their first home, teenagers often save to buy a car, and families might save to take a nice vacation. Parents often save to send their kids to college. In fact, since tuitions at colleges and universities have gotten rather expensive, many savings and investment accounts are now set up specifically for college savings. One of the most important things citizens save for is retirement. When a person "retires" it means that they no longer work. People may retire due to an illness or because they simply don't want to work anymore. The most common reason people retire is age. However, even retired people still need money to live on. If they are not working and earning a salary (money paid by an employer) then this money must come from somewhere else. For many, it comes from **retirement savings**. Many people participate in 401k or pension plans through their employers, which allow them to set aside money for retirement that grows with interest. Others set up IRA accounts, which are individual retirement accounts. Such savings plans allow people to set aside money over time for when they are older, while often offering tax advantages as well. The earlier people set up or participate in such accounts, the longer their money grows and the more they have for retirement.

A lucky retiree

GA lottery ticket: not a reliable financial plan

Many people count on Social Security benefits to provide their retirement income. You may remember reading about Social Security in chapter 7. Social Security is a federal government program that provides monthly payments to retired citizens. In reality, however, Social Security cannot provide enough money for most people to live on and many political leaders and financial experts wonder if it will even exist in a few decades. Therefore, citizens need to save on their own as well. Otherwise, they run the risk of having to work well into their old age or seriously having to reduce their standard of living once they can no longer work. By investing wisely and starting early, citizens can do a good job of saving for retirement.

Practice 14.2 Citizens and Financial Responsibility

1. The amount of money that you owe to lenders is called what?

   A. credit B. interest C. bankruptcy D. debt

2. Which of the following does a person need to know to plan an effective budget?

   A. statewide interest rates
   B. his or her credit score
   C. personal income
   D. adjustable rate mortgages

3. Describe some of the ways people save and give reasons why they do.

4. Why is it important that citizens make wise money-management choices?

CHAPTER 14 REVIEW

Key Terms, People, and Concepts

responsibilities of citizenship
political involvement
voting
elections
secretary of state
political parties
Republicans and Democrats
primaries
run-off elections
independent candidates
third-party candidates
general elections
personal money-management choices
debt
credit
interest rate
foreclose
repossess
credit score
default
bankruptcy
budget
income
expense
financial discipline
consumer society
spending
savings
savings account
investing
retirement savings

Multiple Choice

1. David's willingness to serve on the jury at a criminal trial is an example of what?
   A. running for political office
   B. fulfilling a civic duty
   C. participating in the political process
   D. voting

2. The secretary of state would be **most** concerned about which of the following?
   A. failure of a citizen to serve on a jury
   B. lack of volunteers at a community project
   C. voting machines failing to operate properly during a general election
   D. poor financial planning by citizens

3. Phil, Lisa, Bonnie, and Chuck face each other in the party's primary for governor. After the votes are counted, Phil received 42% of the vote, Lisa 38%, Bonnie 15%, and Chuck 5%. What will happen next in the political process?
   A. Phil will become governor.
   B. Phil will become the party's nominee for governor.
   C. The four candidates will face each other again in a run-off election.
   D. Phil and Lisa will face each other again in a run-off election.

4. Mike is running for lieutenant governor; however he is not part of any political party. Mike is which of the following?
   A. an independent candidate
   B. a third-party candidate
   C. ineligible to run for office until he joins a party
   D. a run-off candidate

5. When someone borrows a lender's money to make a purchase in exchange for paying that lender interest it is known as
   A. savings.
   B. credit.
   C. foreclosing.
   D. investing.

6. Too much debt tends to produce which of the following?
   A. high credit scores
   B. effective budgets
   C. lower interest rates
   D. defaulting on loans

7. Which of the following is a characteristic of an effective budget?
   A. too much income
   B. investing more than you save
   C. spending less than your income
   D. expenses greater than your income

8. Retirement, college education, weddings, a nice trip, and a new truck are all what?
   A. examples of undisciplined spending
   B. things bought on credit
   C. methods of investing
   D. reasons people save

8th Grade Georgia Studies Practice Test 1

The purpose of this diagnostic test is to measure your progress in comprehending Georgia social studies. This diagnostic test is based on the revised Social Studies Georgia Performance Standards and adheres to the sample question format provided by the Georgia Department of Education.

General Directions:

1 Read all directions carefully.

2 Read each question or sample. Then choose the best answer.

3 Choose only one answer for each question. If you change an answer, be sure to erase your original answer completely.

1. James Oglethorpe is BEST described as SS8H2
   - A. a member of Parliament who wanted to establish a colony for debtors.
   - B. a businessman who wanted to establish plantations in Georgia.
   - C. a slaveowner who introduced Africans to Georgia.
   - D. a royal governor who finally convinced the king to make Georgia a royal colony.

2. Money people must pay the government based on their income, property, what they purchase, etc. is known as SS8E4
   - A. taxes.
   - B. fees.
   - C. fines.
   - D. expenditures.

3. Which of the following describes a significant change in Georgia agriculture during the first few years after World War II? SS8H10
   - A. Cotton was no longer produced
   - B. Farmers gave up producing food crops in favor of crops that could be used to produce textiles.
   - C. The state produced a greater variety of cash crops.
   - D. Farmers began to support the Republican Party.

4. The boll weevil reeked havoc on Georgia farmers in the early twentieth century largely because SS8H8
   - A. Agriculturalists failed to produce enough cotton.
   - B. Farmers failed to diversify their crops.
   - C. Farmers tried to raise too many different kinds of crops.
   - D. Governor Talmadge rejected the New Deal

5. The role of Georgia's executive branch is predominantly to SS8CG3
   - A. amend federal laws.
   - B. pass new legislation.
   - C. enforce state laws.
   - D. preside over the state Senate.

6. During the Civil War, the Union decided to blockade the Georgia coast in order to SS8E2
   - A. force Lee's army to abandon Atlanta.
   - B. meet Sherman as he finished his march to the sea.
   - C. engage Georgia's navy in battle.
   - D. disrupt the foreign trade on which Georgia and the Confederacy depended.

7. An advocate of the "New South" would have been MOST excited about which of the following? SS8H7
   - A. increased agriculture
   - B. the Populist Movement
   - C. the International Cotton Exposition
   - D. the rise of the two-party system in Georgia

8. The fact that Georgia politicians often won statewide elections before the 1960s without winning a majority of individual votes is evidence of SS8H12
   - A. voter fraud in most elections.
   - B. the fact that African-Americans did not have the legal right to vote.
   - C. the county-unit system.
   - D. segregation.

9. The Supreme Court's ruling in *Brown v. Board of Education* most affected which of the following? SS8H11
   A. the number of public schools in Georgia
   B. the amount of state funds granted to the University of Georgia
   C. racial policies in public schools
   D. integration in private businesses

10. Most cases reach the Georgia Supreme Court SS8HCG4
   A. as criminal trials.
   B. as civil trials.
   C. as misdemeanor cases.
   D. as appeals.

11. The process of growing plants and trees developed by the late Archaic peoples is called SS8H1
   A. horticulture.
   B. migration.
   C. immigration.
   D. mounding.

12. What does the following list describe? SS8H3
   - Divided Florida into two British colonies
   - Expanded Georgia's territory
   - Angered colonists wanting to settle west of the Appalachian mountains

   A. the Yazoo Land Fraud
   B. the Stamp Act
   C. the Charter of 1732
   D. the Proclamation of 1763

13. The General Assembly passes a law on immigration. However, the governor vetoes the law and the bill dies. This is an example of SS8CG1
   A. separation of powers.
   B. checks and balances.
   C. civil rights.
   D. legislative authority.

14. The amount of money you make each month at work is considered SS8E5
   A. credit.
   B. debt.
   C. interest.
   D. income.

15. What would be the best heading for the following list? SSH5
   - Savannah
   - Augusta
   - Louisville
   - Milledgeville
   - Atlanta

   A. cities Founded by Oglethorpe
   B. cities That Have Served as Georgia's Capital
   C. cities Burned During Sherman's March to the Sea
   D. cities That Have Served as Key Ports

16. Who is the following quote MOST LIKELY referring to? SS8H8

> *"Who knows if Roosevelt's policies would help Georgia, or not? Every time he tries to implement something, the governor is right there waving his defiant fist and yelling that the federal government needs to keep its hands off state matters. It ain't no exaggeration to call him a 'wild man'."*

   A. Lester Maddox
   B. Alexander Stephens
   C. Eugene Talmadge
   D. Alonzo Herndon

17. Which of the following requirements must Patrick meet if he wants to serve in the General Assembly? SS8CG2
    A. He must be at least 30 years old.
    B. Must be a citizen of Georgia for at least 15 years
    C. Must be a legal resident
    D. Must already hold some kind of civil appointment

18. In which of the following cases would a defendant be entitled to a lawyer if they cannot afford their own? SS8CG4
    A. a defendant is sued for $900
    B. a defendant is sued for $100,000
    C. a defendant appeals a civil decision
    D. a defendant is charged with armed robbery

19. Maggie owns her own restaurant. On average she spends $5.00 on every meal she prepares and charges customers an average of $10.00 per meal. The $5.00 that Maggie makes off of each meal she sells is her SS8E3
    A. debt.
    B. profit.
    C. credit.
    D. savings.

20. King George II agreed to grant Oglethorpe and the trustees a charter to found Georgia because SS8H2
    A. he knew a revolution was coming and wanted a new colony loyal to the Crown.
    B. he believed it would help Britain economically while providing military protection for the southern colonies.
    C. he was against slavery and liked the fact that Oglethorpe would not allow it in Georgia.
    D. the trustees promised the king that Georgia would be founded as a royal colony.

21. What impact did Pearl Harbor have on Georgia? SS8H9
    A. It convinced most Georgians to become isolationists.
    B. It caused most Georgians to blame Roosevelt for the war.
    C. It created support for the war and a spirit of national pride
    D. It severely hurt the state's economy as materials were taken out of the state and used for the war effort.

22. Which of the following was an issue of debate at the Constitutional Convention in 1787? SS8H4
    A. whether or not the US should have a king
    B. whether or not anything was wrong with the Articles of Confederation
    C. whether or not citizens had any rights
    D. whether or not slaves should count as citizens

23. A Georgian who supported states' rights and white supremacy would have been MOST supportive of which politician? SS8H11
    A. Lyndon Johnson
    B. William Hartsfield
    C. Herman Talmadge
    D. Jimmy Carter

24. A student in Europe hoping to find Georgia on a globe would need to look SS8G1
    A. in the Eastern Hemisphere above the equator.
    B. below the equator.
    C. in the Northern and Western Hemispheres.
    D. in the Southern and Western Hemispheres.

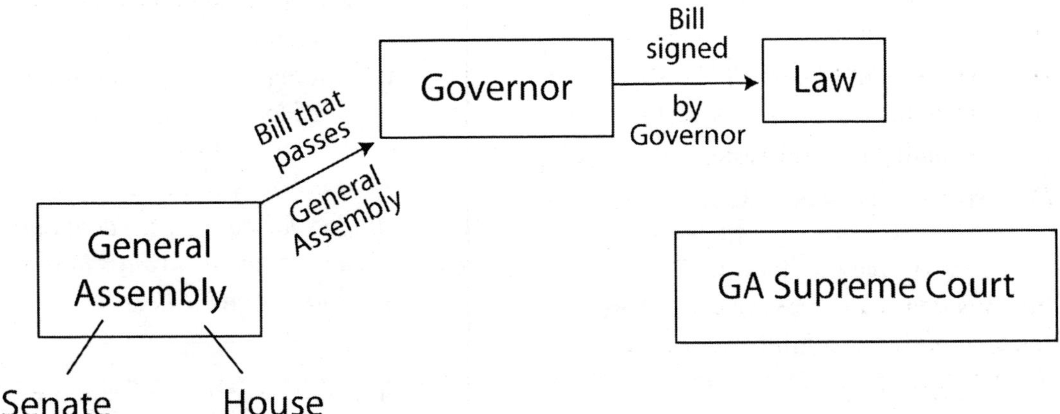

25. The above diagram depicts the process by which a bill becomes a law if the governor signs it. However, if the governor vetoes the bill, then where would you draw an additional arrow? SS8CG2
    A. from the state Senate to the state House
    B. from the governor's office back to the General Assembly
    C. from the General Assembly to the Georgia Supreme Court
    D. from the governor's office to the Georgia Supreme Court

26. A southern politician who believed in the doctrine of nullification would have been MOST supportive of SS8H6
    A. abolition.
    B. a strong federal government.
    C. states' rights.
    D. crop diversification.

27. Laws meant to keep blacks and whites segregated in Georgia were known as SS8H7
    A. grandfather clauses.
    B. Solid South laws.
    C. integration laws.
    D. Jim Crow laws.

28. Hartsfield-International Airport is important to Georgia's economy because SS8G2
    A. it is the only airport in the state.
    B. it makes sure products produced in Atlanta reach other parts of the state.
    C. it makes Georgia accessible to visitors, business travelers, and trade.
    D. it is the busiest deepwater port in the world.

29. Headrights and lotteries in the early 1800s were the result of what? SS8H5
    A. falling cotton prices
    B. debates over slavery
    C. disputes over vast stretches of land
    D. reconstruction

30. A municipality that wants a strong elected executive with lots of power over the council and city matters would likely use a SS8CG5
    A. strong mayor-council system.
    B. weak mayor-council system.
    C. council-manager system.
    D. special districts system.

31. Anything a juvenile does that would be considered a crime even if it were committed by an adult is referred to as SS8CG6
    A. a delinquent act.
    B. an unruly act.
    C. a civil offense.
    D. an informal adjustment.

32. Which of the following did Lyman Hall, Button Gwinnett, and George Walton all have in common? SS8H3
    A. They each signed the Declaration of Independence on behalf of Georgia.
    B. They each served as governor after Georgia became a royal colony.
    C. They each signed the Constitution on behalf of Georgia.
    D. They each served as confederate leaders during the Civil War.

33. Anyone who enjoys watching the Atlanta Braves play baseball owes a debt of gratitude to SS8H10
    A. Lester Maddox.
    B. Jimmy Carter.
    C. Herman Talmadge.
    D. Ivan Allen, Jr.

34. What is the following quote describing? SS8H11

> *"It was amazing to see so many students descending on South Georgia to help register black voters! Even Dr. King offered assistance. Although it did not accomplish all of its goals, it surely opened the eyes of all of us to see what we could accomplish when we gathered in mass demonstration to demand our civil rights."*

    A. the March on Washington
    B. the Atlanta Compromise
    C. the Niagara Movement
    D. the Albany Movement

35. Who is the following list referring to? SS8H12
    - Successful state senator and governor of Georgia
    - Only Georgian to serve as president of the United States
    - Helped draft the Camp David Accords
    - Praised for his diplomatic and charitable work as an ex-president

    A. Newt Gingrich
    B. Bill Clinton
    C. Andrew Young
    D. Jimmy Carter

36. The first Europeans to establish settlements in Georgia were the SS8H1
    A. English.
    B. French.
    C. Spanish.
    D. Dutch.

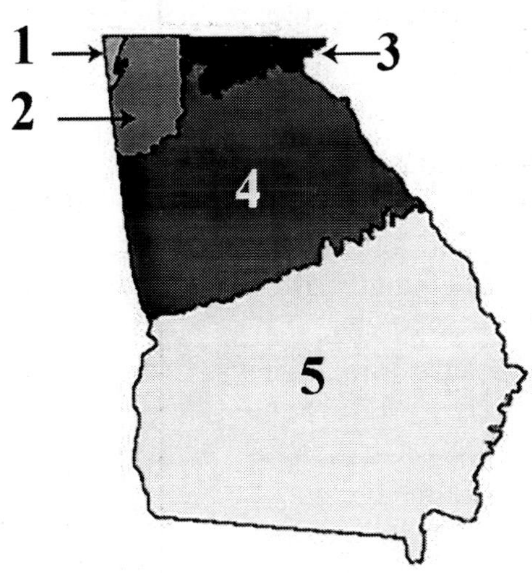

37. Look at the map above. What number corresponds to the region in which one would visit Tallulah Gorge or begin hiking the Appalachian Trail? SS8G1

A. 1
B. 2
C. 3
D. 5

38. What crop dominated Georgia's agriculture from the early 1800s until the 1920s? SS8E1

A. rice
B. tobacco
C. cotton
D. peanuts

39. One way appellate courts differ from trial courts is that they SS8CG4

A. don't have judges.
B. don't hear from lawyers.
C. don't have juries.
D. are not part of the judicial branch of government.

40. How has Georgia's growth in international business impacted the state's economy? SS8E2

A. negatively, because state citizens lose their jobs to immigrants
B. positively, because international business creates jobs for Georgians and pumps more money into the local economy
C. it has had little effect because, although international businesses are located in Georgia, their wealth goes back to their home countries
D. it has hurt population growth as many native Georgians have been forced to leave the state in search of other opportunities

41. Which of the following statements most accurately describes how President Roosevelt felt about Eugene Talmadge leaving office as governor of Georgia in the late 1930s? SS8H8

A. He was devastated because the two were close friends.

B. He was disappointed because Talmadge was a key figure in helping FDR establish the New Deal in Georgia.

C. He was pleased because Talmadge was a Republican and FDR was a Democrat.

D. He was glad to see Talmadge go because he made it difficult for the president to implement the New Deal in Georgia.

42. Shortly after Lincoln's election, Georgia SS8H6

A. remained loyal to the Union.

B. seceded from the Union.

C. abolished slavery to avoid war.

D. seceded from the Confederacy.

43. Governor Vandiver's decision to authorize the Sibley Commission was closely related to SS8H11

A. his campaign promise to integrate schools.

B. his belief that the Supreme Court's decisions were unlawful.

C. his fears that school desegregation could lead to violence in Georgia.

D. his realization that the "solid South" was over.

1-Speaker of the House

2-President pro tempore

3-Chief of Atlanta's Police

4-State Attorney General

5-Georgia's Chief Justice

6-Secretary of State

7-Georgia Congressmen

8-Commissioner of Insurance

44. Which of the positions listed above are part of Georgia's executive branch of government? SS8CG3

A. 4,6,8 C. 2, 4, 8

B. 1,3,5 D. 2,4,6

45. Which of the following areas saw the greatest decrease in population during the Great Depression? SS8H8

A. Northern cities

B. Atlanta

C. Savannah

D. rural Georgia

46. Which of the following BEST describes Richard Russell and Carl Vinson? SS8H9

A. Their efforts helped end the New Deal in Georgia.

B. Together, they helped strengthen the US military and rebuild Georgia's economy.

C. Under their leadership, Atlanta became a progressive city in the 1950s and 1960s.

D. They made sure that the federal government had little influence on what happened in Georgia during the middle part of he twentieth century.

47. The US Bill of Rights SS8H4
    A. was opposed by people who believed in personal freedoms.
    B. was the first part of the US Constitution written.
    C. had to be added to the Constitution before Georgia would ratify it.
    D. consists of 10 amendments to the Constitution intended to protect citizens' rights.

48. The Dahlonega Gold Rush, *Worchester v. Georgia,* and the Trail of Tears all are related to SS8H5
    A. issues involving slavery.
    B. scandalous land deals in Georgia.
    C. the plight of the Cherokee.
    D. disputes over Georgia's boundaries following the revolution.

49. A Japanese firm that wants quick travel back and forth between Georgia and Tokyo would likely use which of the following most often? SS8G2
    A. Hartsfield-Jackson International Airport
    B. Savannah's port
    C. Brunswick's port
    D. I-95

50. In what ways do political constituencies affect state spending decisions? SS8E4
    A. Politicians are not likely to support spending that is unpopular with those who elected them.
    B. They usually demand higher taxes.
    C. If the government has a political constituency then it will not need a state budget.
    D. For every constituency the government has it also has an opportunity cost.

51. Which of the following people would have MOST LIKELY been a "malcontent"? SS8H2
    A. someone who supported James Oglethorpe
    B. a Georgian during the trustee period who wanted more land and slaves
    C. a Salzburger
    D. a Spanish missionary living on Georgia's barrier islands

52. William Hartsfield, Ivan Allen, Jr., and Ellis Arnall can all be accurately described as SS8H10
    A. leaders of the civil rights movement.
    B. progressive politicians in Georgia.
    C. Republicans who ended the "solid South."
    D. Democrats who supported Jim Crow laws.

53. Alonzo Herndon's success was proof that SS8H7
    A. African-Americans were able to succeed in business during the early twentieth century.
    B. the Bourbon Triumvirate controlled Georgia after Reconstruction.
    C. Georgia did better as a royal colony than as a charter colony.
    D. the Albany movement was growing.

54. How would a passionate segregationist have responded to the election of Lester Maddox as governor? SS8H11
    A. with outrage because Maddox supported forced integration of businesses
    B. with excitement because Maddox opposed involuntary integration
    C. with indifference because Maddox cared little about matters involving race
    D. with skepticism because Maddox had never expressed his views on segregation prior to his election

55. Retirement, vacations, emergencies, and college are all reasons why responsible citizens SS8E5

A. save.

B. tax.

C. vote.

D. boycott.

56. Elijah Clarke's victory at Kettle Creek SS8H3

A. boosted the morale of Georgia Patriots and halted British attempts to organize upcountry Tories during the revolution.

B. stopped the Union's first attempt to invade Georgia during the Civil War.

C. allowed Lord Cornwallis to finally invade North Carolina during the revolution.

D. led to the end of Native American resistance to Indian Removal and the Trail of Tears.

57. What was significant about the 1996 Olympic Games? SS8H12

A. They marked the arrival of professional sports in Georgia.

B. They put Georgia on a world stage and boosted economic development.

C. They drained Georgia's economy and resources, causing financial stress for the state.

D. President Carter ordered a boycott of the games because of the Soviet's invasion of Afghanistan.

58. Increased markets, more efficient trade, and the rise of Atlanta can all be attributed to SS8H5

A. conflicts between Georgians and Native Americans.

B. the Yazoo Land Fraud.

C. the establishment of railroads in the 1800s.

D. Sherman's "march to the sea."

59. Which of the following people would have MOST LIKELY supported Radical Reconstruction? SS8H6

A. Alexander Stephens

B. Leaders of the Ku Klux Klan

C. Henry McNeal Turner

D. Joseph E. Brown

8th Grade Georgia Studies Practice Test 2

The purpose of this diagnostic test is to measure your progress in comprehending Georgia social studies. This diagnostic test is based on the revised Social Studies Georgia Performance Standards and adheres to the sample question format provided by the Georgia Department of Education.

General Directions:

1 Read all directions carefully.

2 Read each question or sample. Then choose the best answer.

3 Choose only one answer for each question. If you change an answer, be sure to erase your original answer completely.

1. Under the Charter of 1732, which of the following were not allowed to settle in Georgia? SS8H2
   - A. debtors
   - B. Jews
   - C. Scots
   - D. Catholics

2. In order for the state and local governments to pay public employees and provide government services, they need SS8E4
   - A. debt.
   - B. expenditures.
   - C. revenue.
   - D. entrepreneurs.

3. What role did farm subsidies play in the transformation of Georgia's agriculture during the 1930s and 40s? SS8H10
   - A. They reduced the need for agricultural products.
   - B. They ensured that cotton remained Georgia's predominant cash crop.
   - C. They finally gave farmers the financial motive to diversify crops.
   - D. They encouraged urban African-Americans to return to rural areas and engage in farming.

4. Which of the following was a result of the Great Depression? SS8H8
   - A. prosperity and consumerism
   - B. increased investments in the stock market
   - C. World War I
   - D. a Great Migration of African-Americans from Georgia to the North

5. The governor is elected SS8CG3
   - A. by the General Assembly.
   - B. by popular vote to a term of four years.
   - C. by popular vote to a term of two years.
   - D. to no more than one term of four years.

6. Which of the following describes Georgia's trade prior to the mid-twentieth century? SS8E2
   - A. The state exported lots of textiles and agricultural products.
   - B. The state tended to import agricultural products while exporting manufactured goods.
   - C. The state engaged in very little trade before the twentieth century.
   - D. Ports played a major role in trade, while railroads had little impact.

7. What would be the BEST heading for the following list? SS8H7
   - John and Lugenia Burns Hope
   - Henry McNeil Turner
   - Alonzo Herndon

   - A. Political Leaders During Reconstruction
   - B. Influential African-Americans in Georgia
   - C. Leaders of the Populist Movement
   - D. Sponsors of the Atlanta Compromise

8. Who would have been MOST disappointed to see the end of the county-unit system? SS8H12
   - A. black urban voters
   - B. white urban voters
   - C. rural segregationists
   - D. rural black farmers

9. Which of the following did Herman Talmadge and Lestor Maddox have in common? SS8H11
   - A. They both inherited positions of political power from their fathers.
   - B. They both opposed integration and federal intervention in local affairs
   - C. They both supported the civil rights movement
   - D. They both served as mayor of Atlanta and supported school integration

10. George is arrested and accused of a crime. He is only 14 years old. Which of the following is true regarding George's rights? SS8CG6
    A. He has no rights because he is not a legal adult.
    B. The state must notify his parents but is not required to provide a lawyer.
    C. The state does not have to reveal who the witnesses against George are.
    D. George has the same rights as any adult, plus the right to have his parents present at all legal proceedings.

11. What was distinctive about the Mississippians who occupied the Georgia region of North America from 800–1600 AD? SS8H1
    A. They were the first white settlers in North America.
    B. They originally came from Spain.
    C. They discovered Native American populations in North America.
    D. They represented the last undisturbed Native American culture before Europeans arrived in North America.

12. Georgians' response to the Stamp Act can best be described as SS8H3
    A. supportive and obedient.
    B. indifferent and submissive.
    C. angry and violent.
    D. disappointed but compliant.

13. Charlie, Olivia, and Juwan all want to vote in the next election . Charlie is a native Georgian who is 17 years old. Olivia has only lived in Georgia a year and is 18. Juwan has lived in Georgia for five years and is 21, but he forgot to register. Which of the following statements is true? SS8CG1
    A. All three may vote.
    B. Only Juwan may not vote because he forgot to register.
    C. Only Olivia may vote.
    D. Only Charlie may not vote because he is too young.

14. Barbara bought a $500 dress using her credit card. By the time she finished paying back the credit card company, Barbara paid $575 for the dress. The extra $75 was SS8E5
    A. debt.
    B. credit.
    C. interest.
    D. expenditure.

15. The establishment of the University of Georgia is evidence of SS8H5
    A. Britain's desire to encourage education once Georgia became a royal colony.
    B. the state's commitment to public education after the revolution.
    C. Georgia's willingness to imitate what other states had already done with public universities.
    D. how important Atlanta was becoming during the early 1800s as a center for education.

16. The Agricultural Adjustment Act, Civilian Conservation Corps, and Rural Electrification Administration were all part of SS8H8
    A. the Georgia Platform.
    B. FDR's New Deal.
    C. Reconstruction.
    D. the "New South."

17. A citizen who wants a bill introduced requiring stores near schools to refrain from selling tobacco products would MOST LIKELY SS8CG2
    A. contact their local school board.
    B. contact their state senator or representative.
    C. contact their congressman.
    D. contact the governor.

18. If the state has a great deal of evidence showing that Melissa is guilty of a serious crime, then Melissa's attorney is likely to advise her to SS8CG4
    A. plead not guilty.
    B. plea bargain.
    C. escape.
    D. give up her right to due process.

19. Arthur Blank of Home Depot, Asa Candler of Coke, and C.E. Woolman of Delta are all examples of SS8E3
    A. African-Americans who proved blacks could be successful in business.
    B. leaders of the Niagara Movement.
    C. businessmen who became politicians.
    D. entrepreneurs who started thriving businesses.

20. Tomochichi is MOST associated with SS8H2
    A. the Yazoo Land Fraud.
    B. Native American wars against Hernando de Soto.
    C. the founding of Savannah.
    D. removal of the Cherokee from Georgia.

21. "Liberty ships" were associated with SS8H9
    A. Bell aircraft.
    B. Pearl Harbor.
    C. the Brunswick and Savannah shipyards.
    D. submarine warfare.

22. Which of the following was a weakness of the Georgia Constitution of 1777? SS8H4
    A. It gave too much power to the governor.
    B. It divided the Assembly into too many houses for laws to be passed efficiently.
    C. It was based on drastically different principles than the Declaration of Independence.
    D. It placed too much power in a unicameral assembly without giving enough authority to the governor.

23. The political power of African-Americans in Georgia increased when SS8H11
    A. the white primary and county-unit systems ended.
    B. the white primary was replaced by the county-unit system.
    C. Herman Talmadge became governor of Georgia.
    D. the Supreme Court struck down segregation in schools.

24. 32° , 02' N to 35° N describes Georgia's SS8G1
    A. exact location on the globe.
    B. latitude.
    C. longitude.
    D. region.

25. Before the state of Georgia may raise taxes, a bill authorizing such a change must be introduced by SS8CG2
    A. the governor.
    B. a private citizen.
    C. a member of the state House.
    D. a member of the state Senate

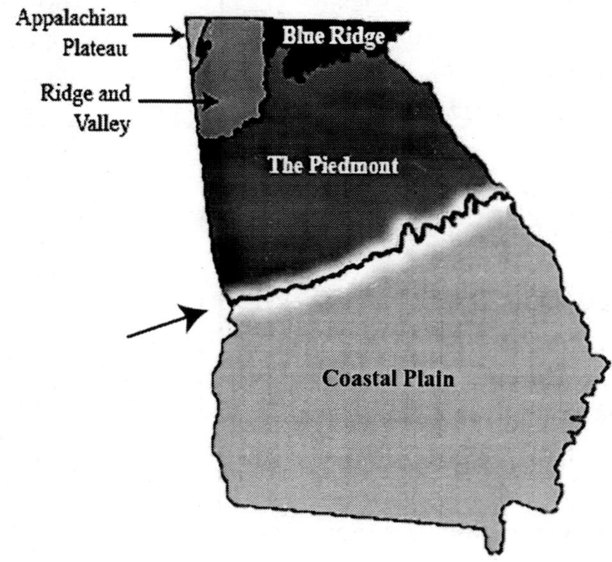

26. Look at the map above. What would be found in the highlighted area? SS8G1
    - A. the Okefenokee Swamp
    - B. Chattahoochee River
    - C. Tallulah Gorge
    - D. Georgia's Fall Line

27. The Leo Frank Case and Riot of 1906 are both examples of SS8H7
    - A. the racial and ethnic tensions that existed in Georgia during the early twentieth century.
    - B. reactions to Supreme Court decisions striking down segregation in the 1960s.
    - C. legal segregation in Georgia.
    - D. outrage in Atlanta's Jewish community over the Holocaust.

28. Which of the following MOST allowed the Baptist and Methodist faiths to grow drastically in Georgia during the years following the revolution? SS8H5
    - A. a willingness to use new methods to reach people on the frontier
    - B. an organized effort by both to convert hundreds of Native Americans
    - C. deep devotion to church traditions and refusal to alter long-established church practices
    - D. their strong stand against slavery

29. The Missouri Compromise was intended to SS8H6

A. outlaw slavery in new territories without ending it in the South.

B. maintain the balance of power in Washington as the US expanded.

C. prevent Missouri from seceding from the Union.

D. end Reconstruction in the South.

30. In a council-manager system of government SS8CG5

A. citizens elect a manager to preside over city affairs.

B. an elected council hires a manager to be the city's chief administrator.

C. an elected manager appoints members of the council.

D. the council elects one of its own members to serve as the city's chief manager.

31. Any act that usually would not be considered a crime if committed by an adult but is illegal for someone under the age of 18 is referred to as SS8CG4

A. a delinquent act.

B. an unruly act.

C. a felony.

D. a lawsuit.

32. Austin Dabney and Nancy Hart represent SS8H3

A. the key role played by missionaries in the founding of Georgia.

B. the roles of women and African-Americans in Georgia during the American Revolution.

C. the gains made by women and blacks under the New Deal.

D. the rise of a two-party system in Georgia after the 1960s.

33. Professional sports in Georgia produced which of the following? SS8H10

A. economic growth

B. agricultural growth

C. end of the "solid South"

D. birth of the "New South"

34. Which of the following has been important to Georgia's interstate and international trade the longest? SS8CG2

A. Hartsfield-Jackson International Airport

B. Savannah's port

C. railroads

D. interstate highways

35. Who is the following list describing? SS8H11

- Acknowledged leader of the civil rights movement
- Believed in non-violence
- Winner of the Nobel Peace Prize
- Assassinated in Memphis, Tennessee
- Arguably the most influential Georgian in history

A. Benjamin Mays

B. Andrew Young

C. Martin Luther King, Jr.

D. Jimmy Carter

36. Someone helping Jimmy Carter run for re-election in the 1980 presidential campaign would likely have tried to highlight SS8H12

A. his handling of the Iran hostage crisis.

B. the state of the US economy.

C. his role in the Camp David Accords.

D. his handling of the Cold War.

37. Spain's first settlements in Georgia were SS8H1
   A. large cities located along the Chattahoochee River.
   B. Catholic missions on Georgia's barrier islands.
   C. forts built along the Tennessee border.
   D. small communities surrounding modern-day Atlanta.

38. Most of Georgia's leaders SS8H4
   A. opposed the Constitution because they feared it did not do enough to protect rights.
   B. supported the Constitution because they wanted a strong central government.
   C. voted against sending delegates to the Constitutional Convention.
   D. refused to support the Declaration of Independence.

- World Congress Center
- Georgia Dome
- 1996 Olympics

39. What would be the best heading for the list above? SS8E2
   A. Facilities and Events that Opened in 1996
   B. The Impact of Sports on Georgia
   C. Economic Disasters for Georgia
   D. Events and Facilities that Have Expanded Georgia's Economy

40. Following World War I, the Ku Klux Klan SS8H8
   A. disappeared because whites appreciated how valiantly blacks had served in the war.
   B. expanded by targeting Jews, Catholics, and immigrants as well as blacks.
   C. shrank from a nationwide organization to a predominantly southern institution.
   D. stopped relying on violence and became more political.

41. Which of the following accurately describes Alexander Stephens? SS8H6
   A. He was a Georgian who served as vice president of the Confederacy.
   B. He was a passionate secessionists who wanted Georgia to leave the Union sooner than most state leaders.
   C. He was a large and intimidating figure who was despised by most southerners.
   D. He was a southerner who remained loyal to the Union and served as vice president under President Abraham Lincoln.

42. Lester Maddox challenged the Civil Rights Act of 1964 because he believed it SS8H11
   A. integrated public schools too quickly.
   B. did not go far enough to guarantee equality to African-Americans.
   C. gave too much political power to blacks.
   D. violated individual property rights.

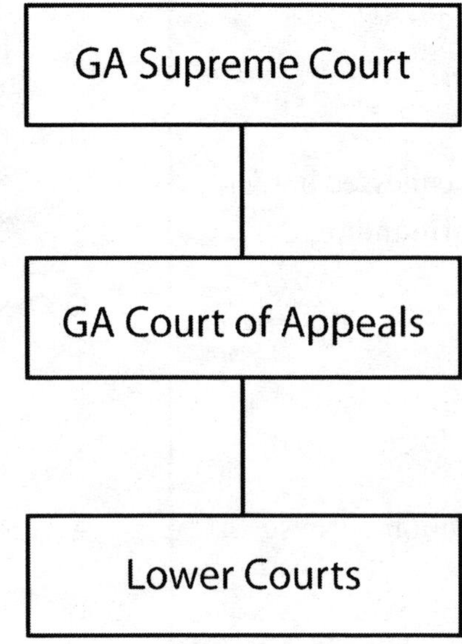

43. The above diagram depicts SS8CG4
    A. the judicial branch of Georgia's government.
    B. the legislative process.
    C. departments of the executive branch.
    D. how bills are assigned to committees.

44. What crop dominated Georgia's agriculture from the early 1800s until the 1920s? SS8E1
    A. rice
    B. tobacco
    C. cotton
    D. peanuts

1-Speaker of the House
2-President pro tempore
3-Chief of Atlanta's Police
4-State Attorney General
5-Georgia's Chief Justice
6-Secretary of State
7-Georgia Congressmen
8-Commissioner of Insurance

45. Which of the officials listed above would be most concerned with making sure state elections are conducted efficiently? SS8CG3
    A. 2 B. 4 C. 5 D. 6

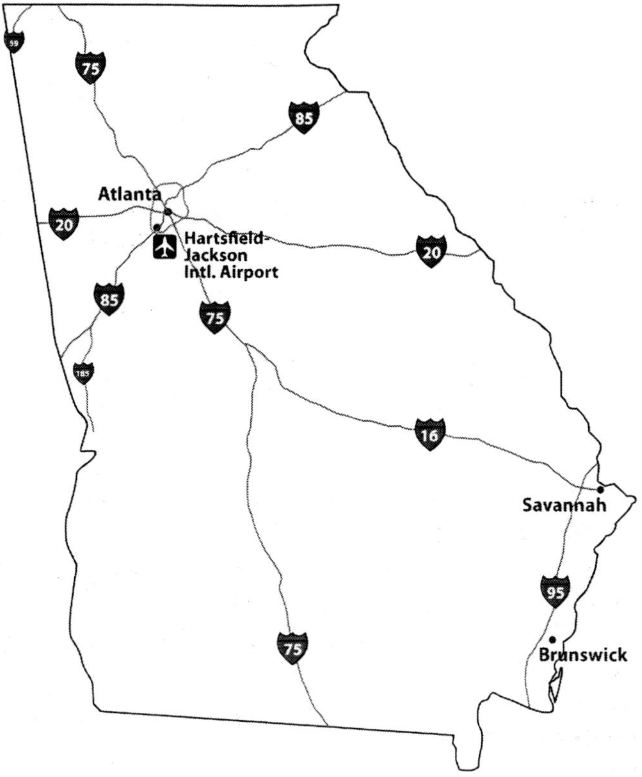

46. Look at the map above. Someone wanting to ship cargo by truck from Florida to Tennessee would MOST LIKELY use SS8G2

A. the port at Savannah.

B. I-85.

C. I-75.

D. I-20.

47. Warm Springs is BEST remembered for SS8H9

A. the presence of a strong Jewish community in Georgia.

B. its role as an important military base during both world wars.

C. its contributions to crop diversification in southern farming.

D. its ties to President Franklin D. Roosevelt.

48. Lockheed is an example of SS8H10

A. new innovations in agriculture following the New Deal.

B. William Hartsfield's abilities to maintain social stability in Atlanta.

C. new industries that boosted Georgia's economy after WWII.

D. businesses that developed from Georgia's shipyards after WWII.

49. The New Deal came later to Georgia than many other southern areas because SS8H8

A. Roosevelt did not like Georgia.
B. Republicans were too powerful in Georgia and would not back Roosevelt's policies.
C. Governor Eugene Talmadge resisted federal intervention in state affairs.
D. Georgia was not hit as hard by the Great Depression as other southern states.

50. What impact did cotton have on Georgia's economy during the 1800s? SS8H5

A. It became the most important crop to the state's economy and ensured that the state remained dependent on slavery.
B. It decreased in importance as more textile mills opened.
C. It decreased the need for slaves because the state had less rice plantations
D. It led to the state's increased dependence on trade as Georgia imported tons and tons of cotton from other states and overseas.

51. The fact that state funds are limited means that Georgia's government will always face SS8E4

A. federal grants.
B. opportunity costs.
C. excessive fines.
D. political constituencies.

52. The legalization of slavery in 1750 contributed directly to SS8H2

A. Georgia's decision to secede from the Union.
B. the growth of rice plantations in Georgia.
C. Oglethorpe's decision to leave the colony.
D. Henry Ellis' decision to become the governor of Georgia.

53. Who is the following list describing? SS8H7

- Social activist
- Supporter of women's suffrage
- First woman ever to serve in the US Senate

A. Nancy Hart
B. Rebecca Latimer Felton
C. Lugenia Hope
D. Rosalynn Carter

54. The fact that more Atlanta city contracts went to black business owners after 1973 is evidence of SS8H11

A. the end of the white primary.
B. the Civil Rights Act of 1964.
C. the impact of Maynard Jackson.
D. the arrival of professional sports in the late 1960s and early 70s.

55. Having a budget, investing for the future, and staying out of debt are all ways citizens SS8E5

A. influence government spending.
B. go bankrupt.
C. manage their money wisely.
D. provide municipal revenue.

56. Which of the following BEST describes how the American Revolution was fought in Georgia? SS8H3
   A. It caused little violence because most of the war was fought north of Virginia.
   B. Slaves and women played no role in the fighting.
   C. Fighting was extremely bloody and bitter because most of the people fighting on both sides were Georgia colonists.
   D. Most of the fighting was between Patriot colonists and British soldiers who had arrived from England after the war began.

57. Immigration, the 1996 Olympics, the growth of Hartsfield-Jackson International Airport, and International Business have all SS8H12
   A. resulted in the end of Georgia's agricultural industry.
   B. led to economic decline.
   C. discouraged people from moving to Georgia.
   D. boosted Georgia's economy and worldwide reputation.

58. Sequoya's GREATEST contribution to the Cherokee was SS8H5
   A. signing a peace treaty with Georgia officials at Indian Springs.
   B. providing his people with their own written language.
   C. challenging laws violating the rights of Native Americans in US courts.
   D. leading Native American forces against Georgia militia in the Dahlonega region.

59. During Reconstruction, some African-Americans in Georgia
   A. were elected to political offic.e
   B. remained in slavery until Compromise of 1877.
   C. quickly obtained equality with whites.
   D. helped establish the "solid South."

Numerics

1996 Centennial Olympic Games, 130

A

Aaron, Henry (Hank), 110
AFLAC, 132
African Methodist Episcopal Church, 70
African-American
    bus boycott, 113
    church, 50
    citizenship rights, 69
    coalition, 109
    demand for civil rights, 113
    desegregation, 110
    draft, 84
    education, 80
    Great Depression, 91
    in Continental Army, 41
    integration in housing, 115
    integration in schools, 115
    Lester Maddox, 117
    migration, 91
    politics, 70, 122
    poll tax, 111
    Populist, 77
    segregation, 79
    sharecropping, 70
    state flag, 112
    transition to freedom, 69
    violence, 71
    vote, 69, 82
    voter, 122
African-American, in army, 65
Agricultural Adjustment Act, 92
Albany Movement, 114
Allen, Ivan Jr., 110
Amendment
    1 through 10, 177
    5, 168
    Fifteen, 69, 81
    Fourteen, 69, 70, 81
    Thirteen, 69, 70
    Twenty-fourth, 114
amendment
    7, 170
Amicalola Falls, 142
Amos, Bill, John, Paul, 132
Anaconda Plan, 64
Andersonville prison, 68
Antietam, battle, 65
anti-Semitism, 103
Appalachian Mountains, 141
Appalachian Plateau, 141
Appalachian Trail, 141
appeal, 168
appellate court, 168
Archaic Period, 13
Archaic Period, late, 14
Archaic Period, middle, 14
armistice, 85
Arnall, Ellis, 111
arraignment, 166
Article I, 150
Article X, 150
Articles of Confederation, 40, 43
Atlanta
    growth, 108
    sports, 110
    transportation, 76
Atlanta campaign, 67
Atlanta Compromise, 81
Atlanta Constitution, 76
Atlanta Race Riot, 82
Atlantic Ocean, 139

B

Baldwin, Abraham, 44
bankrupt, 181
barrier islands, 143
Battle of Bloody Marsh, 29
Begin, Menachem, 126
Bell Aircraft, 100, 107
bench trial, 167
bicameral assembly, 30
Bill of Rights, 45
    Georgia, 150
Black Tuesday, 91
black Wall Street, 81
Blank, Arthur, 131
Bleeding Kansas, 59
blockade runner, 64
Blue Ridge Mountains, 141
Blue Ridge region, 141
boll weevil, 89
Boston Tea Party, 37
Bourbon Triumvirate, 75
boycott, 36
Bragg, Braxton General, 66
Brasstown Bald, 141
Braves, 110
British Florida, 40
Brown v. Board of Education, 115
Brown, Joseph E., 75
Bryan, William Jennings, 77
budget, 181
Bull Run, battle, 64
Busbee, George, 129
buying on speculation, 90

buying on the margin, 90

C

Calloway, Howard (Bo), 123
Camp David Accords, 126
candidate
types of, 179
Candler Field, 109
Candler, Asa, 131
capital offense, 167
Carter, Jimmy, 124, 125
Cathy, S. Truett, 132
Central Powers, 83
charter, 24
Charter of 1732, 24
Chattahoochee River, 144
Cheatham, Owen, 131
checks and balances, 150
Cherokee (Native American), 55, 56
Cherokee Indians, 31
Chickamauga, 141
Chickamauga, battle, 66
Chick-fil-A, 132
Churchill, Winston, 98
circuit rider, 50
citizenship
responsibilities, 177
civil appeals process, 170
civil law, 169
Civil Rights Act of 1964, 114, 117
civil rights laws, 123
Civil Rights Movement, 113
Civilian Conservation Corps (CCC), 93
Clarke, Elijah, 43
Clarke, Elijah Colonel, 41
climate, 138
Coastal Plain region, 142
Coca-Cola, 131
Cold War, 108, 114
Colquitt, Alfred H., 75
Commons House of Assembly, 30
Compromise of 1850, 58
Compromise of 1877, 71
concentration camp, 102
confederacy, 63
Confederate States of America, 59
Congress, United States, 44
conquistador, 17
constituencies, 160
Constitution
Georgia, 149
of the United States, 44
US, 168
Constitution, of 1777, 40, 44
Constitution, United States, 45
Constitutional Convention, 44, 45
constitutional convention, 151
consumer society, 182
consumerism, 90
Continental Congress,, 39
convict lease system, 76
conviction, 166
Cornwallis, General Lord, 42
Cortes, Hernando, 17
cotton gin, 52
Cotton Kingdom, 52
council-manager system, 158
counter sue, 170
county government, 157
county-unit system, 78, 112
court
Georgia, types of, 165, 170
Court of Appeals, 168
Georgia, 155, 170
credit score, 180
credit, 180
Creek (Native American), 54
Creek Indians, 31
criminal law, 165
crop lien system, 77
Cumberland Plateau, 141

D

Dabney, Austin, 41
Davis, Jefferson, 63, 64
de Soto, Hernando, 17
debt, 182
debtor, 25
prison, 23
Declaration of Independence
adoption of, 38
Georgians who signed, 38
deepwater ports, 128
defendant, 166, 169
defense attorney, 166
defensive zone, 15
delinquent act, 172
Delta Airlines, 132
Democrat, 178
disfranchised, 81
district attorney, 166
diversify, 89
doctrine of nullification, 57
draft, military, 84
Dred Scott case, 59
drought, 89, 140
DuBois, W.E.B., 80, 81

E

Early, Mary Frances, 115
Eastern Theater, 64
economic development, 139
economy, 128
Eisenhower, Dwight, 108
El Niño, 139
election, 177
    1860, 59
    1896, 77
    1932, 92
    1980, 123, 126
    types of, 179
Ellis, Henry, 31
Emancipation Proclamation, 65
entrepreneur, 130
equator, 137
expenses, 181

F

Falcons, 110, 131
Fall Line, 142
farming
    drought and boll weevil, 89
    Great Depression, 91
    overproduction, 90
    subsidies, 92
federal grant, 161
felony, 165
Felton, Rebecca Latimer, 79, 84
Few, William, 44
financial discipline, 182
First Continental Congress, 37, 38
Flames, 110
Ford Motors, 107
foreclosure, 180
formal hearing, 173
Fort Argyle, 25
Fort Sumter, 63
Fort Thunderbolt, 25
Forward Atlanta program, 110
Frank, Leo, 82
Freedmen's Bureau, 69
French and Indian War, 31, 35
Fulton County Stadium, 110

G

General Assembly
    Georgia, 151
    qualifications, 151
General Motors, 107
Georgia
    during WWII, 100
    founding of, 24
    Great Depression, 91
    shipyards, 101
Georgia Dome, 130
Georgia Platform, 59
Georgia-Pacific, 131
German U-boats, 83
Gettysburg, battle, 65
GI Bill, 108
Gingrich, Newt, 123
gold rush of 1829, 55
Goldwater, Barry, 123
Gordon, John B., 75
governor
    qualifications, 153
Governor's Council, 30
governor
    powers and duties, 154
Grady, Henry W., 76
grand jury, 165
grandfather clause, 81
Grant, Ulysses S., 66, 69
Great Compromise, 44
Great Depression, 91, 103
Great Depression, 100
Great Migration, 91
Guale, 18
gubernatorial election of 1942, 111
gubernatorial election of 1946, 111
gubernatorial election of 1966, 117
Gwinnett, Button, 38, 40

H

Habitat for Humanity, 126
Hall, Lyman, 38
Harris, Joe Frank, 129
Hart, Nancy, 42
Hartsfield, William, 109, 116
Hartsfield-Jackson International Airport, 127
Hawks, 110
headright system, 50
Hemisphere
    Eastern, 138
    Northern, 137
    Western, 137, 138
Herndon, Alonzo, 81
Herndon, Alonzo, Hope, John, 81
Hideki Tojo, 98
Highland Scot, 27
Hiroshima, 102
Hispanic, 133
Hitler, Adolf, 97
Holmes, Hamilton, 115
Holocaust, 102
Home Depot, 131

Hoover, Herbert, 91
Hoovervilles, 91
Hope, John and Lugenia Burns, 80
horticulture, 14
House of Representatives, 44
hung jury, 168
Hunter, Charlayne, 115
hurricane, 140

I

immigration, 133
immigration, Illegal, 133, 134
income tax, 162
indian removal, 54
indictment, 165
informal adjustment, 173
intake, 172
interest rate, 180
international business, 129
International Cotton Exposition, 76
International Date Line, 138
interstate highway, 108
interstate highways, 127
Intolerable Acts, 37, 38
Investing, 182
Iran Hostage Crisis, 125
isolationism, 98

J

Jackson
    Maynard, 122
Jackson, Andrew, 56
Jackson, Maynard, 130
Jewish community, 103
Jim Crow law, 79
Johnson, Andrew, 68
Juanillo Revolt, 18
judicial appeals process, 171
jurisdiction, types of, 170
jury trial, 167
juvenile code, 172

K

Kansas-Nebraska Act, 59
Kennesaw Mountain, 67
Kettle Creek, battle of, 41
King, Dr. Martin Luther, 122
King, Martin Luther Jr., 113
Ku Klux Klan, 71, 82, 91, 112

L

La Niña, 139
land lotteries, 51
land ownership
    rules of, 28
latitude, 137
lawsuit, 169
Lee, Colonel Harry (Light Horse), 43
Lee, Robert E., 64
legislative branch
    Georgia, 151
legislative process, 152
Lend-Lease, 98
Leo Frank case, 82
Liberty Boys, 37
Liberty Ships, 101
limited government, 149
Lincoln, Abraham, 63, 68
Lincoln, Benjamin, 42
line-item veto, 154
literacy test, 82
Little White House, 103
Lockheed, 107
longitude, 138
Lookout Mountain, 141
Louisville, 49
loyalists, 39
Lusitania, 83

M

Maddox, Lester, 117, 124
Malcontent, 28
March on Washington, 114
march to the sea, 67
Marcus, Bernie, 131
Marshall, John (Chief Justice), 56
MARTA, 122, 159
Mattingly, Mack, 123
mayor-council system, 158
Mays, Benjamin, 113
McIntosh, William, 54
McKinley, William, 77
meridian
    prime, 137, 138
military base, 85
military bases, in Georgia, 100
Milledgeville, 50
Mississippian Period, 15
Missouri Compromise, 58
mistrial, 168
Moravian, 27
Morehouse College, 113
municipal government, 158
Musgrove, John and Mary, 25
Mussolini, Benito, 97

N

NAACP, 81, 123
Nagasaki, 102

National Highway Act, 108
Native American, 13
Cherokee, 55, 56
Creek, 54
disease, 17
Mohawk, 37
removal, 54
naval blockade, 64
naval store, 76
New Deal, 92, 93, 94 103
New South, 76, 89
Niagara Movement, 81
North America, 138

O

office park, 107
Oglethorpe, James, 23
Oglethorpe, John, 24, 27, 29
Okefenokee Wildlife Refuge, 144
Okenfenokee Swamp, 144
Olympic Games, 1996, 122
opportunity cost, 160
overproduction, 90

P

Pacific Ocean, 139
Paleo Indians, 13, 14
parallels, 137
Parks, Rosa, 113
Patriots, 37, 38, 39
Pearl Harbor, 99
Pemberton, John, 131
People's Party, 77
Perdue, Sonny, 123
Pershing, General John, 85
personal money-management choices, 180
Phagan, Mary, 82
Pickens, Andrew, 43
Pizzaro, Francisco, 17
plaintiff, 169
plantation system, 29
plateau
Cumberland, 141
plateau
Appalachian, 141
plea bargain, 166
Plessy v. Ferguson, 79, 115
political involvement, 177
political parties, 178
poll tax, 82
popular sovereignty, 149
Populist movement, 77
preamble, 150
president pro tempore
Georgia, 153
primary, 179
private school plan, 116
probable cause hearing, 173
Proclamation of 1763, 36
property tax, 162
prosecutor, 166
Provincial Congress, 39
public defender, 166

R

racial violence, 82
Radical Republican, 69
railroad
in business, 53
railroads, 128
reapportionment, 121
Reconstruction, 69
Red Cross, 85
region, 137
Blue Ridge, 141
Coastal Plain, 142
Piedmont
Piedmont region, 142
Ridge and Valley, 141
South, 138
religion
Baptist and Methodist, 50
re-possess, 180
Republican, 178
residential zone, 15
retirement, 183
Reynolds, John, 30
rivers, 144
Roosevelt, FDR, 98
Roosevelt, Franklin, 103, 144
Roosevelt, Franklin Delano (FDR), 92
Rules of 1735, 27
Rural Electrification Administration (REA), 93
Russell, Richard, 101

S

Sadat, Anwar, 126
sales tax, 161
salutary neglect, 35
Salzburgers, 26
Sand Mountain, 141
Santa Catalina mission, 18
Savannah
founding of, 25
Savannah River, 144
Savannah, Siege of, 42
savings account, 182
scalawag, 70

Second Continental Congress, 38
secretary of state
  Georgia, 178
Security and Immigration Compliance Act, 134
segregation, 79
segregation laws, 123
Selective Service Act, 84
Seminole, 144
Senate, United States, 44
Seneca River, 144
separation of powers, 150
Sequoyah, 55
settlers
  types of, 26, 27
Seven Deadly Sins, 173
sharecropper, 89
sharecropping, 70
Sherman, William T., 66
shipyards, 101
Sibley Commission, 116
slave trade compromise, 45
Smith, Hoke, 82
Social Security Act, 93
solid South, 71
Sons of Liberty, 36, 37
Southern Christian Leadership Conference, 114
speaker of the House
  Georgia, 153
speaker pro tempore
  Georgia, 153
special-purpose governments, 159
speculation
  buying on, 90
spending choices, 160
Springer Mountain, 141
St. Augustine, 18
Stamp Act, 36, 37
state budget, 160
state flag, 112
states' rights, 57
Stephens, Alexander, 60, 63, 65
stock market crash, 91
subsidies, 92
Sun Belt, 138
Supreme Court
  Georgia, 155, 168
Supreme Court, United States, 44

T

TAG corner, 141
Tallulah Gorge, 142
Talmadge, Eugene, 94
Talmadge, Herman, 111, 123
tenant farming, 70, 89
textile industry, 101
textile mill, 52, 76, 85
Thrashers, 110
Three-fifths Compromise, 45
thunderstorm, 140
Tomochichi, 25
Tories, 37, 39, 41, 42
tornado, 140
totalitarian dictator, 97
trade, 128
Trail of Tears, 56
transportation, types of, 128
Treaty of Indian Springs, 54
Treaty of Paris, 43
trial court, 155
  jurisdictions, 156
trial, types of, 167
Triple Entente, 83
tropical storm, 140
Trustee Period, 29
Turner Field, 130
Turner, Henry McNeal, 70
two-party system, 123

U

University of Georgia, 49, 115
unruly act, 172

V

V-E Day, 102
Vicksburg, siege, 66
Vinson, Carl, 101
Virginia Plan, 44
voir dire, 167
vote, 177
  register, 177
  requirements, 178
voter
  urban, 121
Voting Rights Act of 1965, 114

W

Walton, George, 38
war
  French and Indian, 35
War of 1812, 52
War of Jenkin's Ear, 28
Warm Springs, 103
Washington, Booker T., 80
Washington, George, 43
Watson, Tom, 77, 84, 94
Wesley, John, 27
Western Theater, 64
white flight, 116

white primary system, 112
white supremacy, 76
Wirz, Henry Major, 68
women's suffrage, 79
Woodland peoples, 14
Woodruff, Robert, 131
Woolman, C.E., 132
Worcester v. Georgia, 56
work or fight, 84
World Congress Center, 130
World War I
    and the US, 83
    post, 89
World War II
    beginning, 98
Wright, Governor James, 39
Wright, James, 31
WWI
    post, 91

Y

Yamacraw Bluff, 25
Yazoo
    Act of 1795, 51
    Land Fraud, 51
Young, Andrew, 122, 130
youth detention center, 173

Z

Zimmerman Telegram, 84